WELFARE ECONOMICS AND THE
ECONOMICS OF SOCIALISM
TOWARDS A COMMONSENSE
CRITIQUE

WELFARE ECONOMICS AND THE ECONOMICS OF SOCIALISM

TOWARDS A COMMONSENSE CRITIQUE

by MAURICE DOBB

CAMBRIDGE UNIVERSITY PRESS

Published by the Syndics of the Cambridge University Press
Bentley House, 200 Euston Road, London NW1 2DB
American Branch: 32 East 57th Street, New York, N.Y.10022

© Cambridge University Press 1969

Library of Congress Catalogue Card Number: 74-19594

ISBNS:
0 521 07462 2 hard covers
0 521 09937 4 paperback

First published 1969
Reprinted 1970
First paperback edition 1975

Printed in Great Britain
at the University Printing House, Cambridge
(Euan Phillips, University Printer)

CONTENTS

PREFACE

Although some of the chapters which follow originated in lectures, as may well be apparent, there is little attempt in this work either to fashion novel analytical techniques or to expound precepts for handling particular problems of planning policy (for which the writer would have been insufficiently equipped). For this reason some may regard it as falling between stools and as failing to cater for what is professionally esteemed as being of intellectual interest and of moment. The writer's concern has been with the general framework of thought in which the economic problems of a socialist economy are approached; but with an eye to the economic content of the theorems that economists have propounded rather than to the enunciation of new ones. In this he has been influenced, no doubt, by the extent to which the somewhat tortuous history of Welfare Economics has witnessed formal sophistication serving as a cloak for deficient logic and plain confusion (this being nowhere more evident than in theorems about the welfare-yielding attributes of perfect competition). The humbler task of clarifying meaning and relevance and putting problems in perspective seemed more likely to be 'fruit-bearing', at any rate so far as the building of a political economy of socialism was concerned, with a view to realistic comparison of the modes of operation of different economic systems or to improving the methodology and the practice of planning. Discussion of the latter as well as accumulated experience in the socialist countries of eastern Europe now suffice to allow at least some provisional generalisation to be made where this was scarcely possible thirty or so years ago; although attempt at generalisation has here been limited advisedly to what falls within the bounds of so-called 'optimising' problems. It is, perhaps, hardly necessary to add that the reference to 'commonsense' in the sub-title is intended strictly within the context we have mentioned and must not be taken as having wider philosophical implications.

While the author, not unnaturally, has had the student of economics and the professional economist in mind in writing this, he has tried not to burden the treatment with technicalities more than the subject itself obliges, and has sought to make the main issues at least accessible to the layman who is enquiring enough not to be deterred by a few diagrams and some specialised terminology from finding what the discussion is about in plain words. He even ventures to hope that the result may be to reveal the subject as less tricky and devious than economists have recently tended to make it.

Acknowledgement and thanks are due for advice on special points to Professor K. A. Naqvi, Professor A. K. Sen and Dr L. Pasinetti, and for the benefit of discussion, comment or detailed suggestions also to Professor Leif Johansen, Professor J. Mirrlees, Mr D. M. Nuti and Mr Brian Pollitt. But this must not be held to associate them with the views expressed or with any of the reasoning employed in the following chapters.

M. H. D.

Cambridge, June 1968

PART I
WELFARE ECONOMICS

CHAPTER I

INTRODUCTORY

Modern discussion of what has come to be called Welfare Economics, while it has not been at all lacking in formal refinements, has often been defective in economic content and in relevance, especially in its application to the comparison of different economic systems. The present attempt to re-survey the field makes no claim to add anything new to the former; but it does venture to hope to make some contribution on the side of commonsense and of practical meaning.

It is true that some professional economists today regard the analytical study of welfare as a boring irrelevance. This is largely because discussion of the difficulties posed by the so-called 'denial of interpersonal comparisons of utility' (of which we shall have more to say below) has become over the past two or three decades increasingly restricted in scope and appears now to have reached a dead end. It has become fashionable among economists to assume that no answers about welfare are possible without resort to so-called value-judgements and that everything involving these must fall outside the boundaries of economics treated as 'a positive science'. Economists are advised to stick to the analysis of various types of market equilibrium. Yet questions involving welfare obtrude themselves into almost every discussion of economic policy (including the policy of non-intervention and of 'leaving it to the market'); and if he persists in closing his eyes to such questions, then it would seem that the economist, *qua* adviser, "had better be suppressed completely" (as Sir Roy Harrod once warned his colleagues would be the logical outcome of current tendencies in their thinking).*

At the same time the inclination of socialists, at least those of Marxist persuasion, had been to dismiss the whole subject as part of the delusive heritage of the 'marginal utility' approach inherited from Jevons and the Austrian School, with their

---

* R. F. Harrod, 'Scope and Method of Economics', in *The Economic Journal* (Sept. 1938), p. 397. (For the fuller context of this remark, see below, page 81.)

obsession with justifying free competition and the free market
in terms of the maximising of utility. Such a dismissal is understandable in view of the apologetic uses to which the notion
of utility has commonly been put. None the less, the classical
heritage, with its Smithian dichotomy between 'value in use'
and 'value in exchange', should have reminded them that
propositions referring to the former are not identical with those
referring to the latter, and that maximising a sum of use values
(if that can be given a meaning) is to be distinguished from
maximising either profits or a sum of commercial values. Had
this been remembered, less surprise might have been shown at
certain recent tendencies in economic discussion in the socialist
countries of the contemporary world, where attention is being
increasingly turned towards maximum satisfaction of consumers' needs and towards means of ensuring that optimal as
well as self-consistent plans are chosen. Experience seems to
indicate that a planned economy cannot entirely dispense with
discussion about welfare criteria in some shape or form;*
and whether it can or cannot has nothing to do with the validity
of the 'classical' approach *versus* the 'neo-classical', of the
Marxian theory of value and surplus value as against the
theory of value and distribution of Jevons or Pareto.

* In this connection an article by Y. V. Sukhotin, 'On Criteria of Optimality in
an Economic Plan' in *Ekonomika i Matematicheskie Metodi*, Moscow, 1966, no. 2,
pp. 283–94, is significant in emphasising that "comparison of useful effects of
different means of consumption" (Marx) is essential to any notion of optimality in
the sense of the attainment of a "maximum level of welfare". "The composition of
an optimal economic plan," he writes, "must necessarily include in itself a search
for the best structure of final production, and not start from an already formulated
(in some fashion not known) assortment" (p. 286). He then goes on to define an
optimum assortment as one which expresses "a full correspondence between the
share of each product in total expenditures of social labour and its significance in
the balance of social consumption" (p. 290); quoting the remark of Engels in
Anti-Dühring (to which Oskar Lange long ago drew attention in his *On the Economic
Theory of Socialism*, Minnesota, 1938, p. 133): "The plan will be determined in the
last analysis by a weighing and comparison of the useful effects of various means of
consumption one with another and with the quantities of labour necessary for their
production." *Cf.* also A. N. Efimov (ed.), *Ekonomicheskoe Planirovanie v S.S.S.R.*
(Moscow, 1967), p. 28: "Marxian economic theory has always attached great
significance to the category of social utility. It has criticised and criticises the
bourgeois conception of so-called marginal utility, not for operating with the
category of utility itself nor for using the method of analysis of marginal magnitudes, necessary in every science, including economics. ... But Marxism ack-
nowledges the important role in economic processes of the category of social
utility, consumers' [use] value of goods and social use-value."

It happens (as we shall see) that much of the modern discussion of economic welfare developed out of a debate about economic rationality in a socialist economy, even if the notion of maximising utility (connected with what Marshall called "the Doctrine of Maximum Satisfaction") was first introduced in the context of perfect competition. It is accordingly interesting to find today the Director of the Institute for Mathematical Economics of the Soviet Academy of Sciences (founded in 1963) declaring that "realisation of the principle of economic optimality is characteristic only of a socialist type of economy and presupposes first and foremost the presence of social ownership of the instruments and means of production, planned development of the national economy and socialist forms of distribution".*

There is a particular respect, it is quite true, in which the approach to problems of economic welfare has been biased by those theories which, since Jevons, have analysed exchange-value in terms of the subjective attitudes or the behaviour-reactions of individual consumers. This bias is implicit in the essentially individualist presuppositions of that approach. The individual is treated as the primary atom, and his wants or preferences as the ultimate data of the problem; individuals being regarded as independent units with respect to the influences affecting demand.† It is scarcely surprising that what has been called consumers' sovereignty should be an implicit corollary of this approach—a sovereignty that a free market (under perfect competition) is held to enshrine. *Per contra* it has been held that in so far as planning interferes with, or supplants, the automatic mechanism of a free market, the rule of consumers' preferences over production is replaced by the 'arbitrary' rule of something called 'planners' preferences', or more pejoratively

---

* N. P. Fedorenko in *Ekonomika i Matematicheskie Metodi* (1965), no. 3, p. 313.

† *Cf.* Paul Streeten: "Les interêts des hommes ne sont pas des données ultimes mais sont eux-mêmes le resultat du cadre économique et social qu'elles contribuent elles-mêmes à former; l'utilité, la satisfaction, le bien-être, le bonheur, etc., ne sont pas des entités isolées, autonomes ... Les intérêts sont largement influencés par les activités et les interêts des autres membres de la société et par des valeurs que crée l'activité économique. Cette dépendance des desirs vis-à-vis de l'activité sociale va plus loin que l'influence de la publicité, qu'on cite souvent, ou la volonté que se manifeste dans la demande des diamants" (*Économie Appliquée*, Tome v, no. 4, Oct.–Dec. 1952, p. 449).

by 'dictatorship'"* Some might say that this sort of corollary may be a habit of thought engendered by myopic concentration on indifference-curves or behaviour-lines, but is not a logical inference from this type of approach. None the less, the latter holds a bias, from the very manner in which the problem is framed, towards ignoring the *inter*dependence between individual desires, through the play of social convention, emulation and other Veblenesque factors, as well as their dependence on producers' initiative (notably with regard to new products), producers' propaganda and presentation. Of the social formation, more generally, of individual tastes and of preferences over time Dr Graaff has said: "Little room is left for doubt about the extent to which tastes (and, naturally, especially those of the young) are moulded by social forces."† Such neglect can beget, indeed has begotten, fallacious interpretation. Professor Alvin Hansen has even gone so far as to declare of the present advertising age that "nowadays consumers no longer act on their own free will. The demand-curve is no longer the product of spontaneous wants. It is manufactured ... The consumer is 'brain-washed' ... [and] the process of consumer brain-washing has become a branch of psychoanalysis. Consumer wants are no longer a matter of individual choice. They are mass-produced."‡

To say that individuals and their desires cannot be treated as absolutes in considering the ends of economic activity, and that analysis cannot start from them, is not to say that individuals do not matter at all: this would be to accept the unreal antithesis between 'consumers' sovereignty' and 'dictatorship' that individualist theory itself has formulated. The fact remains that purely individualist conclusions are implied in any approach that ignores the complex social influences which serve to mould the wants and market-behaviour of individuals and which make the demand-pattern of a market so largely a reflex

* *Cf.* Branko Horvat, *Towards a Theory of Planned Economy* (Beograd, 1964), p. 32 : "It would seem necessary to call attention to a dangerously misleading practice, common to many economists, of treating all non-individualist choices as *arbitrary*."

† J. de V. Graaff, *Theoretical Welfare Economics* (Cambridge, 1957), p. 44. Of so-called 'external effects', Dr Graaff adds: "In the main there has been a tendency for professional economists—with notable exceptions—to ignore them" (p. 43).

‡ 'The Economics of the Soviet Challenge', in *Economic Record* (March 1960), p. 10.

of the socio-economic relations of a given society (*e.g.* through the distribution of income and the class conventions and standards associated therewith).

Clearly, there is still a good deal in the modern debate which remains to be clarified; and some of the issues in the discussion among English-speaking economists of thirty years ago have reappeared in recent discussion in socialist countries, if in a more realistic context and within a setting of given institutional constraints. There would seem to be some point, at least, in reviewing the subject again, if only to sort out wheat from chaff and to purge our thinking of confusing formulations and unreal questions. Such positive conclusions as emerge may appear to some unworthy of the machinery by which they are produced and as adding little to what unaided commonsense could discern. Whatever their proper assessment may be, however, the sceptical reader can be assured that no bold claims are made for these conclusions in the sequel, and that as much attention is paid to what can *not* be said as to what can usefully be said and should be observed in the course of formulating policy.

One conclusion of the present study will be that there can be garnered from a discussion of theoretical welfare economics (as this has been conducted in the past) a limited number of conditions, or criteria, for attaining an *optimum*—as necessary conditions for maximising economic welfare; but that such conditions are far from being *sufficient* conditions, and cannot be made to yield a unique maximum without introducing some *deus ex machina* that only *seems* to afford an answer on a purely formal plane without really doing so. It follows that, while we can derive some useful and quite important rules for avoiding certain kinds of *non*-optimality—certain kinds of irrationality or inefficiency in the use and deployment of economic resources—there is no such thing as a unique set of 'rational prices', as many (if not most) economists have apparently supposed, and no such thing as a uniquely efficient production-pattern and allocation of productive resources.* That this is

---

* One should, perhaps, explain forthwith that this must not be taken to imply that, in face of a *given output-plan* (or alternatively a system of weighting the various competing ends of activity) there is not an optimum use and disposal of productive resources to achieve this (with a set of 'shadow prices' relative thereto). Also, as we shall suggest later, with a given rate of growth there is an optimising system of pricing material inputs and products.

the case has no doubt been appreciated by a number of economists taking part in the debate. Yet they seem too often to have remained captive, nonetheless, of accepted habits of thought when formulating conclusions; and the illusion of a unique optimum has at any rate persisted to breed quite a tribe of fallacy. Here as in other fields one could well say, with Lord Keynes,* that "the difficulty lies, not in the new ideas, but in escaping from the old ones, which ramify, for those brought up as most of us have been, into every corner of our minds".

Although such a degree of scepticism as this will no doubt make more difficult the task of those seeking to demonstrate that optimality (in its static interpretation) is "characteristic only of a socialist type of economy", at the same time it draws the sting from the many charges levelled at a socialist planned economy of patent irrationality *sui generis* by comparison with a 'free market system'. In doing so it may enable us to view the actual problems of a socialist economy (to which we shall come in Part II) in fresh perspective and with less clouded eyes.

* In the Preface to *The General Theory of Employment Interest and Money* (London 1936), p. viii.

CHAPTER 2

UTILITY AND PERFECT COMPETITION: WALRAS AND PARETO

The justification in a rigorous form of free trading and free competition on the ground that the resulting situation represented a maximum of utility to the parties concerned was afforded by Léon Walras in 1874, and was afterwards developed by his successor (in the Chair of Political Economy at Lausanne), Vilfredo Pareto. This was something that had been lacking in the case for free trade as presented by the classical economists, which had linked the argument with particular objectives such as promoting the accumulation of capital or "greatest improvement in the productive powers of labour" and "progress of opulence".* Walras, after setting out the general equilibrium-conditions of exchange, first enunciates the proposition that "given two commodities in a market, each holder attains maximum satisfaction of wants, or maximum effective utility, when the ratio of the intensities of the last wants satisfied [by each of these goods], or the ratio of their *raretés*, is equal to the price". Then, after setting out the equilibrium conditions for production in a set of production equations, he concludes that, when "production in a market ruled by competition" takes place, "the consequences of free competition . . . may be summed up as the attainment, within certain limits, of maximum utility. Hence free competition becomes a principle or a rule of practical significance, so that it only remains to extend the detailed application of this rule to agriculture, industry and trade."†

---

* It is true that the germ of the later idea was implicit in Adam Smith, who said that "consumption is the sole end and purpose of all production; and the interest of the producer ought to be attended to, only so far as it may be necessary for promoting that of the consumer" (*An Inquiry into the Nature and Causes of the Wealth of Nations*, 4th edition, London, 1826, p. 620); while Bentham used utility as the touchstone of economic policy. But explicit statement of maximising conditions, or the stipulation of an 'objective function' to be maximised, was absent (*cf.* Hla Myint, *Theories of Welfare Economics*, London, 1948, pp. 53–5).

† L. Walras, *Elements of Pure Economics*, trans. William Jaffé (London, 1954), pp. 125, 255 (*Leçons* 8, 22).

This proposition, while emphasising it as a rule of practical policy ("the conclusions of pure science bring us to the very threshold of applied science"), he was quick to qualify two pages later, firstly with the remark that "this principle of free competition, which is applicable to the production of things for private demand, is not applicable to the production of things where public interest is involved", and secondly by pointing out that "the question of the [original] distribution of services remains open, however"—as he added, "an observation of fundamental importance".* If we substitute here the word "wealth" for "services", which better conveys to our ears the meaning he was intending, we shall see that he was not unaware of a consideration that will recur repeatedly in our subsequent analysis. But the qualification, important as he himself apparently considered it to be, was not emphasised at the time and was more often than not forgotten by those who quoted and made use of his proposition.

This idea that free exchange resulted in a maximum of satisfaction to those concerned in the exchange was developed by Pareto with the aid of Edgeworth's indifference-curves and the notion of tangency of indifference-curves as the condition of equilibrium in exchange. It is in this form that the principle is familiar to students of economics today. He defined a position of maximum (maximum *ophelimité* as he preferred to call it) as one where no further exchange could bring further benefit to *both* parties (or if to one only, then without loss of benefit to the other). As he says in the *Manuel*: "We are therefore led to define as a position of maximum *ophelimité* one where it is impossible to make a small change of any sort such that the *ophelimités* of all the individuals, except those that remain constant, are either all increased or all diminished".† Until such a point was reached in exchange, there would be further possible exchanges of potential mutual benefit; and if the trading process stopped short of this point (owing to inertia or ignorance, for example, or to some artificial barrier such as rigid

* *Ibid.* p. 257 (*Leçon* 22). It would appear that Walras had only in mind here distribution as a question of "justice" between the parties, and not as something that affected and qualified the nature and significance of the 'maximum' reached —the aspect which will be developed below.

† *Manuel d'économie politique* (Paris, 1909; being the French version of the *Manuale di economia politica* of three years earlier), pp. 617–18, also *cf.* p. 354.

prices inconsistent with reaching the maximum position) there would be a loss of (potential) utility to both parties. Until it is reached, some gain of utility is possible to one party at least without involving any loss to the other. This limit beyond which no further mutually beneficial exchange is possible was formally defined by the familiar condition that the ratios of the marginal utilities of the goods in question were equal to the rates of interchange of these goods, or to the ratios of their prices; this condition holding for *both* (or all) parties to the exchange. In the language of indifference-curves it is where the price-line, or exchange-line, is tangential to indifference-curves of the two parties (which are accordingly tangential to one another). Such a point is customarily referred to as a Pareto-optimum, or utility-maximum.

It should be intuitively obvious that, attractive as this notion is at first sight, the maximum that it defines is a conditional one and does not define a unique position. To speak of the best one can do, or the furthest one can go, within the limits of *mutual* benefit, leaves open the area of possible positions where, although further mutual gain is excluded, it is quite possible for one person to gain more than another loses.* No criterion of choice is afforded within *this* area. The Pareto-criterion stops short, as it were, of providing an answer precisely within a region of decision where possibly the most crucial (and in practice the most difficult) decisions may lie. Another way of putting it is to say that it merely expresses how the utility of any one individual can be improved on the assumption that the utilities of all other individuals in the community are held constant at some arbitrary levels.† Indeed, the Pareto-corollary to the effect that free trading results in a maximum as defined might seem to be a quite trivial result, and something pretty close to a tautology. If free trading is conceived of as a process of unhampered exchange between freely acting individuals, each conscious of and motivated by his own benefit, it is obvious that exchange between them will proceed so long as both (or all) parties see a benefit to themselves in proceeding and will stop

---

* *Cf.*: "the subjective optimum defined in the Paretian way has nothing to do with the maximum sum of satisfaction of both individuals" (H. Myint, *op. cit.* p. 103).

† *Cf.* Oskar Lange, 'The Foundations of Welfare Economics', in *Econometrica*, vol. 10, nos. 3–4 (July–Oct. 1942), p. 218.

when any party sees no further net benefit to himself. More abstractly one could define a trading process as the unimpeded swapping of any object at the free will of self-interested individuals, each intent on his own advantage. A condition for the swapping to continue would be that both (or all) individuals saw a chance of improving themselves. *Quod erat demonstrandum.*

This, indeed, was the line of criticism of the Walras–Pareto position that was adopted by Wicksell, and by implication also by Marshall. It amounted to saying that the maximum in question is a purely *relative* maximum : relative, that is, to a range of neighbouring positions and to the initial situation from which the trading starts, in particular the initial distribution of goods between the individuals. The conditions defined as constituting a maximum do not give a unique result : there are numerous positions (indeed an infinity of them) in which the conditions can be satisfied ; and as Professor Boulding has aptly remarked, 'there is nothing in the ... conditions which can differentiate the top of the molehill from Mount Everest'.* This is how Wicksell expressed his criticism :

It is almost self-evident that this so-called maximum obtains under free competition, because *if*, after an exchange is effected, it were possible by means of a further series of direct or indirect exchanges to produce an additional satisfaction of needs for the participators, then to that extent such continued exchange would doubtless take place, and the original position could not be one of equilibrium ... But this is not to say that the result of production and exchange under free competition will be satisfactory from a social point of view or will, even approximately, produce the greatest possible social advantage.†

A few pages earlier (with reference mainly to Walras) he has indicated cases where, for example in the labour market or in an exchange between a rich man and a poor man, "a much greater total utility for both together—and therefore for society

---

* Kenneth Boulding in *A Survey of Contemporary Economics*, vol. II, ed. Bernard F. Haley (American Economic Association, Homewood, Ill., 1952), p. 27.

† Knut Wicksell, *Lectures on Political Economy*, trans. E. Classen (London, 1934), vol. I, pp. 82–3. "It is almost tragic", he remarks of Walras, that one, "usually so acute and clear-headed, imagined that he had found the rigorous proof, which he missed in the contemporary defenders of the free trade dogma, merely because he clothed in a mathematical formula the very arguments which he considered insufficient when they were expressed in ordinary language" (p. 74).

as a whole"—may be attained if exchange "is effected at a suitable price fixed by society, than if everything is left to the haphazard working of free competition."* His terse conclusion is that "Pareto's doctrine contributes nothing."†

In like manner Marshall, rather more cautiously, distinguished between two versions of the so-called 'Doctrine of Maximum Satisfaction' (to which he devoted the greater part of a chapter) : the first and "limited sense" that "so long as the demand price is in excess of the supply price" for a commodity, and in this sense competitive equilibrium has not been reached, "exchanges can be effected at prices which give a surplus of satisfaction to buyer or to seller or to both" (in which sense every position of equilibrium is *ipso facto* one of maximum satisfaction as defined) ; the second, and "not universally true", sense that a "a position of equilibrium of demand and supply is one of maximum aggregate satisfaction in the full sense of the term : that is, that an increase of production beyond the equilibrium level would directly ... diminish the aggregate satisfaction of both parties."‡ He then goes on to deal, as a leading exception, with the case of commodities which "obey the law of increasing returns" (or decreasing costs) : a case that we mention later in a slightly different context.

To press the point further might seem otiose, were it not that one can still hear inflated claims being made, or at least implied, for the Pareto-optimum as hallmark and criterion of economic efficiency and rationality.§ The precise nature of its limitations (as well as of the limited validity it has as a 'relative maximum')‖ can be appreciated by presenting the matter schematically in the form of the well-known 'box diagram' (a form of demonstration that Pareto himself used in the *Manuel*)¶ and adding to it the equally famous 'Contract-curve' of Edgeworth (which Pareto did not himself use).

This representation is constructed as follows. Starting with the systems of indifference-curves (or the 'indifference-maps') of any two individuals, *A* and *B*, we invert one of these (let us

---

* *Ibid.* p. 77. † *Ibid.* p. 83.
‡ Alfred Marshall, *Principles of Economics* (7th edition, London, 1916), pp. 470-1.
§ One recent example of this kind is cited below on p. 60 n.
‖ The term was used by Edgeworth. ¶ *Manuel*, p. 355.

say that of *B*) through an angle of 180° until it confronts and
overlaps that of *A*. The set of indifference-curves of *A* and *B* will
be convex to the origin of its own diagram; and Pareto's
ophelimité, or utility, is conceived of as rising with movement
away from the origin, with each convex curve as a contour-
line* of "la colline du plaisir". Now that the two diagrams
confront one another, *B*'s standing as it were on top of *A*'s, the

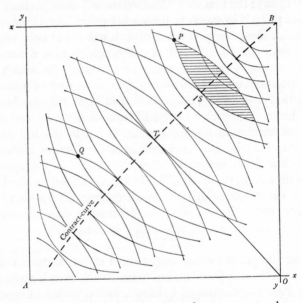

two upward movements stand opposed; movements in a north-
easterly direction representing a rising utility for *A*, but movements in a south-westerly direction representing a rising utility
for *B*. Along the axes of each diagram (now combined to form
a 'box') are measured quantities of two commodities, *x* and *y*,
that are to be the objects of exchange. Along the bottom side of
the box, accordingly, are measured from left to right quantities
of *x* possessed by *A* and along the top side from right to left
quantities of *x* possessed by *B*. (Correspondingly along the left
and right sides we have, respectively from bottom up and from
top downwards, the quantities of *y* possessed by *A* and *B*.) Any

* But without any definite numerical value attaching to them (such as the height
in feet on a contour-map) since he conceived of *ophelimité* as a purely ordinal and
not a cardinal magnitude.

point in the plane enclosed by the sides of the box accordingly represents a given distribution of a (constant) total stock of x and y between the two persons A and B.

Manifestly each convex indifference-curve of A's system will be tangent at some point to some particular indifference-curve of B's system (they can be conceived of, like contour-lines, as being indefinitely large in number, even if no more than a limited number are sketched in on any particular map). If we join up all these points of tangency along the (roughly speaking) middle of the diagram, we have Edgeworth's Contract-curve, as a locus of points for all of which a particular condition is fulfilled : namely, that the *ratios* of the marginal utilities of x and y are equal for both of the individuals, A and B. Since at each such point the two curves share a common tangent, and the inclination of such a tangent can be regarded as a rate of exchange or price-line, it follows that the ratios of the marginal utilities of x and y to A and B respectively are simultaneously equal to the price at that point.*

We can imagine the process of exchange starting from an initial position in which A has all the x's and B has all the y's : namely from the right-hand bottom corner of the box (marked O). The price-line of any given set of transactions will then be represented by a straight line from this point ; and initially any movement inwards from O, provided that it is within the two indifference-curves that pass through O (which we can call curves of zero gain for the two parties) will represent an improvement for both parties—a movement 'uphill' on their several utility-slopes. There are various ways in which one could imagine the process of bargaining, or of mutual 'swapping' of x for y, to proceed. It could proceed along a price-line from O that is a tangent to indifference-curves of the two persons

---

* Edgeworth expressed the condition defining points on his Contract-curve as

$$\frac{\partial P}{\partial x} \cdot \frac{\partial \pi}{\partial y} = \frac{\partial P}{\partial y} \cdot \frac{\partial \pi}{\partial x},$$

where ∂P was the marginal utility (or increment of utility) to one individual and $\partial \pi$ the marginal utility to the other individual (*Mathematical Psychics*, London, 1881, p. 21). This can be seen to imply that

$$\frac{\partial P}{\partial x} \bigg/ \frac{\partial P}{\partial y} = \frac{\partial \pi}{\partial x} \bigg/ \frac{\partial \pi}{\partial y}.$$

at a point (on the Contract-curve) marked in the diagram as *T*—either by a series of exchanges at this rate or in one single transaction. Alternatively one could conceive of one person, say *B*, taking always the initiative in the bargaining process and the other remaining passive. *B* would then try out *A* with a series of offers, each as favourable to *B* as possible but just sufficing to tempt *A* to accept the offer. As the bargaining proceeded, *B*'s offers would have to become increasingly favourable to *A* in order to tempt him further until the final transaction carried them to the point *T*.* In either case the

* This path of successive offers made to *A* could be represented by drawing tangents from *O* to successively higher indifference-curves of *A*'s system until *T* was reached, when *B* could make no further offers acceptable to *A* and advantageous to himself. The path composed of all these points of tangency constitutes *A*'s 'offer curve' (or demand curve)—and correspondingly for *B* if *B* were passive and *A* took the initiative in making successive offers. The two demand curves starting from *O* will intersect at *T*.

But will not the final equilibrium be affected by the *path* whereby it is reached? And if so, why should the two bargainers end up necessarily at *T*? It was the contention of Marshall that when exchange takes the form of direct barter (as in our

example), the process, although it will end up on the Contract-curve, will not necessarily reach equilibrium at a unique point such as *T*. If *A*, for example, gets the worst of the early bargains, he will tend to be in a less favourable bargaining position for the succeeding bargains, so that the final equilibrium reached will be relatively unfavourable to *A* and favourable to *B*. The reason adduced by Marshall for this was that if in those early bargains *A* had to give up a lot of *x* to gain a relatively small quan-

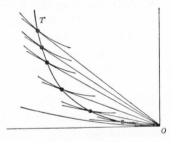

tity of *y*, the relative marginal utilities of *x* and *y* would be affected in a manner likely to render him more keen to obtain *y* in future transactions than if the initial transactions had brought him more of *y* (*cf.* Appendix F on Barter to Marshall's *Principles*). Graphically expressed, this could be represented by supposing that after each successive transaction the origin (*O*) from which tangents are drawn to superior indifference-curves is shifted, and as a result of this shift of origin the offer-curve for future transactions tends to get pushed further to the left.

This indeterminacy would not necessarily be removed by increasing the *number* of barterers on both sides, except to the extent that randomness of the initial bargains could be expected to give those who had made bad bargains a chance of finding persons on the other side who had made equivalently bad bargains for themselves and rebargaining with them to the advantage of both (thus the chance of eventual convergence would be enhanced, but the outcome would still remain uncertain).

Edgeworth, however, maintained that, if 'recontracting' were possible, there would be a tendency to converge on the point *T*; and hence such indeterminacy as

exchange of x's for y's would end up at T (or at any rate somewhere on the Contract-curve), and could then proceed no
further because any movement beyond it in a north-westerly
direction would involve movement on to a lower indifference-
curve for at least one of the parties.

Thus T is a Pareto-maximum relative to the starting-point O.
But it is a maximum relative only to a particular starting point,
representing an initial distribution of the goods, x and y. If
one had started from a different point in the box, representing
a different initial distribution of x and y, one would have ended
up, still on the Contract-curve it is true, but at some *different*
point on it. Moreover, every point on the Contract-curve is
equally a Pareto-maximum relative to neighbouring points
that are off it, in the sense that from the latter it is always
possible by moving on to the Contract-curve for both parties
to improve their positions (or one party to do so while leaving the
other in a no worse position). This is always true for movements
within one of the arcs formed by intersecting indifference-
curves, such as those intersecting at P in the above diagram ;
and a movement from P to S (or to other points on the Contract-
curve within this shaded arc) represents an improvement for
at least one of the parties without loss to the other.

Regarding choice of positions along the Contract-curve the
Pareto-principle is unable to pronounce, since these represent
shifts of distribution between A and B, involving *conflict* between
them in the sense that what A gains must be at the expense of B,
and conversely. It cannot, for example, say anything about
the choice between points T and S on the diagram : it can only
tell one that each is superior to a limited area of neighbouring
positions lying off the curve. Moreover, since it has nothing to
say about income distribution, it cannot pronounce on any
changes involving a mixture of movement *on to* and *along* the
Contract-curve, such as a move from P to T or from P to Q or
from Q to S. It even follows that a point such as Q which is off
the Contract-curve may be superior to a point such as S which
is on it. This turns out to be a serious restriction on the Pareto-
principle, as we shall see, even though Pareto and those who

there might be was *solely* due to lack of competition (*e.g.* the fewness of the bargainers) and not to the influence of the result of early bargains on the marginal
utility of the remaining stocks of commodities in the hands of the bargainers.

followed him conceived it possible to separate the problem of distribution from the problem of production and to propound rules of so-called 'economic efficiency' for the latter *per se*.

The pictorial construction we have used to illustrate exchange of two final commodities between two consumers of them can also be used, *mutatis mutandis*, to illustrate the choice of methods of production. This application of the Pareto-principle may seem more interesting, and its claim to propound an 'objective' criterion of economic efficiency that is independent of income distribution (and of other institutional factors) to be better grounded. The reason, evidently, is that to separate the question of methods of production from that of the relative outputs of different products* is easier than to separate the swapping of commodities between individual consumers from the question of the comparative amounts of those commodities which the individuals possess initially or will possess at the end of the process of re-allocation. In the former one is dealing with maximising an objective quantity, namely the output of a physical product; while in the latter one is speaking about subjective utility (or *ophelimité* or 'revealed preference'), an increment of which from an increment of what is consumed cannot be separated from the total of the things to which an individual has access. We must not let the similarity of formal construction obscure the substantial difference between these cases. Even so, this distinction must not be pressed too far. We shall see that, except in a special situation, the methods of production chosen in accordance with this principle are not independent of the output-pattern and hence of demand.

In this second construction A and B are treated as representing two distinct production-plants or firms producing distinguishable outputs, and x and y as two productive agents or factors of production such as machines and men, land and labour. (The only restriction on generality is that x and y must be regarded as homogeneous entities to the extent of each being unambiguously measurable in some unit of itself.) The collection of indifference-curves belonging respectively to A and B production-units are no longer curves of equivalent consumers' preference or utility, but *equal product curves* or isoquants, depicting different combinations of x and y in production, all of

* *I.e.* leaving aside the special problem introduced by indivisibilities.

which are capable of yielding the same output. Instead of contour-lines of a utility-hill, they are contour-lines of a production-surface, which rises to higher levels of output as one moves (in A's case) in an upward direction from A to B, or (in B's case) from B to A. Moreover, corresponding to the Contract-curve of the consumers' diagram, there will be a series of points of tangency running from south-west to north-east of the box-diagram; and the line connecting them can be called, not inappropriately, a line of efficiency-loci,* because it can be shown (by an analogous demonstration) that movement to any such tangency-point from neighbouring points away from the line will make possible an increase of one of the two outputs without any decrease of the other (or else an increase of *both* outputs).

Here there is no direct equivalent of the problem in our first case about the relativity of the utility-maximum to the initial distribution of goods. What could be held to take its place (but has a different economic significance) is that in reaching any given solution either a price-ratio of the two products or else an output-plan to determine the relative outputs of the two must be postulated. The size, or rather *shape*, of the box will represent the relative supplies available of the two factors, x and y, and will determine the position at which the two sets of isoquants confront one another (and hence the slope of the line of points of tangency and the angle of the lines of tangency themselves). There will be an influence of product-prices on the result to the extent that the production-situations of A and B (in the sense of isoquant-patterns) are different.† But this is the only way in which income-distribution (with its influence upon demand) can have an effect; and this effect will be exerted *via* its effect on the relative outputs of A and B, which we have seen will be one of the data of the problem in any case.

The economic interpretation of the tangency-condition in this case will be discussed later, in the context of so-called 'optimum conditions' considered as a whole. At this stage we will say only that it implies a choice of methods of production in both A and B such that the ratios of substitution between factors x and y are

* The term used by Dr Graaff (*Theoretical Welfare Economics*, pp. 75–7).
† If they were not different (and methods of production were independent of scale) the curve of efficiency loci would be a straight line.

equal (at the margin of production) ;* and that the ratio of substitution expresses the relationship between the additional quantity of x (say, labour) needed to replace a given quantity of y (say, land of a given grade or quality) while leaving output unaffected.

How then are we to sum up the matter of the Pareto-maximum? How important are we to regard it as being? Is it to be treated as of leading importance as a guide to economic policy, or of negligible value as Wicksell seems to have thought it, at any rate in its application to trading in final consumers' goods? There can be no doubt about its initial attraction: to suppose that one can distinguish types of change and lines of policy that cause gain to all, and correspondingly condemn as 'uneconomic' anything which hinders something being done that can bring benefit at no one's expense, immediately commands attention. As Dr Graaff has said, "when it is not attained, everybody can be made better off"†—what could be more objective and apparently universal in its application? Yet, if the principle does not suffice to define a unique result, how far can it take us and how much importance can we assign to it as a policy-imperative? As we have seen, economists' opinion has been far from unanimous, and as regards its 'free trading' corollary opinion has been sharply divided.

Expressed in formal terms the issue is fairly simple. If a movement from Situation 1 to Situation 2 really involves a mutual benefit (at least, more satisfaction to one person without loss to anyone else), it would seem hardly open to question that this represents an improvement from the point of view of welfare and should be binding as a policy-prescription, provided that there is reasonable expectation of other things remaining constant, in the sense that there are no indirect or unforeseen effects of the change in an adverse direction.

As soon as one translates this into concrete terms, however, one has to be very careful to bear in mind what is implied under 'other things remaining constant' and also the sense in which we are here implicitly defining 'more satisfaction'. We are ruling out the type of social influence upon individual tastes that we have mentioned, whether operating through convention,

---

* If one introduces market-determined factor-prices, then the inverse of these ratios will be simultaneously equal to the ratio of factor-prices.   † *Op. cit.* p. 57.

emulation or more generally by social moulding, of which economists have come to speak as Duesenberry-effects or Veblenesque influences or 'external effects in consumption'. To the extent that we admit such influences we can no longer treat an individual's satisfaction as depending *only* on his own consumption : it will depend also on the level and kind of other people's consumption. In this case we can no longer assume that more goods to one person with no less to anyone else will necessarily be an improvement in welfare. Again we have to remember that when speaking in terms of the trading example (swapping commodity x for commodity y) we implicitly identified consumers' satisfaction or welfare with the market behaviour of the individuals concerned in expressing a preference. This in turn implies that in exhibiting their preferences individuals know what best contributes to their own welfare, and (in Professor Alvin Hansen's words)* "act of their own free will" in the sense of not being deflected from their purpose by the wiles of the 'adman'. Many would call in question both of these assumptions. For the moment, however, let us brush these difficulties aside, and for the sake of the argument accept *both* of the above conditions provisionally. Then we can accept that Situation 2 is better than Situation 1, as illustrated in our diagram by a movement within one of those arcs, such as the shaded arc within which lies a movement from P to S and with Situation 2 lying on the Contract-curve.

To postulate, however, that 2 is better than 1 does not exclude the possibility (as we have already shown) that there is another Situation 3 that puts the Pareto-optimum Situation 2 in the shade; and this it may do even though it is *not itself a Pareto-optimum*. Thus we shall have :

3 ← preferred to 2 ← preferred to 1.

If, however, Situation 3 is not itself a Pareto-optimum (*i.e.* not on the Contract-curve), then the theorem enables us to infer that there is some Situation 4 which is preferable from a welfare-standpoint to Situation 3 itself and hence to the others. So (if we put in bold those situations that correspond to a Pareto-optimum) we are left with the following type of preference-series :

4 ← 3 ← **2** ← 1.

* See above, p. 6.

In other words, if we are in a position which is *not* a Pareto-optimum (like 1 and 3), we can know that there is some conceivable situation that is still better. At a purely abstract level there is nothing to cavil at in such a proposition; and if all Pareto-theorems were to be taken at this level, we could accept them and pass on. But when they are translated into propositions of applied economics (see Walras's "conclusions of pure science bring us to the very threshold of applied science"), it is crucial to know what sorts of movement are in practice available. In any actual situation of which one is speaking some kinds of movement are apt *not* to be. If, then, it happens at all commonly that the kind of move we have depicted as from 3 to 4, though 'conceivable', is not available,* then one may very well quarrel with a Pareto-theorem translated into the form: "optimising consists in always moving to a Pareto-optimum" (since this would sanction choosing 2 in preference to 3). What we are here confronted with is a confusion of levels or of categories of statement. Yet much sophisticated special pleading in this subject has consisted in simple confusion of this kind.

Disagreement starts, accordingly, when one comes to apply this notion to actual alternatives and to consider what practical corollaries can and cannot be inferred. Clearly it will make all the difference whether in practice the move from 1 to 2 and a move to 3 are mutually exclusive or whether one is quite free, having first moved to 2, afterwards to consider moving to 3 or, better still, to 4. If the two moves *are* mutually exclusive, the advice implied in this kind of optimum can be regarded as not only trivial but positively misleading. To put it differently: it will make all the difference whether the policy-alternatives that arise in practice are of the simple sort that we have depicted by our move from *P* to *S* (within one of the arcs) on our diagram, or are apt to be of the more complex type, such as *P* to *T* or *P* to *Q*, involving a loss to some as well as gain to others —a *distributional* change as well as a change in relation to the Contract-curve. Disagreement is then about the *relevance* of the Pareto-optimum, either to the sort of question to which it is being applied in any given context (such as free trade and free competition) or for the actual policy-alternatives to which one is likely to want to apply it in the real world.

* Or can only be made available by sacrificing some other desirable end.

The crux of the matter would seem to be whether the question of income-distribution can in practice be separated from questions of production and exchange. In asking such a question we need to distinguish the two cases that we have mentioned to which the notion of a Pareto-optimum has been applied: exchange of final goods between individual consumers and choice between alternative methods of production. In the latter we have suggested that such a separation can legitimately be made (at any rate if we frame the problem as being the choice of how best to produce a given output-pattern),* and to this case we shall revert later. Economists have traditionally assumed that such a separation is justified in the former case as well. Their procedure has usually been to assume that the distribution of money income is independently determined, and then to regard an application of optimum conditions (however defined) as maximising welfare *relatively* to this predetermined income-distribution. To say that a certain position is optimum relative to a certain distribution presumably means that to move towards this position necessarily represents an improvement. If it does not mean this, the statement is, surely, meaningless; and the term 'optimum' applied to such a situation is misplaced. But the attempt to apply optimum conditions involves changes in price-policy or tax-policy, with consequential effects on the outputs of different products. How then can we be sure that its effects are exclusively of the sort represented in our diagram by a move from P to S? Indeed, we can be fairly sure of the contrary: that a shift in relative prices and in relative outputs will *not* be entirely neutral in its effect on distribution when looked at in *real* terms.† One can put the matter shortly by saying that a given distribution of *money* income between

---

* Even here, to be consistent, we have to assume that the shift in methods of production *per se* will have no appreciable effect on real income-distribution (*e.g.* by causing a shift from wages to profits).

† Pigou, indeed, in the first edition of his work, drew attention to this possibility, although he did not at the time develop its fuller implications. In his discussion of index numbers as a measure of a change in national income he remarked that where the community is "made up of two parts containing, respectively, very rich people and very poor people", "the relation between the amount of satisfaction purchasable with the representative man's sovereign at two different times . . . will be largely determined by the distribution of the price movements which have taken place among things chiefly consumed by the rich or by the poor" (*The Economics of Welfare*, London, 1920, p. 87).

persons or classes will have a different welfare-significance—
will yield a different pattern of distribution of *real* income—
for every different structure of relative prices. This is obvious
once it is stated ; but one is surprised how often economists have
let it slide out of sight. If necessaries are cheap compared with
luxuries, this will *per se* improve the welfare-position of the poor
relative to that of the rich, whatever the distribution of money
income. The classic example of where the application or non-
application of the Pareto-condition can certainly not be separated from distribution-effects—indeed is dominated by the
latter—is that of rationing in war-time (or other situations of
acute scarcity). This manifestly offends against the Pareto-
condition because it is a limitation on free trading (in the sense
of free consumers' choice). Yet the alternative would be to
allow the price of scarce necessities to soar, and to reach equilibrium between demand and supply through so-called rationing
by the purse. The result would obviously be a drastic worsening
of the welfare-situation of the poor compared to the rich, perhaps with widespread starvation. In the case of any particular
price-change this distribution-effect may be too small to be
worth noticing or it may be large. Economists have no right to
assume that it will always be negligibly small.

The conclusion seems to be that one is only justified in applying the notion of a Pareto-optimum unreservedly to situations
(or in ways) where at least no change in relative outputs is
involved ; and this essentially means to the case of free consumers' choice among the products (and product-quantities)
available, since this in effect amounts to collective trading
among consumers, and allows each individual to adapt his own
consumption-pattern to the relative prices* that emerge—
as we shall again see later. Even so, one has always to remember
that a superior result† could possibly be reached by directly
effecting a redistribution of quantities through some form of
rationing, *i.e.* with constrained choice. One is only justified in
going beyond the case we have mentioned where there is good
reason to suppose that any output-shifts involved (with consequential price-shifts) will have negligible distribution-effects
(or else exclusively beneficial distribution-effects).

---

* Assumed to be flexible demand-determined equilibrium (or clear-the-market)
prices. † Though not 'the best *conceivable*'.

An alternative, and in a sense more sophisticated, device adopted by some economists has been to assume that any such distribution-effects are somehow offset by simultaneous and compensating shifts in money-income—usually in the form of so-called 'lump-sum transfers'. By doing so it is supposed that the measures designed to shift the economy to an optimum can be appropriately isolated. But however plausible this device, and designed to catch the unwary, it is scarcely more valid than the previous, more *simpliste*, assumption; and is just another question-begging way of postulating distribution in real terms as given and then proceeding as though output-shifts could not affect it. In the first place it assumes that one can isolate and measure the 'distribution-effect' and separate it from the effect on production of the measures in question. But this is the converse and complement of the notion that one can measure the production-effect of a change independently of distribution, which we shall consider later in the context of compensation-criteria generally.* The latter notion we shall see is invalid; and accordingly the idea that one can hold distribution constant

---

* More precisely one can express the difficulty in this way. If a certain change consisted *only* of a change of relative prices, it would be enough (given sufficient information about individual expenditure-patterns and reactions in them to price-changes) to calculate the changes in individual money-incomes needed to enable each individual to purchase exactly the same commodities as he had previously done. But the changes we are concerned with are not solely in prices: if shifts in allocation of resources are involved, they are changes in relative *outputs*, of which price changes are the resultant; and what price-changes result from a given output-change will depend on demand, which will depend in turn upon the compensation-payments or money-transfers that are made.

The root of the difficulty actually lies deeper. If relative outputs change, individuals cannot purchase the same, but at best an 'equivalent', assortment of commodities. If it happened that the new output-total just sufficed to maintain everyone on the same indifference-curve as formerly, this would provide a definition of 'maintaining distribution unchanged'. It would then be at least conceivable that (given knowledge of individual indifference-maps) some combination of money-income transfers and of price changes could be reached which would achieve this result. (This result, in other words, could be taken as simultaneously defining a constant *total* income and a constant *distribution*.) But in all other cases where the new output-total failed to fulfil this condition (and by what right could we assume its fulfilment when productive resources are reallocated?), what expenditure-patterns of various individuals would one aim at as constituting the same relationships between real incomes of individuals as had prevailed in the original situation? In other words, there would seem to be no sure way of keeping distribution constant (or alternatively at some ideal level) other than by keeping relative outputs constant (or conforming to some postulated pattern of real income).

(or prevent its deterioration) by compensating and offsetting through lump-sum money-transfers in face of changes in a production-total is invalid in principle.* There is also a more practical objection. The supposed point of using lump-sum transfers is that they shall have no marginal effects, or incentive-effects, which might interfere with the Pareto-condition and movement towards it. But this is probably an illusion. A poll-tax is a most inflexible instrument of redistribution (*per se* it is scarcely equalising) ; and if it be used merely to finance money grants or social expenditures, the latter must be graduated in some way, and graduated according to some criterion (probably an income- or expenditure-criterion). There may well be no practicable way of transferring money income that will not affect the supply of something (*e.g.* the supply of effort and the demand for leisure).

This is what Dr Graaff has in mind when he forcibly sums up as follows:

By far the simplest way of securing the distribution of wealth we desire is *through the price system*. In this I include income-taxes which affect the price of labour (or leisure). Much of orthodox welfare theory lacks realism precisely because it assumes that the desired distribution of wealth has already been attained (and is somehow maintained), and then proceeds to regard the price system as a highly specialised resource-allocating mechanism which exercises no influence whatever on the distribution of wealth.†

* Someone may wish to retort here that in most cases it should be possible to compensate losers sufficiently accurately to keep distribution *approximately* constant, and that for practical purposes this is the most that is needed. This may well be true, but is beside the point at the moment. What we are discussing is the claim that an optimum can be rigorously defined and embodied in precise rules of conduct. If it cannot, its significance as a criterion of rationality and an imperative for policy is appreciably changed—a point we shall return to later.

† *Op. cit.* p. 155 and *cf.* pp. 77–9.

CHAPTER 3

PIGOU AND THE MEASUREMENT
OF TOTAL PRODUCT

To survey Pigou's classic enquiry into economic welfare and its causes does not directly advance the argument on which we have embarked. But it can do so indirectly. Not only is it unequalled in its judicious and comprehensive survey of the field, but being based as it is on a separation of production from distribution in the course of postulating conditions most conducive to economic welfare, it confronts us both frankly and very clearly with the difficulties involved in this traditional dualistic approach. Logically as well as chronologically, it is accordingly a natural sequel to our discussion of Pareto-optima, even if what emerges may seem to some extent a repetition of issues that we have already met. This will happen again, moreover, when we come to the *soi-disant* 'new welfare economics'; and inevitably so, since the same fundamental difficulty, simple enough once it is exposed to view, has dogged all the various attempts to formulate a unique General Optimum. In each case, however, the same (or analogous) problem is revealed in somewhat different perspective, so that something new is gained by its recognition.

What we have termed the dualistic approach was given more plausibility by Pigou's treatment because he was less concerned with formulating maximum conditions than Walras and Pareto had been, and more with specifying the main causes of an increase in welfare with a view to indicating the direction in which and the ways by which improvement could come. The picture it presented was one of simultaneous movement along different roads; and there was no necessity for showing that advance along one was completely independent of advance along the other in order to demonstrate that progress was possible and that theory could enlighten practice. A characteristic virtue of Pigou was that he was more concerned that his disquisition should be "fruit-bearing", contributing "to practical results in social improvement", than he was to create a new formalism.

[27]

The two different ways in which economic welfare could be increased were summed up by him in two crucial propositions (which we shall refer to subsequently as Propositions 1 and 2, relating to production and to distribution respectively). These were as follows:

1. "Any cause which, without the exercise of compulsion or pressure upon people to make them work more than their wishes and interests dictate, increases productive efficiency, and, therewith, the average volume of the national dividend [income], provided that it neither injures the distribution, nor augments the variability of the country's consumable income, will, in general, increase economic welfare."*

2. "Any cause which increases the proportion of the national dividend received by poor persons, provided that it does not lead to a contraction of the dividend and does not injuriously affect its variability, will, in general, increase economic welfare."†

The latter proposition he held to be "fortified by the fact that, of the satisfaction yielded by the incomes of rich people, a specially large proportion comes from their *relative* rather than their *absolute* amount, and, therefore, will not be destroyed if the incomes of all rich people are diminished together".‡ Hence the existence of the type of 'external effect' emphasised by Veblen and later by Duesenberry was expressly indicated by Pigou and held not to weaken but on the contrary to strengthen his second proposition about distribution.

It was, of course, the first proposition that corresponded to Pareto's problem of seeking a maximum relatively to a given distribution; and chief among the "influences affecting the magnitude of the national dividend" (which had been Marshall's name for the national income) were "those associated with the distribution of the productive resources of the community among various uses or occupations".§ To give it any precision, some independent meaning had to be given to the national income as a magnitude: *i.e.* a meaning that would make it independent of income-distribution. For this reason

---

* A. C. Pigou, *The Economics of Welfare* (London, 1920), p. 47.
† *Ibid.* p. 53.　　　‡ *Ibid.* p. 53.　　　§ *Ibid.* p. 108.

Pigou introduced at an early stage of the book a chapter entitled 'Measurement of Changes in the Size of the National
Dividend' (chapter v in the first edition and chapter vi of Part I
in the third), to which we shall come in a moment. This opens
up the question of index number theory, which has occupied
a prominent place in discussion about economic welfare in
recent decades, and centres upon the question of how much
one can infer about changes in total production or national
income, measured in terms of consumers' satisfaction or utility,
from the sort of market data about prices and quantities that
form the stuff of index numbers. Were the national income a
homogeneous aggregate like sacks of potatoes or a gigantic cake,
there would be no problem, of course. No doubt would ever
arise as to whether in total it had increased or decreased or
remained the same: one would need only to weigh it or to
count it. There can, I think, be little doubt that most of us
instinctively think of the national income, or total national
product, in terms of the cake-analogy; so that commonsense
scouts the idea of there being any serious problem about defining or calculating a change in its size. But since the national
income is in fact heterogeneous in character, composed of a
number of diverse items, there always *is* a problem, except in a
case where all things change *in the same direction* (and, if the
change is to be measured, in the same degree)—or at least,
when some things change in one direction, all other things
remain constant and none of them changes in the contrary
direction. For, if some change in one way and some in the other,
any measurement of the total will depend on how much weight
is assigned to the various items. Even if only one thing has
decreased while everything else has increased in like degree, the
result can show itself as a fall in total magnitude if enough
weight be assigned to the item that has declined. Since the
weights in question are prices, this is equivalent to saying that
there is always *some* system of relative prices at which such a total
will be shown to fall between the two dates and another system
of relative prices at which that total (its composition changing
in the same way) can be shown to rise. *Which* system of prices
can be held better to reflect the change in the utility-content
or welfare-content of the total?

But before we start on this problem of measurement, let us

see how economic welfare is defined for the purpose of the two Pigouvian propositions.

After postulating "more or less dogmatically", first that "the elements of welfare are states of consciousness and, perhaps, their relations", secondly that "welfare can be brought under the category of greater or less", Pigou proceeds to define the part of welfare that is the province of the economist, or *economic* welfare, as being "that part of social welfare that can be brought directly or indirectly into relation with the measuring-rod of money". Only when in this way "there is present something measurable" can the economist's analytical machinery "get a firm grip".* This is admittedly no more than a *part* of total welfare (which obviously includes non-economic elements in large or small degree), and cannot be separated "in any rigid way" from other parts. Nor can it be taken even as "a barometer or index of total welfare". Yet this is held not to be an objection to regarding economic welfare as a worthwhile object of study so long as it is generally true that the promotion of economic welfare does not *compete* with other elements in welfare, in the sense of having effects on the latter which cancel the effect on the former. While admitting that there are exceptions and that doubt is possible, he deems it reasonable to fall back on "a judgement of probability", to the effect that "unless there is specific evidence to the contrary", the effect of any course of action upon economic welfare is "*probably* equivalent in direction, though not in magnitude, to the effect on total welfare", "the burden of proof" lying upon "those who hold that the presumption should be overruled".†

To study that part of welfare which "can be brought into relation with the measuring rod of money" amounts to treating economic welfare as essentially consisting of "satisfactions" enjoyed by consumers (*minus* "dissatisfactions", or Marshallian subjective "real costs", suffered by producers) so far as these can be gauged from their market-behaviour : as measured, that is, by "the money which a person is prepared to offer for a thing". Here one faces an immediate difficulty. As is very frankly pointed out, "the money which a person is prepared to offer for a thing measures directly, not the satisfaction he will get

* *Ibid.* pp. 11–12.   † *Ibid.* pp. 12, 20.

from the thing, but the intensity of his desire for it". Evidently these two things often diverge: many advertisers, as we know only too well, would have to go out of business were it not so. Pigou took the view, however, that "in a broad general way", and with the important exception of desires over time (the choice between present pleasures and future ones), the assumption could be made that things are "desired with intensities proportioned to the satisfactions they are expected to yield", and that (at any rate in the case of things of wide consumption required for direct personal use) "not much harm is likely to be done by the current practice of regarding money demand price indifferently as the measure of a desire and as the measure of the satisfaction felt when the desired thing is obtained".* As we have suggested, this remains a questionable assumption, especially in this age of the 'adman'. It is the more questionable, the more importance is attached to those various elements of social convention, of which we have spoken and shall speak again, in the formation of consumers' demand. The more one is inclined to question it, the less faith will one place in any postulation of optimum conditions that relies on such an identification.

One further difficulty is connected with a type of problem that we shall also meet later. This is that market behaviour, even if it can be treated as an index of satisfaction, only indicates changes of satisfaction at (or close to) the margin, and is not an index of *total* satisfaction.† This could be dismissed as unimportant to the extent that the problems with which the welfare economist is likely to be concerned are *marginal* problems, in the sense of being concerned with the effects of small changes at various margins, such as step-by-step transfers of resources from one industry to another or from one set of persons to another. Here it may be said that the *sign* of the difference in effect is what matters. The fact remains that this is a restriction on the field of application of such theorems, and a restriction that may be easily overlooked. It means that the method cannot be applied to a direct comparison of different *states* of

---

* *Ibid.* pp. 23–4.

† This is, of course, Marshall's problem of so-called 'consumers' surplus'. Pigou noted this difficulty in the 3rd. edition of *The Economics of Welfare* (London, 1929), pp. 60–1.

the economy, as distinct from comparatively small displacements from an initial position; and it remains a crucial difficulty in problems concerned with substantial 'indivisibilities' (where change has to be by substantial jumps). Here the marginal method breaks down; and it is in this guise that we shall meet the problem again.

It is perhaps worthwhile adding (since there has been so much loose talk in recent years about so-called 'value judgements') that once economic welfare and its increase have been defined in this way, the Pigouvian study of what will increase or decrease it becomes as much a *non*-normative study of causes and effects as is any other branch of economics. What the two main propositions are stating is that certain changes in the allocation of resources and in the distribution of income will have certain effects on welfare as defined. Any ethical or normative judgement enters in only when it comes to deciding whether or not economic welfare as defined is a desirable goal of policy. This falls outside the Economics of Welfare as such; and if the question be answered affirmatively (as Pigou assumed it to be), the economic enquiry in itself is as positive in character as is an enquiry about whether the effect of a certain tax or subsidy will be to raise or to lower price.

Consideration of the principles associated with Pigou's first proposition will be reserved for a later chapter concerned with optimum conditions. For the present let us revert to the problem of how an increase in national income, or total production, can be measured and defined, since this is manifestly a necessary preliminary to giving any such principles a clear meaning.

Pigou's method can be described as being the equivalent of dealing with the matter in terms of a representative individual in the community, and then generalising from this individual to the totality of individuals composing the community as a whole (*i.e.* from individual income to national income). This is done on the assumption that the distribution of income between those various individuals is constant. On this assumption, what is true of a representative individual can be held to be true of the totality: if certain price and quantity changes can be shown to amount to an increase of real income in the relevant sense for the individual, they can be held to amount to an increase of social income, or national income. If, however, the assumption is dropped, and the pattern of income-distribution between the individuals composing the community is allowed to change between the dates in question (between which comparison of national income is being made), then such a generalisation from individual to society is invalid, and no conclusion about change in social or national income can be drawn.

It may be noted that an assumption that tastes are constant, or that the underlying system of wants and preferences is given, has also to be made. But this is common to all treatments of the subject and is not peculiar to Pigou.

Regarding the definition of what it is that one is trying to measure, he started by defining the national income as an "objective thing", which if we could, we should like to measure in terms of "some objective physical unit and without any regard to people's attitude of mind towards the several items contained in it". This, he held, was "the point of view which everyone intuitively takes".* The national income, however, consisted of heterogeneous things, some of which were apt to increase with a decrease of others, and it was impossible to find any satisfactory physical unit in terms of which the increases in some and the decreases in others could be weighed in the balance so as to determine whether the aggregate had increased or diminished. (This was for the reason that no physical measurement such as length, area or weight, had economic significance outside special cases: a truth of which there are familiar examples, such as making nails, tools, kitchen utensils or bedsteads heavier which may diminish rather than augment their economic usefulness.) Accordingly he adopts as the standard of measurement the use-values of the various constituent items composing the national income. In other words, he estimates the size of any given aggregate in terms of the utility or "the economic satisfaction (as measured in money)" which that total yields. As evidence of this he had necessarily to appeal to "people's attitude of mind" as expressed in their market behaviour. This meant that any possible difference between "desires" and "satisfactions" had perforce to be ignored, and "satisfaction measured in money" to be taken as equivalent to "the amount of money which" people are "prepared to offer" for

* *The Economics of Welfare*, 3rd edition, p. 54.

a particular thing or for any aggregate of things (this, of course, being on the assumption that total *money* income is constant, or with allowance made for any change in it).

To this end he takes a representative individual with constant tastes and constant money income confronted with a certain real income in Period 1 and in Period 2 respectively: "we say that his dividend [income] in Period 2 is greater than in Period 1 if the items that are added to it in Period 2 are items that he *wants more* than the items that are taken away from it in Period 2".*

It remains to relate such a definition to the actual price and quantity data afforded to us by the market. This is the problem of index numbers and of what can be deduced from them about changes in real income. In reproducing his argument we shall undertake some translation of his notation into the more familiar form of p's and q's; and we shall subsequently supplement his exposition with some conclusions of index number theory that have been developed since Pigou wrote.

After dismissing the measurement of consumer's surplus as being, though desirable in principle, impossible in practice, he comes to "the quantities and prices of various sorts of commodities" as affording "the only data which there is any serious hope of organising on a scale adequate to yield a measure of dividend changes". ("There is nothing else available", he adds, "and therefore if we are to construct any measure at all we *must* use these data").† First let us make the simplifying assumption that the money income (or expenditure) of the community of individuals at the two dates is the same, which may be expressed as:

$$\frac{\text{Total money expenditure of Period 2}}{\text{Total money expenditure of Period 1}}, \quad \text{or} \quad \frac{\Sigma p_2 q_2}{\Sigma p_1 q_1} = 1.$$

This enables us to focus attention upon the effect on consumption of price-changes between the two periods in question. Of the price-change we have two alternative measures, called respectively the Laspeyres and the Paasche price-index. The former, in summing the price-changes of the various individual products (the various p's of the different q's), weights them with the quantities of those products available and consumed in the *first period*; the latter weights them with the quantities available and consumed in the *second period*. Thus we have as measures of the (weighted) average price-change respectively:

$$\frac{\Sigma p_2 \, q_1}{\Sigma p_1 \, q_1} \, [L] \quad \text{and} \quad \frac{\Sigma p_2 \, q_2}{\Sigma p_1 \, q_2} \, [P].$$

It can easily be seen to follow that if the ratio of money expenditures (which we have assumed for simplicity to be unity) is divided by the *Laspeyres* index of the price-change, we reach a so-called product-index in which the quantities of the two periods are severally summed and compared in terms of the prices prevailing in the *second* period (and referred to for this reason as the *Paasche product-index*). Thus we have:

$$\frac{\Sigma p_2 \, q_2}{\Sigma p_1 \, q_1} \div \frac{\Sigma p_2 \, q_1}{\Sigma p_1 \, q_1} = \frac{\Sigma p_2 \, q_2}{\Sigma p_2 \, q_1}.$$

Obviously, if the first expression (ratio of money expenditures) is unity, a *fall* in the price-index will mean that the product-index on the right-hand side will be greater than unity: *i.e.* that the quantities available and consumed in the second period, when weighted by the prices prevailing in the second period, are greater than the quantities (so weighted) available and consumed in the first period.

Comparably, if one divides the ratio of money expenditures by the *Paasche* index of price-change, we reach a product-index in which the quantities of the two periods are severally summed and compared in terms of the prices prevailing in the *first* period (and referred to for this reason as the *Laspeyres product-index*). Thus we have:

$$\frac{\Sigma p_2 \, q_2}{\Sigma p_1 \, q_1} \div \frac{\Sigma p_2 \, q_2}{\Sigma p_1 \, q_2} = \frac{\Sigma p_1 \, q_2}{\Sigma p_1 \, q_1}.$$

We are confronted, therefore, with two measures of the change in real income (or of quantities), namely

$$\frac{\Sigma p_2 \, q_2}{\Sigma p_2 \, q_1} \, [P] \quad \text{and} \quad \frac{\Sigma p_1 \, q_2}{\Sigma p_1 \, q_1} \, [L].$$

The question is: can these two measures yield contradictory results, and if they do what can we conclude to be the correct answer?

It is quite possible, of course, that the alternative measures will yield contradictory results; and Pigou held that in such cases no certainty was possible. Only if there was agreement between them as to the direction of change could one speak of an increase or decrease of real income "in an absolute sense". In the contradictory case, however, he thought that a judgement of probability could be made by taking the square root of the result of multiplying the two measures (this according with an idea of Irving Fisher of what consituted an 'ideal index number'). This notion is one upon which serious doubt has been subsequently cast; so that we are absolved from doing more than mention it as an historical curiosity, and we shall not follow Pigou further in this question.

It is now generally recognised that (strange as at first sight it may seem): (*a*) the Paasche product-index is decisive for an *increase* of real income, so that one can regard as irrelevant whether this result is supported or not by the Laspeyres product-index; (*b*) the Laspeyres product-index is decisive for a *decrease* of real income, and it is irrelevant whether this result is supported or contradicted by the Paasche product-index. This narrows down the possibility of genuine contradiction to the case where the Paasche index shows a rise and the Laspeyres a fall: a head-on collision between them where each is claimed to be decisive. The question as to whether this contradictory case is possible we shall consider in a moment.

Let us first examine the reason for our propositions (*a*) and (*b*): a quite simple reason that can be expressed in terms of plain commonsense. Consider the case where the Paasche product-index shows a rise in real income. We have seen that this index can be broken down into the ratio of money income (or expenditure) and the Laspeyres *price*-index, thus:

$$\frac{\Sigma p_2\, q_2}{\Sigma p_1\, q_1} \div \frac{\Sigma p_2\, q_1}{\Sigma p_1\, q_1}.$$

If the first ratio be taken as unity (meaning that total money income or expenditure is constant), then we have said that a *fall* in the price-index means that what can be bought with this money-income in Period 2 yields more satisfaction to consumers (representing accordingly a larger real income) than what could be bought with it in Period 1. Why can we be so sure of this as to hold it to be true even though the rival product-index points in the contrary direction?

What exactly does a fall in the Laspeyres price-index really tell us (when combined with knowledge that total money income is constant)? It tells us that consumers could if they wished in Period 2 buy *more* of the same bundle or basket of commodities (composed of the same items in the same proportions) as they had chosen to purchase in Period 1. In actual fact they are probably not buying this commodity-basket (which we will write as C_1) but a somewhat differently assorted one (which we will write as C_2) because relative prices have altered. But it was still open to them to go on buying C_1 if they had preferred to. If, therefore, they have in fact substituted C_2 for it in Period 2, this must be because they preferred C_2 to C_1 at prevailing prices (the p_2's)—because they felt they would get more satisfaction for their money by spending it according to the new pattern rather than the old. The comparison can be represented accordingly like this (we put square brackets round C_1 in the second period as a reminder that it is a hypothetical and not an actual pattern of consumption) :*

Period 2 $[C_1] \rightarrow C_2$
               $\uparrow$
Period 1 C_1

Since C_2 is preferred to (or yields more satisfaction than) $[C_1]$, and we know (from the price-index) that $[C_1]$ represents more of the same goods than did C_1 in Period 1, we can conclude that $C_2 > C_1$, in the sense of yielding greater consumers' satisfaction than did consumption or real income in Period 1.

If, however, the Laspeyres price-index, instead of showing a fall, had shown a rise between Periods 1 and 2, we should have been able to conclude *nothing* about the comparative magnitudes of C_2 and C_1. The comparison afforded would have looked like this :

Period 2 $[C_1] \rightarrow C_2$
               $\downarrow$
Period 1 C_1

* The arrows represent directions of preference, or of superiority from the standpoint of consumers' satisfaction.

We should know that what was actually consumed (C_1) in Period 1 was greater than what could be consumed in Period 2 of the same basket of commodities as were previously consumed in Period 1. But since the latter is *not* (in all probability) what is actually being consumed in Period 2, but instead a different and preferred basket, we can infer nothing concerning the relative satisfactions yielded by C_1 and C_2. The result is consistent with either $C_1 > C_2$ or with $C_1 < C_2$.

By parity of reasoning it can be shown that when the Laspeyres product-index registers a fall of real income between the two periods, it is decisive; whereas it can tell us nothing decisive when it seems to indicate a rise. We may indicate the main lines of the analogous demonstration as follows.

This index can be broken down, as we have seen, into the ratio of money income (or expenditure) and the Paasche *price-index*, thus:

$$\frac{\Sigma p_2\, q_2}{\Sigma p_1\, q_1} \div \frac{\Sigma p_2\, q_2}{\Sigma p_1\, q_2}.$$

A *rise* in the Paasche price-index tells us that in Period 1 consumers could have enjoyed more of the basket of commodities that were being consumed in Period 2 (C_2). But in fact not this basket but another one (C_1) was being bought in Period 1 : it was being bought (when both were available) presumably because consumers preferred C_1 at the prices prevailing in Period 1 (p_1). The information afforded to us can accordingly be represented in this way :

Period 2 C_2
                    $\downarrow$
Period 1 $C_1 \leftarrow [C_2]$

from which we may deduce that $C_2 < C_1$.

Were the Paasche price-index to show a *fall*, however, between Period 1 and Period 2, we should have, instead, this picture :

Period 2 C_2
                    $\uparrow$
Period 1 $C_1 \leftarrow [C_2]$

from which we could infer nothing about the comparative magnitudes (in terms of consumers' satisfaction) of C_1 and C_2.

One can generalise the matter by saying that a product-index, to be decisive in the change that it indicates, must have the following form:

$$\Sigma p_x\, q_x > \Sigma p_x\, q_y$$

(where x and y may stand for either 1 and 2 or conversely). In other words, the comparison of quantities must be made in terms of the prices prevailing in the period when real income is greater. The reason for this is not far to seek. It is that, to reach a conclusion, one has to combine two pieces of evidence: the evidence afforded by a price-index and the evidence afforded by the market upon which consumers register their preferences (at a given set of prices). Only if the two pieces of evidence have the same sign, or point in the same direction, will they be congruent and yield a definite conclusion. Consumers will be better-off when prices have fallen (and conversely), and will be better-off if they shift their expenditure towards things that have fallen in price most. From this it can be seen to follow that the prices in terms of which consumers' market-behaviour is registered (in opting for one basket of commodities rather than another) must be those of the period in which prices are lower and hence real income greater (when the ratio of money expenditures is equal to unity).

Reasoning of a rather similar kind about consumers' behaviour in face of price-changes also leads to the inference that normally

$$L > P:$$

an inequality which applies to both the product-index and the price-index, and means that the Laspeyres index of either kind will usually register a larger positive difference (*i.e.* a rise) between one period and the next than will the Paasche index; whereas, in the case of a negative difference (*i.e.* a fall), the Laspeyres index will usually register a *smaller* fall than will the Paasche.

The reason for this can again be put quite simply, and more shortly; using again C_1 and C_2 to represent the consumption-patterns (or the q_1's and q_2's) of the two periods that one is considering, and assuming money income or expenditure to be constant, as before. To the extent that C_2 differs in composition from C_1, it is likely* to consist more of things that have risen in price *less* than the things principally composing C_1—or alternatively, in the case of a general price-fall, to consist of things that have fallen most. Hence in the case of a general price-rise, a price-index weighted in accordance with C_1 (*i.e.* Σq_1) will usually register a larger rise than a price-index weighted with C_2. Conversely, when prices have fallen, the former will usually register a smaller fall than the latter (or show a higher price-*level* after the fall by comparison with another date).

It can immediately be seen to follow that a Paasche *product*-index, which uses a Laspeyres, or q_1-weighted, price-index as divisor of the ratio of money-expenditures, will register the bigger *fall* in real income (and hence a lower *level* after the fall) when prices rise; but in the converse case will show the smaller *rise* in real income (and hence a lower *level* after the rise). In other words, the Paasche product-index can be expected to yield the more conservative measure of any rise of real income, and the Laspeyres product-index the more conservative measure of any fall.

What is not excluded is that the Laspeyres product-index may indicate a *rise* of real income and the Paasche simultaneously a *fall*. This is not inconsistent with the inequality $L > P$. But it is only an apparent contradiction, not a real one, since the Laspeyres cannot be decisive when it indicates an increase, nor can the Paasche be decisive when it indicates a decrease. In this case we can conclude nothing about the change in real income.

What then of the opposite sort of contradiction, where the Paasche claims an increase and the Laspeyres claims a decrease? Here there is a head-on clash between the two in a case where each can speak with a decisive voice (if our previous argument is valid). Is such a case really possible, or does our argument mean that it cannot in fact occur? The answer is, indeed, that it is impossible if consumers behave consistently† and if tastes (and distribution) remain unchanged. But this does not mean, of course, that it cannot possibly occur in the real world, where as we know consumers may well behave inconsistently and

---

* Ignoring some special and 'peculiar' effects in a contrary direction of income-elasticities of demand.

† Consistency here means that if consumers choose A in preference to B and choose B in preference to C, they must also choose A in preference to C and not the converse.

both tastes and distribution quite commonly change. If, therefore, we meet such a contradiction in practice, it is an indication that one of these three things has happened.

This brings us back to Pigou's assumption of constant income-distribution on which we have seen that the possibility of giving an unambiguous meaning to a change of (real) national income depends. Pigou was quite frank in recognising the Achilles's heel of his definition. If, he says, "tastes and distribution of purchasing power were really fixed", this definition of changes in real income would be "free from ambiguity" and entirely satisfactory. If, however, tastes or distribution vary, then "our definition leads in certain circumstances to results which, in appearance at least, are highly paradoxical". It is quite possible for the production of Period 2 to appear greater from the standpoint of the tastes or distribution of one year and at the same time smaller from the standpoint of the tastes or distribution of another year. "The only escape" from this contradiction is "to admit that, in these circumstances, there is no meaning in speaking of an increase or decrease in the national dividend in an absolute sense."*

How seriously does this restriction matter so far as making sense of Pigou's First Proposition is concerned and giving to its corollaries some clear operational meaning? At first sight it might seem that the restriction is not very serious; and many (if not most) writers on the subject seem to have supposed that both sense and importance can be assigned to this proposition and its corollaries, despite the fact that it can only be unambiguously stated when distribution is assumed to be given and constant. As we remarked earlier, it seems at first sight to make sense to speak of maximising social (or national) income as a way of enabling a given income-distribution to yield as much utility or welfare as it is capable of doing. If it does make sense, then one can surely speak of the two Propositions together as presenting two independent policy-objectives, each to be pursued by measures appropriate to itself, unaffected by whether or not simultaneous measures are being taken in pursuit of the other. No fallacy of composition will be involved in treating the appropriate measures under each head as separate and additive contributions to social welfare.

* *The Economics of Welfare,* 3rd edition, p. 56.

Such an answer is convincing up to a certain point. But it breaks down at the very point at which precise definition is required of the goals that are severally implied by the two propositions. The assumption of independence can then no longer be reasonably maintained, and without it vagueness and essential relativity replace and exclude precision. What may appear as movements towards one of the goals (as postulated in isolation) may well shift, and hence compete with, the other. The two goals of policy can accordingly no longer be independently defined and pursued separately. Autonomy of the First Proposition, on the one hand, would *appear* to be quite justified so long as one is content to define 'given income distribution' or 'constant distribution' in terms of *money* income. But for the reasons we examined at the end of the last chapter, this is by no means sufficient; and the enduring belief in its sufficiency turns out to be an example of nothing more sophisticated than the so-called 'money illusion'. When we speak of distribution in real terms, this is something that will be affected by the very quantity-and-price adjustment involved in moving to a maximum in terms of Pigouvian Proposition One; and it is quite possible that the distributional effects of these 'maximising' adjustments will be such as to more-than-cancel out the intended increase in welfare. It may be noted that Pigou himself was expressly guarded on this point: his formulation does *not* sanction optimising unreservedly under his Proposition 1, but only in so far as it does not "injure the distribution". On the other hand, if changes in distribution of money income in furtherance of the goal defined by Proposition 2 proceed conjointly with the aforementioned quantity-and-price adjustments in furtherance of Proposition 1, the Pigouvian notion of a 'representative' individual crumbles; and it is quite possible as a result to have precisely that sort of contradiction between the Paasche and Laspeyres indices which leaves us with "no meaning in speaking of an increase or decrease" of social income "in an absolute sense". Of a change involving such a contradiction we shall give an example in a later chapter, when we shall return to this question in another guise.

We have noticed above a passage* in which Pigou showed

* Above, p. 23 n.

himself aware of the possible interaction between price-quantity changes and distribution. The reason we have suggested why he did not consider it an objection to his manner of stating his two crucial propositions is that he was less concerned with a statement of optimum conditions than with indicating the general direction in which improvement lay. This concern is apparent particularly in his treatment of Proposition 2 where the emphasis is on movement towards greater equalisation as a way of augmenting welfare, and there is no discussion (as there was later to be in Professor Abba Lerner's work, for example) about whether absolute equality or something short of it is likely to maximise the welfare yielded by any given income (or alternatively, allowing for differences between individuals, such a distribution as will equalise the marginal utilities of all individual incomes). To this extent Pigou's method of approach can be held to have been justified. But if one wishes to lay down optimum conditions for maximising national income with any degree of precision (as was later to be done), then the difficulty we have mentioned is crucial, since talk of maximising requires clear and unambiguous definition of the maximand.

NOTE TO CHAPTER 3 ON PROFESSOR HICKS ON
INDEX-NUMBER DATA AND THE MEASUREMENT
OF REAL INCOME IN TERMS OF
INDIFFERENCE-CURVES

It may be convenient to summarise an analogous demonstration of the significance of Index-Number data provided by Professor J. R. Hicks in terms of indifference-curves. This first appeared in an article on 'The Valuation of the Social Income' in *Economica*, May 1940 (esp. pp. 108–10). That part of Professor Hicks's analysis that is summarised here is confined, however, to the level of the *single individual*, and accordingly does not raise immediately the problems confronting Pigou when considering the social group.

In place of Pigou's definition of a change of real income in terms of additive Utility or Satisfaction, we have here an increase of real income defined as "moving to a higher 'indifference-curve'". The analysis is conducted in terms of the familiar two-commodity case; these commodities x and y being joined between the two axes by the familiar system of n indifference-curves expressive of the individual's attitude (of preference and indifference) towards them. Such a system is characterised by two properties that are crucial to the argument. For reasons that are sufficiently well known all such curves must be *convex* to the origin, and individual curves of the system cannot intersect one another. But this is *all* that we know about the system of curves, or the shape of the indifference-map : we have no knowledge *a priori* of the curves themselves, apart from their *general* shape in the immediate neighbourhood of particular points, such as the Q_1 and Q_2 in which we are interested (such points representing certain combinations of the two commodities x and y).

Let us take the *Paasche* product-index and see what it can tell us when $\Sigma p_2\, q_2 > \Sigma p_2\, q_1$. The diagrammatic representation of $\Sigma p_2\, q_2$ is fairly obvious : if a combination of commodities represented on

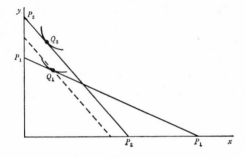

the diagram as Q_2 is purchased at price p_2, this implies an income when measured in terms of either x or y sufficient to purchase Q_2, and hence a price-line passing through Q_2 at an angle representing the relative price in question. How then is $\Sigma p_2\, q_1$ to be represented? Evidently this must be by a (hypothetical) price-line parallel to the former one, but passing instead through the point Q_1 (the commodity-combination of the first situation). If the two points in question are to be considered points of equilibrium (in the sense of the individual consumer in question being in the best, or most preferred, situation possible with the income available to him), the (actual) price-line at each point must be tangent to *an* indifference-curve (of which we know only that it is convex in shape ; hence we can only sketch it in tentatively in the immediate neighbourhood of the point in question).

It can be seen to follow from the properties of indifference-curves that we have mentioned (convexity and non-intersection) that all points to the *left* of a price-line tangent to the indifference-curve of one of the positions in question *must* be on *lower* indifference-curves. The converse, however, does not apply : not all points to the right of the price-line P_2–P_2 are of necessity on higher curves than the one that is tangent to P_2–P_2 (one can only be sure of their being on higher curves if they are points within the north-east quadrant that hinges on the position Q_2).

The inequality $\Sigma p_2\, q_2 > \Sigma p_2\, q_1$ evidently means that the price-line representing the former is 'outside' that of the latter, which in turn means that the point Q_1 must be to the *left* of the price-line P_2–P_2 on which Q_2 is situated. Accordingly Q_1 is on a lower in-difference-curve than Q_2; thus representing a lower 'real income' than Q_2. (It is to be noted that the indifference curve on which Q_1 is situated is *not* tangential to the (imaginary) P_2–P_2 line, but to the price-line actually prevailing in the first situation, namely P_1–P_1.)

But if we reverse the inequality and write $\Sigma p_2\, q_2 < \Sigma p_2\, q_1$, since Q_1 is now to the *right* of the P_2–P_2 line passing through Q_2, this is consistent with Q_1 being on *either* a higher *or* a lower indifference-

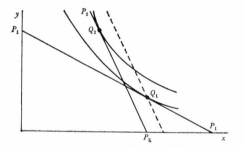

curve than is Q_2. The attached diagram could be taken as illustrating a case where the indecisive form of the Paasche index was consistent with Q_1 being on a lower indifference curve than is Q_2. This very asymmetry, it may be noted, follows from the convexity of indifference-curves.

By analogous reasoning it can be shown that the *Laspeyres* in-equality, if it has the form $\Sigma p_1\, q_1 > \Sigma p_1\, q_2$, implies that Q_1 is on a higher indifference-curve than is Q_2; while the reverse form of the inequality is indecisive. The former case can be illustrated dia-grammatically in the manner of the third diagram. (Here, it will be noted that $\Sigma p_1\, q_2$ is represented by a price-line through Q_2 parallel to the P_1–P_1 price-line through Q_1.) Since Q_2 is to the left of the P_1–P_1 price-line through Q_1, Q_2 must necessarily be on a lower in-difference curve than is Q_1—as is illustrated in the third diagram.

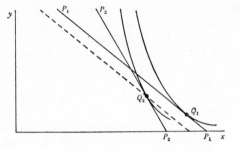

What is true of the two-commodity case is evidently true also of the *n*-commodity case with an indifference-curve system in *n*-dimensions.

These results, however, can*not* be transferred from the level of the individual to that of society as a whole, for the simple reason that social or 'community indifference curves' do not share the convenient property of non-intersection, which we have seen was crucial to the above argument. A 'community indifference-curve' is arrived at by weighting and aggregating individual curves; the weighting of the latter being given by the distribution of income. Hence to each different distribution there is a different set of community indifference-curves. While the family of community-curves characterised by any *given* distribution shares the properties both of non-intersection and convexity belonging to its constituent individual curves, this ceases to be true of community-curves of mixed families, *i.e.* of different distributions. (It is true that Professor Hicks in the above-mentioned article *does* transfer his results to the social level; but this is on a special definition of "an increase in real social income", which we shall discuss—and criticise—later, in chapter 6.)

CHAPTER 4

OPTIMUM CONDITIONS FOR
MAXIMISING WELFARE

The maximising corollary which Pigou attached to his First
Proposition is perhaps too familiar to need requoting. It was that
in any given situation as regards the supply of economic
resources and the state of technique, these resources should be
so allocated between various productive uses as to equalise
(in terms of money value) the *social* net product of a unit of
these resources at the margin of all uses. The significance of
social net product here is that it was designed to include the full
return of utility or welfare to society as a whole from any given
productive activity, and was not confined to the value-return
to the individual owner of the resources in question—to the
individual *entrepeneur* or firm responsible for investing those
resources. The immediate use he made of the corollary was a
critical one in relation to what Marshall had termed the
Doctrine of Maximum Satisfaction; to disclose the leading
cases of divergence of individual from social net product, and
hence as a theoretical critique of the doctrine of *laissez-faire*.

Expressed in this form the condition had a very general
character: one that was appropriate enough for his immediate
purpose, but one that called for particularisation in the context
of more detailed discussion of price-policies and of the relation
between their proximate effects and the macro-configuration
of inter-industry relations. Such a shift of focus occurred both
in the course of further analysis of the Pigouvian cases of divergence between individual and social interest during the
later twenties and also in the course of the debate about
wirtschaftsrechnung and pricing-policy in a socialist economy
during the decade of the thirties. Pigou's more general corollary
was accordingly broken down and particularised in a set of
optimum conditions (as they came to be called) for maximising
national income. These necessary and sufficient conditions for
an optimum were variously stated; but the diverse statements

were capable of translation into common terms. We shall here adopt a form of statement that enables us to relate it to the issues reviewed in the last chapter and also to some of those raised in the discussion about so-called rationality and efficiency under socialism. The classification adopted will distinguish a Consumers' Condition applying to the retail market for final consumers' goods (Menger's 'goods of first order') and a general Production Condition, affecting the actions of firms and industries in making decisions about production; with the latter of these subdivided into two separate conditions embracing respectively choice of methods of production and of the output-pattern or relative scales of output. We shall then show how these two sub-conditions can be (and commonly are) combined in a single, more general condition, similar to Pigou's but variously formulated; in which general form an important qualitative distinction between the two sub-conditions tends to get lost.

The first, our *Consumers' Condition*, will be familiar from the Paretian box-diagram of chapter 2 as the tangency of a consumer's indifference-curve and price-line (in the case of any pair of commodities); the condition stating that this must hold true for each and every consumer. For shortness of identification we shall refer to this hereafter as the consumers' tangency-condition. It can be alternatively stated (for any number of commodities) in the form that the consumers' marginal rates of substitution are proportional to the price-ratios of goods; or yet again that the ratios of the marginal utilities of the various goods are equal to the ratios of their prices.

The commonsense of this condition is that unless the consumer is in this position—has distributed his expenditure among commodities so that the required equalities prevail—he can always secure a gain in satisfaction by redistributing his expenditure: spending less on things from which the satisfaction obtained (at the margin) is small compared to the price and more on things from which the satisfaction obtainable is large compared with their price. The position in question is described as being an optimum because a consumer who is away from it will be in something less than the most preferred position and obtaining less satisfaction or utility for his money than is possible. This condition affords a justification of free consumers' choice in spending their income as they best please, by contrast with rationed expenditure or with payment of wages in kind instead of in general purchasing power. Were it not for the cumbrousness of any barter-system, one could even imagine the condition being fulfilled when wage-payments were made in kind, provided that each recipient of the goods-quota or ration was able to exchange with others less favoured portions of it for more favoured, to enable each to end up with an assortment more in accordance with his taste.*

That, while being a necessary condition for any optimum, it is not a sufficient condition becomes clear from the fact that it is capable of being fulfilled at *any* set of prices. It is only necessary for consumers to adapt their individual expenditure-patterns to the pattern of supply-prices confronting them on the market. (A reciprocal reaction upon prices will, of course, be exercised, as we have said earlier, by any aggregate demand-shifts involved in this adaptation, but only within the limits of individual willingness to trade one expenditure-pattern for another at the current prices, and hence within the limits of mutual benefit.)† This indicates the restricted significance of the Consumers' Condition *per se*. Yet at the same time it is the pivot on which more general formulations of the Production Condition (or the *second half* of the latter condition as we shall state this) crucially depend, in the sense that without it the latter would be lacking in significance.

The limitation of this Consumers' Condition *per se* may be illustrated in another way by emphasising that its significance consists in adapting the consumption-patterns of consumers *to the extent that there is a variation of individual tastes or of demand*. Each individual makes his own particular selection from the general pool according to his own peculiar pattern of preferences, with the price-structure at any given time treated as a parameter. For that mythical being the 'average consumer', or in the hypothetical case where consumers' tastes were uni-

---

* *Cf.* J. E. Meade, *The Stationary Economy* (London, 1965), pp. 201–2.

† Even this statement is, however, subject to the qualification that where, because of inelasticities of demand, the resulting price-changes (and hence differential income-effects) are large, the adverse distribution-effects of fulfilling the tangency-condition, in face of a given supply-pattern, may more than offset the benefits; whence the type of 'exception' referred to above, p. 24, exemplified in rationing of necessities in times of scarcity.

form, the condition would lose its significance, since the available supplies (and hence the *aggregate* consumption-pattern) at any one time would be given; prices being the dependent variable which equated actual consumption to what there was to buy. Only if producers responded appropriately would shifts in aggregate demand do anything more than modify the price-structure.

In a world in which individual variation is both important and considerable, at least as regards the micro-composition of tastes, this limitation, while being clearly recognised, should not be exaggerated. The tangency-condition, despite this limitation, has been regarded as sufficiently important to support a leading corollary in the theory of index numbers (together with the kind of reasoning that we examined in the last chapter): namely, the corollary that output should be valued at final (retail) market prices, and not at any other price-level, whenever welfare considerations are involved. Of this Professor J. R. Hicks has written as follows.

The reason why we use prices as weights when measuring the social income as an index of economic welfare is because prices give us some indication of marginal utilities, because the slope of the price-line at a point of equilibrium is the same as that of the indifference curve through that point. The particular prices chosen must always be those which will correspond most closely to relative marginal utilities; this usually means that we must take those prices which actually confront the consumer. We must take retail prices not wholesale prices, prices after tax or subsidy, not before, and so on.*

A still sharper (if ambiguous) way of putting this justification is to say that if the tangency-condition is fulfilled, equal value-increases of various commodities (when valued at consumers' prices) represent equal increases of utility.† This is valid for small marginal increases and for consumers treated severally. But this form of statement has the disadvantage of seeming to imply that it makes no difference to social welfare whether more of one commodity is produced or more of another. Such

---

* J. R. Hicks, 'The Valuation of the Social Income', in *Economica* (May, 1940), p. 113.
  † *Cf.* D. R. Hodgman, *Soviet Industrial Production 1928–1951* (Cambridge, Mass., 1954), p. 19 : "The comparability of value units rests on the implied identification of equal value units with equal amounts of consumer satisfaction."

a conclusion amounts to illicit aggregation and is inadmissible. Different persons will consume commodities in very different proportions, for a variety of reasons including differences in their incomes. A rich man may consume much wine and relatively little bread, a poor man consume them in opposite proportions; and the benefit to the latter from the last shilling spent on bread will be very much greater than to the former. It would be quite absurd to conclude from the above statement that to produce additional wine costing a shillingsworth of productive resources and additional bread costing the same amount represented equal increments of utility to the community. The fact is that if more bread were produced and less wine, there would be an effect, *ceteris paribus*, on relative prices favourable to bread-consumers, and hence to the poor; and conversely if more wine were produced and less bread.

No such fallacy of aggregation is implied in Professor Hicks's justification, which is valid on its own grounds so far as it goes, and does not need any condition *other* than the consumers' tangency-condition to support it.* Yet one has to remember that this justification remains as limited by the assumption that changes to which the measure is applied are neutral in their effects on distribution as we have seen that Pigou's measure was; and in face of this limitation some may feel inclined to question whether this justification can carry us very far.

* Professor Hodgman, however, has suggested otherwise. Starting apparently from the notion that 'equal value increases represent equal utility-increases' can be aggregated, and that this is necessary for the use of market prices as a measure, he claims that "free consumers' choice" is not enough and needs to be supplemented by what he calls "consumers' sovereignty" (by which he seems to mean fulfilment of the full Producers' Optimum Conditions as well). Believing that the latter is absent in a planned economy but is fulfilled in a "free market system", he proceeds to deny the validity of using market-price valuations as a measure of national income changes in a planned economy, and chooses a "factor cost" basis of valuation instead (*ibid.* pp. 21–2). There would seem to be a similar implication in Professor A. Bergson's *Real National Income of Soviet Russia since 1928* (Cambridge, Mass., 1961), p. 39, in his statement that "under Soviet conditions where consumers seemingly have only limited sway over resource allocation ... the proper valuation of such goods in terms of the consumers' utility standard must be a matter of opinion." And what are we to make, in this connection, of the same author's statement, in *The Economics of Soviet Planning* (New Haven and London, 1964), pp. 67–8: "Conformity to clearing levels is no longer in order, however, if the system's directors are entirely indifferent to differences in intensity of desire"? (Are we to take "no longer in order" to mean "no longer have any point"?)

It is because of the pitfalls into which interpretations of this tangency-condition can lead that we have laboured the restrictions on it to an extent that some may deem otiose or unwelcome. We shall witness these pitfalls again in the sequel.

To come, secondly, to our *Production Condition*, and to deal initially and separately with its first half. This is that methods of production are so chosen in each industry or production-unit that no increase in production can be obtained by changing the proportions in which various productive agents or resources are used in any line of production. This is a condition for choice of optimum methods of production from among feasible methods, and can be seen to be the same as that production-version of the Pareto optimum which we considered above, in chapter 2, expressed in the two-factor-two-products case as the points of tangency of production-isoquants. In the textbooks it is often expressed as the equality of the ratios of factor substitution in all industries.* It follows that so long as this ratio is different in different lines of production a mere swapping of factors between them (with no change in the total amount of the factors used) can bring about an increase in output. For example, let us suppose that in one industry, say Linen, this ratio of substitution of capital goods for labour (assumed to be expressible severally in common units in both industries) is 1:2, and in another industry, say Cotton, it is 1:3. Then a transfer of one unit of capital from Linen to Cotton will release (because it is a sufficient substitute there for) three units of labour in Cotton for transfer in the opposite direction from Cotton to Linen. In Linen these three units of labour will *more* than make up for the unit of capital lost, and hence will enable an increase in output of Linen while leaving the output of Cotton unchanged. When, but only when, the substitution-ratio is uniform in different lines of production will further gain of this kind from the swapping of factors be no longer possible.

---

* This means the ratio in which, at the margin, factors have to be substituted for one another in order to leave the product unchanged. Reflection will show that equality of this ratio in different industries is the same thing as equality of the ratios of marginal productivity of the factors; since the latter ratio is simply the inverse of the former. For example, if the marginal product of a unit of capital goods (*e.g.* a particular type of machinery) relatively to the marginal product of a unit of labour is as 2:1, then it will need *two* units of labour to replace the loss of one unit of machinery while leaving output unchanged, and conversely.

It is worth-while noting that this condition can be stated in purely product terms (in the case of Linen in terms of physical units of output of Linen and in Cotton in terms of physical units of output of Cotton). It is independent of the product values: *i.e.* in our example it can be expressed without taking account of what the market prices of Linen and Cotton may be.* Consequently it does not depend for its validity upon the prior fulfilment of the Consumers' Condition: in this sense it is a pure Production Condition, which tells us that the most is being made of existing resources (with given technical knowledge), and is worth fulfilling in its own right.

But while the form of *statement* of the condition itself is independent of product-prices, this does not mean that the methods of production to be chosen in accordance with it are independent of the relative quantities of final outputs that are produced, and hence of the pattern of demand.† That the equality itself can be stated independently of prices finds its significance in the fact that the methods chosen would also be independent of prices if (but only if) technical conditions in the various industries were uniform, in the relevant sense so as to render factor-proportions uniform when substitution-ratios were equal. In all situations other than this factor-proportions will be non-uniform; and from this it follows that (with given quantities of factors or inputs) the proportions in which they are combined in any industry will need to change appropriately with every change in output-pattern of final products.

One should also observe that to make sense of the condition as stated requires that the several productive resources or factors that are being combined must be comparable, as between different lines of production; which means that they must be measurable in terms of physical units of themselves. To assume this is realistic enough in the case of labour or of land of homogeneous quality that can be turned to a variety of productive uses; also in the case of particular inputs such as coal or oil

---

* This is presumably what Professor A. P. Lerner had in mind when he referred some time ago to equal ratios of marginal factor-productivity as being an 'objective' efficiency-criterion (*Review of Economic Studies*, 1934, vol. II, no. 1, p. 53; *cf.* the present writer's comment in the ensuing issue, Feb. 1935, p. 146). It remains true, however, that the actual result—the precise ratio at which equalisation occurs—is *not* independent of the structure of demand, and hence of income-distribution. † *Cf.* above, p. 19.

or electrical energy, or a special metal or flour or cotton or wool fibre. It is much less realistic (if realistic at all) in the case of most capital equipment, which is apt to be *sui generis* in each industry. To reduce various and heterogeneous capital goods to a common *genus* labelled 'Capital' (as the marginal productivity theory has traditionally done) involves the introduction of *values* (of the diverse capital goods), including product-prices generally on which *inter alia* the prices of capital goods themselves depend. (This is of course the now well-known problem of the measurement of capital, with its attendant allegation of circular reasoning against marginal productivity as a general theory). For our maximising condition to be *relevant* to actual problems, there must exist alternative ways of producing the same product: *i.e.* alternative combinations of inputs, rendering these inputs *substitutes* for one another. In any one industry, in any given technical situation, the alternatives may be limited, at any rate as regards capital equipment and labour and especially as regards raw material inputs.* Although a limited amount of variation may be possible, it will be far from continuous variation along a smooth substitution-curve, as textbooks like to depict.

Sometimes one finds this condition stated differently in terms of cost: in the form that the method of production, or combination of inputs, is (or should be) chosen that results in a given output being produced at minimum cost. This can be shown to be an equivalent statement. But it has the disadvantage for our present purpose that, in order to give a meaning to 'least cost', the introduction of factor-prices is necessary: moreover, the prior assumption of given factor-prices where these are not only (in part) derived from product-prices, but also mutually determined by the latter in combination with the conditions of supply of factors and with the choice of factor-combinations itself. Since, however, to yield a particular solution—a set of methods of production in terms of which the equalisation of substitution-ratios takes place—the postulation of final product-quantities (and hence by implication prices) is necessary, this difficulty associated with the least-cost form of statement may possibly be regarded as more apparent than real.

---

* A classic example of fixed coefficients is the amount of iron ore and coal needed (with given technique) to produce a ton of pig-iron.

Expression in terms of least cost (and hence of input-prices) might seem to be the only way of formulating a condition for choosing methods of production if all inputs for a given product were entirely specific, in the sense of having no productive use elsewhere (like highly specialised labour or machine-tools, iron ore or bauxite or raw cotton), while at the same time there was some scope for variation in the relative quantities of these inputs that were used. Here there are two possibilities. First, it is possible that among the inputs used in the production of these inputs there may be resources that are used in other lines of production as well as in this one; in which case we can formulate our condition about equal substitution-ratios in terms of them, without bringing in prices (whether of final products or of the inputs or factors themselves). Secondly, and alternatively, it is possible that no inputs at any stage of the vertical production-process whereby the final product is turned out have any use in other lines of production (concerned with other final products). Then, if at any stage the inputs are available only in given quantities,* their availability will determine the proportions in which they are combined (although it is possible that no feasible combination exists which employs all of them to the full). If, however, they can be produced in any quantity (without using any non-specific inputs), then so far as non-human factors are concerned the choice of input-combinations *per se* is devoid of economic significance, since to use more of any input involves no social cost. In so far as human labour (even though specialised and specific to the industry) is involved as a factor of production, then there will be one set of methods, presumably, in the vertical chain of productive processes which minimises the quantity of labour needed to produce a given quantity of final product. Since minimising human toil is socially desirable, this will be the socially optimum set of methods to be used. Again our condition can be expressed without introducing prices.

The second half of our Production Condition, *per contra*, can only be expressed in values, and essentially depends on the postula-

---

* *I.e.* either they are *not* what we shall later call 'produced inputs' (below, chapter 8), or, if they are, they are not reproducible within the relevant time-horizon of the decisions that are in question.

tion either of given product-prices or of a given structure of demand (by which product prices are assumed to be determined in conjunction with variations in supply). It is concerned, no longer with the proportions in which productive factors are combined in various industries, but with the total amount of them in any given industry—the way in which a given quantity of any factor in existence is allocated between industries. For this reason the problem involved is often spoken of, as the allocation problem. It is quite possible that the proportions in which productive resources are combined may be optimal (in the sense of the first half of our Production Condition), but at the same time there may be, in some sense, 'too many' resources of all kinds in industry A and 'too few' of them in industry B. In Professor Lerner's words, "there is not an optimum division of resources among different *products*".*

Here we come back to Pigou's corollary of equalising the net product of resources at the margin of all uses. This can be applied severally to each input or ultimate factor of production that is transferable and has various economic uses; and if it applies to each of them severally, it must apply also to any 'dose' of combined factors (as Pigou called it). If any factor is producing more in one use than elsewhere, then it is obvious that there is a gain to be made in the total situation by transferring some factors from the margin of industries where their productivity is relatively low and adding them to the margin of industries where their productivity is greater. Only when, in consequence of such transfers, productivity at the margin is equalised, will there no longer be any advantage obtainable from such transfers; and for this reason the position in question can be regarded as optimum. In this context producing more or less means more or less in *value*; and since comparison of productivity is in terms of qualitatively different products, it can be interpreted in no other way. To make sense of this proposition the prices of final products (though not necessarily factor-prices) have to be immediately introduced.

It follows that this half of the Production Condition is not a Pareto-optimum in the sense in which our former half was. In so far as it defines a unique production-pattern, it does so by

---

* A. P. Lerner, *The Economics of Control: Principles of Welfare Economics* (New York, 1944), p. 122.

reference to a specific pattern of demand (*via* the influence of
the latter on prices), and hence is relative to a certain distribution of income, with the 'weighting' or relative 'pull'
given by this distribution to individual demands in composing
the aggregate demand of the market. It is commonly held to
derive its significance as an optimum from the Consumers'
Condition (tangency of indifference-curves to price-line),
and accordingly to presuppose fulfilment of the latter (which
we have seen to be true). But we have also seen that the consumers' tangency-condition can be fulfilled at *any* set of prices,
and its fulfilment by no means implies that the resulting pattern
of aggregate demand is independent of income-distribution.
The welfare-significance of such an equilibrium-position, if it is
truly distribution-relative, would seem too dubious to justify
the name of 'optimum'.

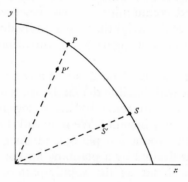

The different character of the qualitatively distinct halves of
the Production Condition can be illustrated in terms of the now-
familiar Production-Possibility Curve: a curve which in a
simplified two-commodity case depicts the possible (and
maximum) combinations of the commodities that are producible with given productive resources (and given technical
knowledge).* Thus any point P on the curve represents the

* This curve will be concave in shape to the extent that the technical situations
of the two industries differ in the sense of rendering factor-combinations different
when substitution-ratios are equalised. When they are sufficiently uniform to
render factor-combinations uniform the curve will become a straight line. As one
extends the number of products beyond two, the curve will, of course, become a
surface or plane in multi-dimensional space.

maximum quantity of commodity x that can be produced consistently with the production of a given quantity of commodity y, and conversely. The first half of our Production Condition will simply provide a guarantee of being *on* the curve, or production-frontier, not somewhere inside it—of getting the most production from existing inputs irrespective of the output-combination. The point P can thus be said to be superior to points *inside* the curve to the south-west of it because at P there is more of *both* commodities, x and y, than at these other points. But the second half of our Production Condition (assuming fulfilment of the first half) defines a precise position on the curve—whether at P or S or at some other point that happens to be consistent with given relative prices (and hence presumably with given demand-conditions). Diagrammatically this position can be defined as the point of tangency between the Production-Possibility Curve and one of a set of so-called community-indifference-curves (these composed by supposedly weighting each individual set with its appropriate income and aggregating these individual sets so weighted).

What is commonly overlooked is that any point on the curve that is consistent with feasible demand-variations can be made optimal in the present sense by arranging the appropriate distribution of money income* We may call these various output-combinations production plans, and imagine them to be alternative plans drafted by a planning authority in a socialist economy. Then so far as the supply-pattern of consumers' goods is concerned, each plan can be regarded as representing a different distribution of real income between the individuals (with differing tastes and preferences and money incomes) who compose the community. To choose a certain plan is *ipso facto* to choose a certain distribution, and no one production plan is

* If individual tastes and preferences were uniform, inequality of money income would cause differences in relative demands to the extent of differences in the income-elasticity of demand for different commodities. But to the extent that individual tastes diverge, any one distribution of income will yield a different aggregate demand-pattern from others by giving a different weighting to some individual preferences compared with others : for example, the demand for beer will be increased compared with that for soft drinks or for tea and cocoa if the distribution of income is shifted in favour of beer-preferers, or the demand for classical music compared with that for pop-music if distribution is shifted in favour of groups with a taste for the former.

more optimal than another independently of a postulate about optimum distribution.*

Dr Mishan seems to be almost alone among economists in appreciating, or at least in emphasising, this point; and one can agree wholeheartedly with his conclusion that "for each point on the production-possibility curve, representing as it does a combination of goods, there corresponds a unique distribution of those goods which invests it with the properties of an optimum and therefore a unique community-indifference-curve ... Far from an optimum allocation of resources representing some kind of ideal output separable from and independent of inter-personal comparisons of welfare, a particular output retains its optimum characteristics only in so far as we commit ourselves to the particular welfare-distribution uniquely associated with it."† From this he concludes that what he terms "top-level optima", which are equivalent to those defined by the second half of our Production Condition, are "in general no improvement actual or potential as compared with a non-optimum position". To this Dr Mishan has elsewhere added for good measure that "a bias in favour of the *status quo* enters whenever one aims to bring the economy closer to an optimum using the existing set of prices, since this set of prices itself emerges from the existing distribution. Unless we have special reasons to be satisfied with the existing distribution of income the optimal position corresponding to the existing set of prices has no more claim on our attention than any other 'efficiently produced' collection of goods. For each of these...could be made optimal by some appropriate distribution of income."‡

Thus there is no reason to conclude that point P on the curve in our diagram is more optimal than S, even though the second half of our Production Condition happens to be fulfilled at P and not at S. Nor can we conclude in the converse case that S is more optimal than P and that a movement towards S is desirable. For the reason we have mentioned, both P and S can

* Cf. I. M. D. Little, *A Critique of Welfare Economics* (Oxford, 1950), p. 182: "The question of income distribution is logically prior to the question of the ideal output."

† In *Economica*, 1957, pp. 335–6. Cf. also Dr Graaff (*Theoretical Welfare Economics*, p. 70) on positions on the so-called "welfare frontier" being "a matter of ethics not of competition".

‡ E. J. Mishan, *The Costs of Economic Growth* (London, 1967), p. 49.

be treated as superior respectively to P' and S' to the south-west of them;* but this does not justify the statement that S is superior to P' because the former is on the curve and the latter is not, or alternatively that P is superior to S'.† It is quite possible to have these inequalities:

$$S' < S \quad and \quad P < S$$

$$or \quad P' < P \quad and \quad S < P$$

* Strictly speaking perhaps this should be: to the south-west and on the line joining P and S respectively to the origin.

† Yet this seems to be what Dorfman, Samuelson, Solow in their *Linear Programming and Economic Analysis* (New York, 1958, pp. 410–12) are claiming when they say that a marriage of the 'efficiency condition' (the first half of our Production Condition) with a Paretian welfare-condition (our Consumers' Condition) —of which they speak as "the production and consumption configuration" being "Pareto-optimal" (p. 410)—"provides the fundamental welfare argument against monopoly, against indirect taxation and against tariffs", with the implication that a position reached under the latter is necessarily inferior to any competitive position. (Of this they also speak boldly as a "fundamental theorem" which "provides the backbone of welfare economics").

What their argument seems to amount to is that unless relative prices of producers' goods as inputs are suitably aligned with the prices confronting consumers, methods of production appropriate to producing the output-assortment or production-plan in question will not be adopted. ('Suitably' here being definable as such an alignment of prices as will make prices equal or proportional to marginal costs, thus equalising marginal value-products.) In this sense the non-competitive point is not a Pareto-optimum—in the sense that there is *some* point P superior to P', and analogously for S'. But this is a matter of non-fulfilment of the first half of our Production Condition. It does not follow from the fulfilment of the Consumers' Condition and does *not* imply that a competitive position is always superior to any other.

As we shall see below (pp. 70–1), the fallacy of supposing that when the consumers' tangency-condition is fulfilled a divergence of the ratio of prices to consumers from the ratio of marginal costs implies a potential gain of utility from a shift of output (and hence that equality of these ratios must *ipso facto* define a welfare-optimum) consists in ignoring the real-income-effect of any output-change (with its accompanying price-change)—an income-effect that will raise the marginal utility of income to those adversely affected by the change (and conversely lower it for those who benefit).

Putting the same point differently: if what is meant by the above "theorem" is that when price-ratios are unequal to marginal cost ratios (*e.g.* under monopoly) there always exists *some* point that is (potentially) superior to it, then this is *not* the same as the proposition that competition will result in such a superior point being reached, since the latter would require a certain distribution of money income (with its appropriate pattern of demand). To say that the latter proposition is implicit in the theorem about "every Pareto-optimum being a competitive equilibrium" is hard to distinguish from verbal jugglery.

Cf. E. J. Mishan in 'A Survey of Welfare Economics 1939–59', in *The Economic Journal* (June, 1960), p. 210, as to why "perfect competition is neither a necessary nor a sufficient condition" for optimum allocation.

and from this to be able to conclude nothing about the comparative magnitudes of S' and P or P' and S. We could only do so if the inequalities were of this kind :

$$S' < S < P.$$

But then we should be basing the statement that $S < P$ on some postulate about income-distribution and *not* on the fulfilment of the second-half of our Production Condition at P and its non-fulfilment at S. Indeed the statement could be true *despite* the fulfilment of the latter condition at S and not at P.

The conclusion follows of some importance to the sequel—and we shall return to it—that if one finds in a certain planned economy that marginal net products are not equalised in various lines of production of consumers' goods, this does not necessarily mean that the production-plan is not optimal and consumers' welfare is being ignored, as welfare-economists so commonly* and perversely assume. It may mean merely that attempts are being made to improve income-distribution through the price-system instead of (or perhaps as well as) through the structure of money-incomes. (This choice of method for improving distribution may be good or bad; but we have no right to assume that it is always bad, and we shall see later that there may often be good reason for it and that some kinds of inequality may be more easily corrected through prices than through money-incomes.)

A warning, however, is perhaps timely against concluding from what has been said that the second half of our Production Condition is totally devoid of sense and to be ignored. Complete nihilism in this matter of relating the productivities of resources in alternative uses (or of aligning prices with costs—which comes to the same thing) would be as mistaken as is the uncritical admiration of it as defining a unique optimum that welfare economists have been prone to affect. It is not only a matter of

* *Cf.* Professor A. Bergson, *Economics of Soviet Planning*, chapter 8 *passim*, especially the references to failure to conform to "marginal cost pricing". There may or may not be something wrong with the retail price pattern and/or the price-pattern of producers' goods in the U.S.S.R.; but the question cannot be decided *a priori* in terms of some proportionality (or equality) of price to marginal cost rule. To give another example: even Professor Wiles's well-known reference to hair-brushes and toothbrushes (which we shall cite below) takes it for granted that the proportions between them will be "more nearly right in a capitalist economy" than in a socialist (*Oxford Economic Papers*, Oct. 1953, pp. 315–16).

the consumption-pattern as *between* individuals, but also of the consumption pattern of each separate individual; and in this sense the problem of shifts in consumption has two aspects or dimensions, which in actuality are not separable but neither of which must be lost from sight. The commonsense kernel of the idea of aligning prices with costs is that, if there is a shift in consumers' preferences in a particular direction, independently of any shift of income-distribution, it is more desirable (from the standpoint of consumers' welfare) that this should be met by corresponding shift in the production-plan rather than by a simple adjustment of prices—although both reactions are consistent with a continued fulfilment of the Consumers' Condition. Let us suppose that there has been an aggregate shift in taste for beer as compared with soft drinks, either because beer-drinkers have become more confirmed in their habits or because more people have acquired the habit. Provided that the shift in taste is 'rational' (in a sense to be discussed later), and is not the product of intensive 'depth-approach' propaganda by the brewing interest, it seems reasonable that more beer should be supplied and less soft drinks.* The decision to make this shift in the production-plan would properly be subject to a consideration of whether beer-drinkers as a social group were already too much favoured under the prevailing price- and income-structure or would be too much favoured if their whims were further catered for. But in the absence of any such counterbalancing reason, it is scarcely to be doubted that in due course the production-shift should be made—to the extent of balancing (at the margin) additional utility-benefit with additional social cost. Another example would be where the demand for household durables and motor cars had risen because skill-differentials had widened in favour of higher earning groups. To increase the output of the things which these higher earners were now more capable of demanding would be (with given re-

---

* An aggregate *shift* of this kind is to be distinguished from a mere shift in consumers' tastes in the direction of less uniformity and more divergence. If, for example, beer-drinkers became more attached to this preference while at the same time soft-drinkers on their side became even more confirmed in their relative contempt for beer, neither a production-change nor a price-change would be called for : what would happen would be, in effect, more 'swapping' of more-preferred and less-preferred beverages between the two groups, which in view of the two-sided shift of preferences would take place at existing prices.

sources and techniques) at the expense of the output of other things consumed by lower-earning groups. This might well give cause for hesitation about an appropriate adjustment of the production-plan. Yet if the widening of skill-differentials was in some sense 'right' and not fortuitous, failure to do so would frustrate* the purpose of the new wage- and salary-scale and contradict its *rationale*. Income-policy can be as little divorced from price-policy as can price-policy from income-policy.

One could put the matter more generally in this way by supposing that in a socialist economy the government and/or the planning commission had drawn up a general production plan which it judged to be about 'right' so far as distribution between main social groups and strata and so far as incentive-needs were concerned. It then found that certain lines of consumers' goods went into short supply, so that to avoid queues, etc., the prices of these deficit lines had to be raised. At the same time other lines piled up on the shelves of retail establishments and could only find buyers at knock-down prices. Obviously there would be strong reason for the planners adjusting their initial plan in the direction of producing more of the former lines and less of the latter. Even so, they might be reluctant to do so automatically and without reflection, in case some of the subsequent output-shifts affected its judgement about the rightness of the overall production-pattern from the standpoint of distribution.

Yet another way of putting the point in general form would be to say that, when faced with two alternative ways of influencing real income-distribution, changing the structure of prices and changing the structure of money-incomes, policy-makers need always to remember that there is a possible disadvantage attaching to the former method (failing to give consumers' preferences sufficient influence on output) that is absent from the latter.

We have to add the consideration, noted above, that if choice of methods of production that are optimal in relation to any given production-pattern is dependent on an 'appropriate' relationship between prices of final output and of inputs, this would be an additional reason for observing the second half of our Production Condition. But we have seen that choice of

---

* It would do so at any rate apart from the existence of a 'money illusion'.

efficient methods of production could be done (in theory at least) in purely physical terms—by shifting the allocation-pattern of productive factors until their substitution-ratios (expressed in each line of production in terms of a particular product) were equalised. This might be a difficult jig-saw puzzle to do—easy enough, perhaps, if done in terms of a few broadly-defined groups of factors, but more difficult to work out in more detail, broken down into categories that admit of measurement in homogenous physical units. To the extent that the problem *can* be handled in terms of physical allocation, the choice of efficient methods of production can be separated from the pattern of final retail prices. Even if prices are used in the choice of productive methods, what is relevant is the relation of prices paid to producing units to the prices of inputs ; and this relation may be such as to secure a choice of inputs that is most efficient for the output-pattern *actually being produced*, whether or not money incomes and demand are such as to bring the ratio of retail prices into line.

The practical upshot seems to be that, while it is *simpliste*, even absurd, to insist on an equalising of marginal products as a necessary condition of maximum welfare, any pronounced *in*equality in factor productivities should be a *prima facie* ground for concern. If no adverse distribution-effects seem likely, then a change of production-plan in the direction of greater equalisation seems called for. But this will be a matter of judging particular cases, not of *a priori* deduction from a general rule: of estimating probabilities about the likely direction of improvement (as we have seen was Pigou's primary concern), not of magisterial pronouncement about a unique and precisely defined optimum. None of the answers can be simply read-off from market data, even if such data may be relevant to an answer. Still less can the answer be left for the market to determine 'automatically'.*

To this one may add the consideration, stressed by Professor Baumol, that consumers' preferences are not always character-

* Some welfare-economists (mostly transatlantic) have sought to claim, whether innocently or with guile, that the verdict of the market has a virtue in itself as the expression of 'consumers' voting'. This is called a value judgement in favour of 'consumers' sovereignty', from which all else follows. But how can one attach much value to a voting-procedure in which votes are allotted with a pronounced bias or by a purely random process?

ised by a high order of precision in their definition. As Professor Baumol has said, "the desires of the individual are often nebulous", with the result that "rather a considerable range of possible output combinations . . . may be regarded for practical purposes as equally preferable". It follows that "only extreme deviations from the ideal output are likely to be of any substantial importance".* This is highly relevant to the degree of 'tolerance' that we allow in the application of any optimising rule.

Perhaps it would make for more precision if one could be sure that distribution of income was already ideal from a welfare-standpoint, or at least close to it? Could not equalising marginal products then be enthroned as a ruling principle, and with it 'market autonomism'? One can at least concede that the problem would be much simplified and uncertainty as to the correct answer in a particular case would be less. But how can one be sure both that distribution is ideal and that it will remain ideal in face of the output-shifts that are contemplated? If one cannot be sure, uncertainty and imprecision will remain, so long as distribution-shifts matter, and one cannot expect answers to be read off from a slide-rule. Here we are back at the kind of difficulty that we met at the end of chapter 2. First, what does it *mean* to be sure that distribution is ideal? Does one make one's judgement on the basis of the structure of *money* income? Then, unless consumers' tastes and consumption-patterns are uniform, this will have a different *real* meaning for every price-structure, since a change of relative prices will affect different consumers differently.† Does it mean that one has judged it to be ideal all things considered (*e.g.* on the basis of actual data about consumption) in an initial and existing situation in which the equality of marginal products may not prevail? If so, how is one to be sure that the situation will remain ideal when one has shifted prices and outputs so as to

---

* W. J. Baumol, *Welfare Economics and the Theory of the State* (London, 1952), p. 61.

† If one were entitled to assume the government to be in possession of full knowledge of the preferences and tastes (or the indifference maps) of all consumers, one could suppose a government capable *in theory* of knowing what distribution of money-income would yield the ideal distribution of real income at relative prices equal to relative costs. But this is, surely, about the last thing one is entitled to assume.

apply the equalising rule (*i.e.* moved to *another* position on the Production-Possibility Curve)? If it is unlikely to continue to be so, there may be little or no point in applying the equalising rule and moving. Does it mean that by some process of intuition one has guessed the situation to which one *will* move by applying the equalising rule to be ideal when one has reached it? Of this one can scarcely be certain until one has actually experienced it; and if the application of the equalising rule *per se* does prove sufficient to achieve the desired result, this will be something of a fluke. Perhaps movement towards an ideal position can be imagined to occur as a process of successive approximations in which both equalising price- and output-changes and money-income changes play a part (an answer that would by no means imply an automatic application of an 'efficiency condition'). Here one meets a second kind of difficulty of which more will be said in a later chapter: that there may be constraints upon the use of shifts in money-income as offset to the distribution-effects of changes in the pattern of output and prices. Restriction, for example, upon changes in money income might well be imposed by incentive-reasons;* and to this extent it might prove desirable to employ an incomes-policy that diverged from the ideal in combination with a price-policy other than one that brought relative costs and prices into alignment. There would remain the more general difficulty (partly of definition, partly of identification) as to how sure one could ever be that any complex situation was exactly right rather than only approximately right. To plump for absolute equality of money incomes (as Professor Lerner did in his *Economics of Control*)† would not be to treat all individuals

---

* It has to be remembered that in a growing economy (as we shall see later), one may have to relate income-differentials to desired *rates of change* (*e.g.* of skilled labour and trained personnel), and that to this extent they may have to diverge appreciably at any one time from what would suffice, in a static situation, to *maintain* existing numbers in various grades and occupations: *e.g.* differentials corresponding to Adam Smith's principle of 'equal net advantages'. It follows that the former type of differential has to be treated as belonging to incentives geared to (and necessitated by) growth and change, and distinguished from such as may be fitted into optimising conditions about relating individual incomes (and hence enjoyment of utilities) to disutilities involved in work.

† Pp. 31–2. Professor Lerner suggests that one can "identify" money income-distribution with real income-distribution on the assumption that there is "an optimal allocation of goods". It is possible that he may mean "identify" in a purely operational sense (that in any given situation one could derive the latter

equally if consumers' tastes varied and hence their consumption (since, as we have seen, a consumer's utility at the margin of his spending would be dependent on the prices of the commodities which bulked largely in his consumption-pattern). If one sought to adjust this by appropriate price-shifts, one would be applying a different criterion for price-policy (and a different production-plan) from the equalising-marginal-products criterion.* Absolute equality would also fail to treat individuals equally if the work done by them differed appreciably (and hence the disutility incurred by them).† Can there be serious doubt that one would be left, not with a single position, but with a whole range or area of positions of roughly equal probability of being 'the best': with the welfare optimum, in other words, constituting a fairly broad plateau rather than a sharp peak or summit? So long as one was somewhere on the plateau, the precise position on it would not seriously matter. Marked inequalities, as regards the marginal rule, would call for correction, but rigid and precise equalisation as a policy-rule would be out of place. Unimportant though the distinction may appear at first sight when abstractly stated, it can have very considerable significance in the actual conduct of policy, in the context of which we shall return to it.

To show that in emphasising this distinction between the two halves of our Production Condition we have not been tilting at windmills, we may cite the definition of 'economic efficiency' afforded by Professor T. Scitovsky in his well-known textbook entitled *Welfare and Competition*. Professor Scitovsky starts by defining this in terms of a Paretian optimum: "We shall say that any change of economic policy or institutions capable of making some people better off without making anyone worse off

---

from the former by means of this assumption). If, however, he is using "identify" in a more general sense than this, such as would deny what is said above in our text, the argument seems to be circular.

* If, on the other hand, one tried to adjust money-incomes so as to 'equalise the marginal utility of incomes' of individuals, one would have to estimate the degree of differences in tastes in their effect (with a given price-structure) upon consumption-patterns and hence upon utility enjoyed at the margin of spending (together with some allowances for difference of need?) and to match these different effects with compensating income-differences. Can one conceive this being done in practice other than quite roughly and approximately?

† See further below, pp. 229–30.

is a change that improves economic efficiency."* As such this
is an impeccable definition. It is equivalent to defining 'efficiency' as being on the Edgeworthian 'contract-curve', or in
production-terms on the 'line of efficiency loci'.† But having
done so he immediately extends it to include "an economically
efficient distribution of consumers' goods", in the sense of "one
that distributes a given quantity of goods in best conformity
with consumers' preferences", which he later on defines as
requiring the ratio of market prices to "equal the ratio of
marginal costs for every pair of products".‡ This is to include
in his definition of efficiency the *second* half of our so-called
Production Condition, and to make efficiency refer to a
particular *point* on a 'Production-Possibility Curve', not merely
to being somewhere *on* this curve or 'frontier'. This is far from
an untypical example. Indeed this kind of treatment is extraordinarily common, especially in the writings of American
economists : so common that it may seem invidious to single out
Professor Scitovsky's estimable textbook for comment. What
makes it surprising in this case is that the author is at the same
time most emphatic about the need to take account of what he
calls "equity" (affecting income-distribution) as well as
"efficiency" and is at pains to warn his readers that an
efficient point may be far from ideal from a welfare standpoint.
(The very separation in this way of "equity" and "efficiency"
may suggest that distribution is not properly the province of the
economist ; but we may let that pass.) Yet he includes under
his 'positive' and 'objective' criterion of efficiency something
that cannot be separated from considerations of income-
distribution. What has gone wrong? Some might feel inclined
to regard this as due to carelessness or (with some other authors)

---

* *Welfare and Competitition : The Economics of a Fully Employed Economy* (New York
and London, 1952), p. 55.

† See above, p. 19.

‡ Scitovsky, *op. cit.*, pp. 55, 352. This marginal cost condition he states as a
necessary condition for "different products to be produced in the proportions
that best conform to society's preferences". If the sentence, "distributes . . . in best
conformity with society's preferences" is taken by itself, it is of course unimpeachable ; but it remains an implicit definition, of little or no operational significance (what are "society's preferences" in the abstract, independently of a
particular distribution?). If it is taken, however, in conjunction with the sequel, it
has an operational meaning which can be no other than the welfare significance of
so adjusting production and supply as to bring these two ratios to equality (a
condition which is, of course, distribution-relative).

as intellectual sleight-of-hand. Actually the point involved is a more subtle one than at first would appear.

What Professor Scitovsky evidently has in mind is that when his condition (equality of ratios of market prices to marginal costs) is not fulfilled, there is some conceivable arrangement (within the constraint of the given conditions of the situation) that would represent an improvement in the Paretian sense that the satisfaction accruing to some consumers (at least) can be increased without detriment to others. In *this* sense a position where his condition remains unfulfilled cannot be a full Paretian optimum: there remains *some* attainable position that would be better. What is *wrong* is to conclude from this that the pattern of money-income-distribution must be taken as the 'given' and that any adaptation of the production-pattern to it must yield an improvement in consumers' welfare (in which conclusion all the fallacious corollaries about the optimum character of competition are implied). This conclusion can only *appear* to follow from what we referred to above as an illicit aggregation of the Consumers' Condition (applying to individual consumers severally),* or, what comes to much the same thing, from an illegitimate use of a community-indifference-curve.† What makes it obscurantist is the implied corollary that relative outputs should be so adjusted as to equalise price-ratios and cost-ratios, even when to do so would have seriously adverse effects on distribution—advice parading

* Is not Professor Scitovsky's argument, *op. cit.* pp. 161–3, where he generalises an argument applied to a single individual consumer to all consumers, guilty of what we have termed illicit aggregation? (True, the passage starts by cautiously describing the result as "the output most highly valued by the consuming public", but very soon, on the next page, this becomes identified with what is "socially most desirable".)

† The argument by which Dorfman, Samuelson and Solow (*Linear Programming and Economic Analysis*, pp. 411, 414) seek to justify their contention that because "every competitive equilibrium is a Pareto optimum" every non-competitive-equilibrium—where price-ratios diverge from ratios of marginal cost—must be inferior thereto, is a compensation-argument (from which it would seem to follow that any move to a competitive equilibrium must be an improvement). But we shall see in a subsequent chapter that compensation arguments can be treacherous: not only may they involve themselves in contradiction when income-distribution changes, but they speak at most in terms of *potential* welfare and tell us nothing about change in *actual* welfare unless compensation is actually paid. (True, the *form* of their argument applies to a typical consumer, treated individually; but to be valid their argument must apply to the *group*, and hence to compensation *between* individuals.)

in the guise of an 'objective' efficiency-criterion. The gain from shifts in the consumption-patterns of individual consumers may be more than offset by the consequential shift in real-income-distribution, due to the reduction of output (and rise in price) of things that bulk large in the consumption of some people (*e.g.* the poor). In such a case it would be more reasonable, of course, to seek improvement by taking the production-pattern of consumers' goods as the 'given' and adapting money-income-distribution (if this be practicable) thereto, or by some mutual adaptation of each to the other. This is quite obscured by laying the emphasis on the "distribution of consumers' goods" (*i.e.* the production-pattern, or production-plan) as what is efficient or inefficient.

If it is not labouring unduly what should by now be obvious, a simplified example should serve to clinch the matter. Let us again take the homely two-commodity case of bread and wine, where wine is largely consumed by the rich and bread is largely consumed by the poor. Suppose that, in face of the prevailing distribution of money-income between rich and poor, 'too much' bread is being produced compared with wine for the ideal (or 'efficient') price-cost relationship to prevail, since to dispose of the available supply bread-prices have to be lowered and equivalently wine-prices to be raised (because of the shortage of wine relatively to the money-demand of the rich). As a result of this the poor would clearly be better off and the rich less well-off than an initial look at the distribution of money-income would suggest. In conscious pursuit of 'economic efficiency' (or under the 'beneficent' influence of competitive market-forces) this initial position is then rectified by transferring resources from producing bread to producing wine, with a consequential shift in relative prices (in face of an unchanged structure of demand). If all persons consumed bread and wine in roughly similar proportions, all would be compensated for the bread they gave up by the additional wine they were now able to obtain—and some, indeed, if not all, could be better off.*

---

* Since the slope of the production-transformation (or production-possibility) curve over the relevant range is such that the cost (marginal) of obtaining more wine when measured in terms of the bread given up in order to obtain it is *less* than the bread-equivalent of the additional wine in terms of utility, as measured by the price-line (and hence by individual indifference-curves tangential thereto when the Consumers' Condition is fulfilled).

But in fact the poor whose consumption is predominantly of bread will suffer an adverse 'real-income effect' from the rise in their cost of living: an adverse effect which may considerably outweigh any benefit to the rich from the extra wine they are now enabled to enjoy.*

A common form in which the Production Condition is stated, and the two parts into which we have separated it are combined, is in terms of the proportionality (or in stricter form, equality) of the marginal products of various factors with their prices. Thus in the simplified two-factor case we have this overall condition:

$$\frac{\text{marginal product of factor } X}{\text{marginal product of factor } Y} = \frac{\text{price of } X}{\text{price of } Y}$$

(where X could stand, *e.g.*, for labour and Y could stand for land). It will be clear that fulfilment of the first half of our Production Condition is implicit in equality of ratios, since if the ratio of marginal products (and hence its inverse, the ratio of factor-substitution) is in each and every industry made equal to the ratio of factor-prices, they must be equal to one another. Here one has to introduce factor-prices as well as product-prices, and to assume that the former have been 'appropriately' determined in relation to the latter. But in order to make things equal to one another, it is not necessary to make them equal in the first place to something else. (Whether for practical purposes this latter may be a convenient way of achieving one's object is another question.) An advantage of stating the condition in the way we have hitherto done is that this has not explicitly introduced factor-prices, and has accordingly served to indicate how far one can go (in principle, at least) without assuming that factors are appropriately priced in the general

---

* In the technical jargon, the rise in price of bread will shift the poor onto a lower indifference-curve than they were before: a move calculated to swamp the compensating effect of any shift *along* a given curve in consequence of the price-change, and one that is capable of resulting in less of *both* bread *and* wine being consumed by the poor than previously. In Pigouvian language, the loss represented by the sharp rise in the marginal utility of income to the poor may outweigh the extra consumption of the rich measured in terms of the *lower* marginal utility of income of additional income to them.

pricing-process (whether by an actual market-process or as the 'dual' of a set of linear programming solutions).

Since, when one is concerned with comparing marginal products of a productive factor in different industries, the qualitatively different products have to be compared in terms of their prices, and since the marginal product of a factor is the inverse of the marginal cost of the product in question in terms of that factor,* it follows that the above condition can be stated in terms of the equality of the ratios of prices of products to the ratios of their marginal costs, thus:

$$\frac{\text{price of a unit of product } A}{\text{price of a unit of product } B} = \frac{\text{marginal cost of a unit of } A}{\text{marginal cost of a unit of } B}.$$

Again, one has to assume that factor-prices are given *as well* as product-prices to endow this statement with any meaning, since the cost of producing a unit of B is arrived at by summing up the factors required as inputs to produce the output in question.

Combining the above condition with our Consumers' Condition (and remembering that the latter can be stated in the form of the equality of the ratio of marginal utilities to the ratio of prices), the so-called 'General Optimum' is summed-up in the global condition:

$$\frac{\text{marginal utility of product } A}{\text{marginal utility of product } B} = \frac{\text{price of a unit of } A}{\text{price of a unit of } B}$$

$$= \frac{\text{marginal cost of } A}{\text{marginal cost of } B}.$$

* If, say, a unit of labour can produce x yards of cotton cloth, then the cost in labour of producing a yard of cotton cloth is $1/x$ units of labour; and similarly with linen, if a unit of labour produces y yards of linen, its cost per yard will be $1/y$ units of labour.

Further, it is obvious that if the value-productivity of labour is to be equal in terms of cotton cloth and linen (in each case a yard being multiplied by its price), the *prices* per yard of the two must be directly proportional to cost in labour, and hence *inversely* proportional to the physical productivity of labour. (Similar reasoning can be applied to any other factor; and, if the ratio, at the margin, of products per unit of the factors is equalised, to the combined 'dose' of factor-inputs and to cost in terms of this.)

Combining the above two considerations, it is evident that marginal costs (since they are the inverse of the net products of factors) must be directly proportional to product-prices if net products of factors are to be equalised (since the latter are inversely proportional to prices).

This is sometimes spoken of as the equality of the consumers' marginal rate of substitution between A and B and the marginal rate of transformation of A and B in production. (On the diagram it becomes the point of tangency of two curves depicting rates of substitution and of transformation.) This equality, it has been held, defines a position where it is impossible to obtain (in existing conditions) more of commodity B without sacrificing (in order to release resources for the production of more B) an amount of A of equivalent utility to that of the additional B to be obtained—and conversely. Thus the position once reached cannot be improved upon. (From what has already been said it should be obvious that this proposition is a consummate example of illicit aggregation.)

What one may, perhaps, call 'purist' writers have maintained, however, that equality of ratios, or simple proportionality between costs and prices, is not enough, and that for a complete all-round optimum one must have equality in each individual case. Thus the price of A must *equal* the marginal cost of a unit of A, and similarly for the price and cost of B. It follows that, correspondingly, the marginal product of each factor must be *equal* to the price of that factor. In this light our own earlier statement of the second half of the Production Condition would be regarded as inadequate. We shall refer to these two forms of stating the Production Condition as the Proportionality and the Equality Versions, or the Lenient Version and the Strict.

Again the commonsense of the issue in dispute can be expressed quite shortly. If the problem under consideration is how to make the best use of an existing and *given* quantity of (ultimate) productive resources, the Lenient Version is manifestly sufficient. All that one is concerned with is the pattern of their allocation, and hence at most with their *comparative* productivities. Since a proportionality condition as stated above is sufficient to define such a comparative relationship, this is as far as one needs to go.

Those insisting on the Strict Version, however, have wished to treat the supply of productive factors (at least some of them) as being variable and in their variation being governed by the maximising principle. For this purpose proportionality is not enough, and equality is insisted on (in the overall condition equality between marginal utility and marginal cost in the case of each product and equivalent equalities in the constitutent conditions). Alternatively it could be said that, while proportionality may suffice when it is a matter of allocating impersonal factors, it cannot suffice in the case of the human factor the use of which involves a human cost in the shape of *dis*utility of work. If, for example, the supply of labour is in question and is treated as a variable, equality between the marginal disutility of extra work and its wage (and hence with marginal utility of the additional product of that work to consumers, if the wage is equated with net product and the consumers' tangency-condition is fulfilled) could not unreasonably be insisted upon as essential to any *welfare* optimum embracing both consumption and human productive activity. Similarly with the labour supplied to each industry or occupation, in so far as disutility associated with work in various occupations differs. Regarding changes in the supply of capital, one finds some statements of optimum conditions including as one of the conditions equality between the marginal productivity of new investment and the so-called marginal rate of time-preference of savers. But the reason for this is less compelling, if not dubious.*

The economic implication of this insistence on the Strict Version was persuasively put by Pigou without any attempt at formal sophistication. Supposing that "the whole community was compelled by law to work for 18 hours a day", the result might be an increase in the national income, which would seem to recommend this compulsion as economically sound. But "it is practically certain that the satisfaction yielded by the extra product would be enormously less than the dissatisfaction caused by the extra labour".† In other words, since men are both producers and consumers, one must not have an exclusively consumers' point of view. The logical complement of allowing free choice in spending his income to the consumer and adapting the pattern of production to the pattern of his demand is to allow free choice of occupation and between work and leisure to the working producer.

Since in modern industry the requirements of technique always place restriction on the hours of work that any individual can choose, some have been inclined to regard insistence on

---

* See below, p. 217.
† A. C. Pigou, *The Economics of Welfare*, 3rd edition (London, 1929), p. 87.

the Strict Version as rather pointless. The same is not true of choice of occupation, although custom and opportunity can be powerful limiting factors. But to picture any general fulfilment of the Equality Condition requires quite a feat of imagination, since it implies the absence of any marginal taxation, whether direct or indirect (with a poll tax independent of income and of almost any individual attribute or circumstance as the sole source of government revenue). To insist on the Strict, or Equality, Version, while it can be said to have some point, does seem to be unduly perfectionist.

Professor L. W. McKenzie has added, however, a further string to the perfectionists' bow. If all lines of production were vertically integrated and costs consisted entirely of 'original' factors, proportionality of marginal costs to prices might suffice for the economical choice of inputs. But to the extent that this is not so, and inputs at various stages include produced (and hence output-priced) goods as well as so-called original factors, anything other than the Equality Version in the relation between costs and prices will occasion some distortion in the use of the two kinds of input. "The prevalent error which has led to false theories on Ideal Output" (in the shape of the Proportionality Version) "is to pay inadequate attention to the fact, which is a commonplace, that firms (and industries, however delimited) sell goods to each other and not merely to consumers."*

Enough has been said to indicate that the Equality Version of the principle is most unlikely to be universally realised. Yet it is apparently an all-or-nothing rule. If the rule is not applied at some points, it may even be damaging to the proper allocation of resources to attempt to apply it at others. Does it follow that partial application of the rule is better than nothing? When it is only partially applied, does the principle tell us anything at all as to the relationship to be aimed at in any particular case? A widely accepted conclusion is that it does not, and that one cannot even know the *direction* in which a correct answer lies (the so-called theory of the second best).† Although this may

---

* L. W. McKenzie, 'Ideal Output and the Interdependence of Firms', in *Economic Journal* (Dec. 1951), p. 785 *et seq.*

† *Cf.* E. J. Mishan, 'A Survey of Welfare Economics, 1939–59', in *The Economic Journal* (June 1960) : in such a case "there are no general rules to fall back upon ... in particular we cannot suppose that more conditions fulfilled are better than less" (p. 212, also p. 245).

hold at a certain level of generality, it remains true (as Dr. Mishan has pointed out) that in many cases, at least, the particular circumstances of the case in conjunction with the principle may yield some answer ("we may still be able to indicate certain easily conceived conditions that permit us to say something useful").* Such an answer, however, would belong, it seems, to the category of commonsense empiricism and not of optimising 'automaticity'. Since, however, we have seen that there are other reasons for not taking the application of any such general principle too seriously, it is scarcely necessary to pursue this matter of second-best solutions at the moment.

* E. J. Mishan, 'Second Thoughts on Second Best', in *Oxford Economic Papers* (Oct. 1962), p. 205.

CHAPTER 5

DISTRIBUTION OF INCOME AND INTERPERSONAL COMPARISONS OF UTILITY

It might appear from what has been said that if Pigou's Second Proposition were to be severely impugned and jettisoned, the task of those wishing to formulate an optimum principle on the basis of his First Proposition, and to derive policy-implications therefrom, would be greatly facilitated. Not only would egalitarian conclusions, distasteful to so many, be banished from sight, but considerations about distribution, so disturbing as we have seen to clear and precise formulation of theorems about allocation of resources and relative outputs, could apparently be banned from intrusion if not totally ignored. The fact that nothing of economic significance could be said about distribution would at least encourage an agnosticism about it; carrying the implication that no great importance need be attached to whatever distribution happened to be at the moment, since there was nothing about it that had any clear and direct relation with economic welfare, or if it had there was nothing the economist was constrained to do about it in his capacity as an economist. If and when the moralist or the sociologist with strong views on the matter came along and managed to convince policy-makers that such-and-such a distribution-pattern was valuable on non-economic grounds, the economist *qua* economist would not wish to stand in the way. In propounding his 'positive' and *wertfrei* theorems, he would have done nothing to interfere with the reaching of such conclusions or the establishment of this or that income-policy, whether egalitarian or the reverse. He would merely have demonstrated how to make the best from an economic stand-point of whatever income-distribution God or Mammon or the State ultimately devised; in the meanwhile establishing his right to speak as an economist about his own scientific province without contradiction from outsiders who did not belong and who owed allegiance to other disciplines. This apparently happy result, as we shall see, is very close to what was destined to happen within two decades of the publication of *The Economics of Welfare*.

It has sometimes been supposed that Pigou's Second Proposition about distribution of income stands or falls with the notion of utility or welfare as a cardinal magnitude, capable of being subjected to the process of addition and subtraction. This, however, is not the case. The Pigouvian proposition was derived directly from what was known as the Law of Diminishing Utility of Income, which amounted to saying that as an individual's income increased, since the more urgent and important wants were presumably satisfied and only the less important (in decreasing order of importance) remained, the utility or satisfaction to be derived, while it rose with rising income, rose *less* than proportionately: in other words, the *marginal* utility of income fell. Hence to transfer £100 from a rich man to a poor man would deprive the former of the satisfaction of less important wants than it bestowed on the latter: and since it would enable "more intense wants to be satisfied at the expense of less intense wants, must increase the aggregate sum of satisfaction".* Provided that this tendency applied to every individual, no addition of the utilities of individuals was needed to reach the Pigouvian corollary about the beneficial effect of reducing inequalities of income.

For this purpose all that is needed is to be able to compare *differences* of utility or satisfaction; and this one can do even if numerical values cannot be assigned for lack of a zero and a definable unit. Cardinal utility, accordingly, in any full sense does not have to be assumed. As Mr I. M. D. Little has said: "If one moves money about until a pound makes the same difference to everyone, one has maximised happiness. The addition of happinesses is never required. The addition of differences in happiness may, however, be necessary."† This is what is called 'measurability up to a linear transformation', which implies knowledge of the signs of second differences as well as of first differences, and hence some knowledge of the *intensity* of satisfaction as well as, simply, the direction of pre-

---

* A. C. Pigou, *The Economics of Welfare*, 1st edition (London, 1920), p. 52.
† *A Critique of Welfare Economics* (Oxford, 1950), p. 54.

ference. In this connection mathematicians may like to recall a passage from Russell's *Principles of Mathematics* where he says that "the quantitative relations of magnitudes have all the definiteness of which they are capable", provided that *difference* between magnitudes can be compared.*

Little's summing-up seems an eminently sensible one, and it is hard to see how this could provoke much dissent: "There is little doubt that we do, in fact, make rough comparisons which, if they were precise, would imply the addition of satisfactions. It makes sense to say, for instance, that the difference between A's and B's increments of happiness is greater than C's increment; in which case we can also say that A's increment is greater than that of B and C put together."†

But in the Pigouvian equalising corollary there was implicit an assumption that he was to call that of "equal capacity for satisfaction" among human beings: that at least this applied as between the average individuals of any given social groups or classes, even if not as between any two particular individuals of diverse temperament. While he admitted that there might be innate differences between individuals, Pigou relied on the random character of such differences in large groups for the validity of his corollary when applied to distribution of income between social groups. This is the manner in which he argued in a restatement made in 1951,‡ which is worth quoting in view of the numerous attempts to evade this type of conclusion in the last two or three decades: "If we take random groups of people of the same race and brought up in the same country, we find that in many features that *are* comparable by objective tests they are on the average pretty much alike; and, indeed, for fundamental characters we need not limit ourselves to people of the same race or country. On this basis we are entitled, I submit, to infer by analogy that they are probably pretty much alike in other respects also. In all practical affairs we act on that supposition. We cannot prove that it is true. But we do not need to do so. Nobody can prove that anybody besides himself exists, but nevertheless everybody is quite sure

---

* *Principles of Mathematics* (Cambridge, 1903), pp. 182–3.

† Little, *op. cit.* p. 55.

‡ 'Some Aspects of Welfare Economics', in *American Economic Review*, vol. XLI, no. 3 (June 1951), pp. 287–302.

of it . . . Unless we have a special reason to believe the contrary, a given amount of stuff may be presumed to yield a similar amount of satisfaction, not indeed as between *any* one man and any other, but as between representative members of groups of individuals, such as the citizens of Birmingham and the citizens of Leeds. This is all that we need to allow this branch of Welfare Economics to function."* And then in summary (and now speaking of rich and poor as the two social groups) : "if we agree that representative members of the two groups are probably by and large pretty much alike, the argument from the law of diminishing utility holds".†

It was, in effect, this essential prop of the Pigouvian proposition about distribution that came under attack with the revival in the late thirties of Paretian scepticism about so-called 'interpersonal comparisons of utility'.‡ The grounds for such scepticism were persuasively (though not, I think, convincingly) argued by (then) Professor Lionel Robbins. But it is hard to believe that the persuasiveness of his advocacy alone explains the alacrity with which scepticism spread and became the current fashion. Can it have been that there was relief (perhaps unconscious) at ridding the subject of the tarnish of provocative egalitarian precepts—or merely that a current of solipsism was in the air?

Professor Robbins expressed his doubts in a much-quoted article in the form of a parable : a story attributed to Sir Henry Maine about a discussion between a Brahmin and a Benthamite, in the course of which the former sought to clinch the argument against human equality with the assertion : "I am ten times as capable of happiness as that untouchable over there." Reflection led Professor Robbins to the confession : "I could not escape the conviction that, if I chose to regard men as equally capable of satisfaction and he to regard them as differing according to a hierarchical schedule, the difference between us was not one which could be resolved by the same methods of demonstration as were available in other fields of social judgement." He was led to conclude that interpersonal comparisons could tell one

* *Ibid.* p. 292.   † *Ibid.* p. 300.

‡ Pigou's restatement of 1951 that we have just quoted was, indeed, an attempt to reply to this scepticism by putting the assumption in a form in which it did not rely directly on comparison of individuals—only on observations about large groups of human beings.

nothing on the question (approvingly quoting Jevons: "I see no means whereby such comparison can be accomplished. Every mind is inscrutable to every other mind and no common denominator of feeling is possible"); and that one ought "frankly to acknowledge that the postulate of equal capacity for satisfaction came from outside", as an ethical precept or value judgement, incapable of scientific demonstration. This he was ready to affirm despite being fully aware that, not only would Pigou's Second Proposition be a casualty of such scepticism, but a number of other precepts for policy of which economists had previously been proud, such as the classical argument for free trade (depending as this did on balancing the gain to consumers in general against the loss to rent-receivers) or for competition as against monopoly.* That the wreckage of propositions would be more widespread than Pigouvian Proposition 2, and could not be confined to this, had been made plain, indeed, by Mr (now Sir) Roy Harrod in the preceding number of *The Economic Journal*, when he had warned that "if the incomparability of utility to different individuals is strictly pressed, not only are prescriptions of the welfare school ruled out, but all prescriptions whatever. The economist as an adviser is completely stultified."†

In this condition of nihilism that the subject had reached on the eve of the Second World War Pigouvian Proposition 1 had become a casualty as much as Pigouvian Proposition 2. Not only could nothing be said about income-distribution (except by introducing a so-called value-judgement as to what was a 'good' distribution), but nothing could be said about whether a policy that seemed to augment the national income would be welfare-yielding in any case where gain to some was accompanied by loss to others (as was possible at least, even if not likely, whenever the production of some things rose while that of others fell). With no way of comparing the utilities or satisfactions of different individuals there was no way, it would seem, of balancing gain to some against loss to others and finding whether the result came out at a *plus* or a *minus*. This was a severe restriction upon generality. What was urgently needed

* 'Interpersonal Comparisons of Utility', in *The Economic Journal* (Dec. 1938), pp. 635–41.
† 'Scope and Method of Economics', in *The Economic Journal* (Sept. 1938), p. 397.

by most economists, if their subject was not to disintegrate, was some way of squaring the fashionable scepticism about interpersonal comparisons with an ability to formulate propositions of the type of Pigouvian Proposition 1, and hence to pronounce on what was an efficient and welfare-maximising course of policy, or system of economic arrangements, and what was not. Yet to do so involved finding a way of unambiguously defining an increase of social income, in the sense of an increase of *potential* welfare* at least, without comparing individual gains and losses and hence adding them together in order to weigh one set against the other.

To resolve this riddle was what Mr (now Professor) Nicholas Kaldor sought to do by enunciating his so-called Compensation Principle. Despite the intricate and recondite discussion that has developed out of it, and around its implications and its application, the idea is a remarkably simple one and makes an immediate appeal to commonsense. In any change that is undertaken or in contemplation it should be possible to assess (at any rate in principle) what is needed to leave the potential losers from the change in exactly the same position as they were before. If, after making this compensation, something remained on the credit side—something from which some persons or all persons in the community could benefit—the change could be defined as an increase in social income. If the process of (hypothetical) compensation was impossible without absorbing the whole of the prospective gain, it could not be defined as an increase of social income. Thus, in the example of the repeal of the Corn Laws in England in the 1840s, consumers generally stood to benefit from the cheapness and plenty of corn with free import, whereas landowners stood to lose from a fall in rents of agricultural land. Said Mr Kaldor: "But it is always possible for the Government to ensure that the previous income-distribution should be maintained intact: by compensating the 'landlords' for any loss of income and by providing the funds for such compensation by an extra tax on those whose incomes have been augmented. In this way, everybody is left as well off as before in his capacity as income-recipient; while everybody is better off than before in his capacity as a consumer."

* This convenient phrase was Professor Sir Dennis Robertson's (*Utility and All That and Other Essays*, London, 1952, pp. 31, 35).

Generalising from this case, he then concluded: "In all cases, therefore, where a certain policy leads to an increase in physical productivity, and thus of aggregate real income, the economist's case for the policy is quite unaffected by the question of the comparability of individual satisfaction; since in all such cases it is *possible* to make everybody better off than before, or at any rate to make some people better off without making anybody worse off. There is no need for the economist to prove —as indeed he never could prove—that as a result of the adoption of a certain measure nobody in the community is going to suffer." In this way he hoped to rehabilitate Pigou's division of "'welfare economics' into two parts: the first relating to production and the second to distribution"; the first remaining 'positive', scientifically objective and unconcerned with value-judgements, the second being inevitably 'political' in the sense that value-judgements about the relative worth of different persons or classes inevitably enter.[*]

This suggestion was quickly endorsed by Professor J. R. Hicks as a basis for defining the conditions for "an optimum organisation of the economic system": conditions which "are universally valid, being applicable to every conceivable type of society", and affording in particular "a means of criticising or testing the efficiency of production by private enterprise". "The position is not optimum so long as such reorganisation is possible" as would "allow of compensation being paid, and which will yet show a net advantage." By means of this line of analysis he held it "possible to put welfare economics on a secure basis and to render it immune from positivist criticism".[†]

At first sight this would seem an unimpeachable escape from the *impasse*. On examination and further analysis is it quite so unimpeachable as at first it appears to unreflecting common-sense? One thing that can be said immediately is that, if it is to have the universality claimed for it (*e.g.* in the statement of Professor Hicks we have just quoted), it must be capable of affording a definition of an increase of social income that admits

---

[*] 'Welfare Propositions and Interpersonal Comparisons of Utility', in *The Economic Journal* (Sept. 1939), pp. 549–52 (reprinted in N. Kaldor, *Essays in Value and Distribution*, London, 1960, pp. 143–6).

[†] J. R. Hicks, 'The Foundations of Welfare Economics' in *The Economic Journal* (Dec. 1939), pp. 696–712. Professor Hicks adds, however, that "there will be an indefinite number of possible optima" distinguished by differences in distribution.

of no exceptions, and certainly not of self-contradiction. This is
something different from being a practical test; since unless
we can give a clear and unambiguous meaning to social income and its increase or decrease, it is absurd to suppose that
we can hang upon it a maximising theorem and endow such a
theorem with universal validity.* If all that one was seeking
was a practical test or indicator as to whether a course of action
would probably yield desirable results, we could be more
lenient: indeed, we should not expect it to give us an answer
in every conceivable case, and should be content, no doubt,
with an answer to the common cases that occur in daily life.
But what we are concerned with here is something that has to
be the fulcrum of a whole branch of economic theory, and we
need to be much more exacting. A rule about maximising
something the quantitative nature of which becomes unclear
and ambiguous in certain situations is immediately suspect.

A cloud soon appeared on the horizon of what was coming to
be called rather prematurely the "new welfare economics"
when Professor Scitovsky two years later pointed out that there
were two possible kinds of compensation—two distinct definitions of it—and not one as had been at first supposed; that
the kind suggested by Professor Kaldor could involve one in a
contradiction; and that to avoid this possibility it was necessary
to speak of 'an increase of social income' only where compensation of *both* kinds was possible, and not when one of them alone
was possible.† The compensation of which Professor Kaldor
had originally spoken was that of potential losers by gainers,
so as to leave the former with at least the same real income as
they had enjoyed under the *original* distribution of income
before the change. The second and new kind of compensation
introduced by Professor Scitovsky (to which we shall refer
in the sequel as the Scitovsky-criterion) has been conveniently
called‡ that of 'losers bribing gainers', and was concerned with

* *Cf.* on this distinction Professor Charles Kennedy, 'Welfare Criteria—A
Further Note', in *The Economic Journal* (June 1963), p. 341.

† T. Scitovsky, 'A Note on Welfare Propositions in Economics', in *Review of
Economic Studies* (Nov. 1941) (reprinted in *Papers on Welfare and Growth*, London,
1964, pp. 123–38).

‡ By Mr Little. Some writers have used the term 'Scitovsky-criterion' to refer
to the *double* condition, embracing both his own and the Kaldor-type of compensation. We shall not follow this usage here.

the payment of a compensation or bribe by those likely to be damaged by a change to the gainers from it: a payment adequate to dissuade the latter from advocating the change and still leave the potential losers better off than they were destined to be if the change were to be made. If this could be successfully done, the change did not qualify for designation as an 'increase in social income'. If on the other hand it was impossible for potential losers to bribe potential gainers so as to dissuade them from making it, the contemplated change qualified as an increase. We shall see that this kind of compensation (or bribe) was equivalent to reproducing the distribution of income (and hence a minimum real income for the potential gainers) equivalent to what would prevail in the second and later situation after the change had been made.*

For the moment it seemed that the difficulty had been overcome by adopting the stiffer definition in terms of the potential fulfilment of both kinds of compensation; and it is true that (at the cost of some restriction and loss of generality) this new double Kaldor–Scitovsky condition precluded the particular case of contradiction from arising to which Professor Scitovsky had drawn attention. But the story of contradiction was not at an end; and it was to transpire that the adoption of the double condition was insufficient to exclude the possibility of contradiction from arising. An incidental disappointment was the amount of practical help that index number data were able to afford in demonstrating the possibility or impossibility of compensation, which turned out to be comparatively small. To this extent the *impasse* remained unresolved. The nature of these further difficulties, and of the essential problem which they revealed, will be the subject of analysis in the next chapter.

---

* This was, indeed, pointed out by Professor Scitovsky at the time: (when using *both* kinds of compensation) "For we compare the first welfare situation with what general welfare would be if the satisfaction yielded by the physical income of the second situation were distributed as it was in the first; and contrast the second situation with the welfare that the first situation's physical income would yield to each person if it were so distributed as to make the distribution of welfare similar to that of the second situation" (pp. 87–8; *Papers*, pp. 136–7).

CHAPTER 6

THE COMPENSATION PRINCIPLE

Before analysing the difficulties in which discussion of the Compensation Principle was to become involved, it may be convenient to restate the two main versions of it (the Kaldor and the Scitovsky) rather more rigorously. Both of these forms or variants of the main principle can be conceived of as analysing any given change into two halves or stages. In the first of these stages the situations before and after the change are looked at from the standpoint of a constant income distribution, irrespective of whether the distribution has actually been affected by the change or not (in most cases of course it will have been affected). To ensure this constancy is the rôle of the hypothetical compensation; and one could regard its function as being to enable one to measure and to define a change in national income along Pigouvian lines, as considered above in chapter 3. In the second stage the quantities of the two situations (we shall refer to them as Q_1 and Q_2) are compared in order to discover which of them is the greater.

Thus in the Kaldor-version 'constancy of distribution' was in effect redefined as 'leaving everyone on the same indifference curve as before' (i.e. as in Situation 1), compensation to losers being (hypothetically) paid until this was achieved. If, when it had been done, Q_2 proved to be greater than Q_1 (as measured e.g. by some relevant index-number comparison), so that at least some people could be placed on higher indifference-curves than before, the result of the change was declared to be an increase of social income, or of potential (if not actual) welfare; and conversely where Q_2 proved to be smaller than Q_1. This Kaldor-version, accordingly, is sometimes spoken of as a method of (hypothetically) redistributing the Q_2's so as to compare Q_2 with Q_1, or the new situation after the change with the initial situation, from the standpoint of the income-distribution prevailing in Situation 1 before the change.

The Scitovsky-version, per contra, can be regarded as redistributing in the first stage the Q_1's so as to make their distribution among individuals (again, hypothetically) in the initial situation the same as they will be in the new Situation 2 after the change has been made. Then Q_2 is compared with Q_1 (thus redistributed) from the standpoint of the new income-distribution that will prevail in Situation 2. If the redistribution (merely) of the Q_1's could *not* suffice to make everyone as well-off (in the sense of being on the same indifference-curve) as he is destined to be in the new Situation 2, the real income of the latter is said to be larger than that of Situation 1. It is larger because the situation reached with Q_2 could *not* have been reached solely by redistributing the Q_1's.* In the converse case the change from Situation 1 to Situation 2 involves *per definitione* a *fall* in social income.

It should, perhaps, be emphasised, to avoid misunderstanding, that this use of compensation in either of its variants was an attempt to define a change of social income independently of whether welfare had actually increased or decreased. It was intended that income should be definable as increasing even though welfare was smaller than before owing to adverse changes in distribution (indeed, for those who denied the possibility of interpersonal comparisons no statement about total welfare could be made when the welfare of different individuals moved in opposite directions). Compensation, as we have shown, was merely a theoretical device for *supposing* distribution to be held constant, so that the same kind of conclusion could be drawn about changes in national income as we have seen earlier that Pigou tried to draw (on the assumption of constant distribution). Only if the compensation (in the Kaldor case) were *actually* to be paid would a change involving an increase in income (in terms of the definition) represent at the same time an increase in actual welfare. If it were not in fact paid there might be distributional effects, involving a loss of welfare to some and a gain to others—changes which (if

* Although in this case Q_2 can be regarded as representing greater 'potential welfare' than Q_1, if appropriately distributed between individuals, one must be careful not to identify this with the statement that, as distributed in Situation 2, it represents a greater *actual* welfare than Q_1 as this was distributed in Situation 1. Similarly, one must be careful not to identify the redistribution of the Q_1's, so as to make each individual as nearly as possible on the same indifference-curve as he would be in Situation 2, with that redistribution of the Q_1's which would make the *total* welfare of all individuals a maximum (assuming that individual welfares can be aggregated).

interpersonal comparisons were allowed) might amount to either a net gain or a net loss in welfare.

For a change of social income, defined in such a way as this, to be capable of practical verification, it must evidently bear some relation to the kind of data about price and quantity changes of which index numbers are made. Since the second, or Scitovsky, variant of the definition conducts the comparison in terms of the distribution (and hence prices) prevailing in the second situation, it may be intuitively evident (at any rate we shall develop the point later) that the inequality $\Sigma p_2 q_2 > \Sigma p_2 q_1$ indicates that the Scitovsky criterion for an increase (the 'impossibility of potential losers bribing gainers' not to make the change) is fulfilled.* Similarly the inequality $\Sigma p_1 q_2 < \Sigma p_1 q_1$ indicates the *im*possibility of fulfilling the Kaldor-criterion for an increase ('gainers compensating losers'), since the latter conducts its comparison between the two situations in terms of the distribution (and the prices) prevailing in Situation 1.†
Unfortunately there is no equivalent index-number inequality to demonstrate the *possibility* of fulfilling the Kaldor-criterion. This would *seem* to require that $\Sigma p_1 q_2 > \Sigma p_1 q_1$. But for the reasons we have examined above, in chapter 3, this form of the Laspeyres product-index is indecisive, and is consistent both with an increase and with a decrease of real income between Situation 1 and Situation 2.

Indeed, the inequality $\Sigma p_1 q_2 < \Sigma p_1 q_1$ that we have just used as evidence of the impossibility of gainers compensating losers in a change from Situation 1 to Situation 2 can also be regarded as the Scitovsky-criterion being fulfilled for a *reverse* move from Situation 2 back to Situation 1. The quite possible case (of which we shall later give an example) where *both* $\Sigma p_2 q_2 > \Sigma p_2 q_1$ *and* $\Sigma p_1 q_2 < \Sigma p_1 q_1$ can, accordingly, be regarded in our present context as representing a self-contradiction in the Scitovsky-criterion for an increase in real income, since it can be fulfilled *both* for a change from Situation 1 to Situation 2 *and* for the reverse change from Situation 2 back to Situation 1.

If we can know, however, in any particular case that the

* For those desiring a rigorous proof of this statement, one has been given by Professor Charles Kennedy in *Oxford Economic Papers*, N.S. vol. 6, no. 1 (Feb. 1954), pp. 98–9, to whose proof reference may be made.

† *Cf.* the present writer, 'A Note on Index Numbers and Compensation Criteria', in *Oxford Economic Papers*, N.S. vol. 8, no. 1 (Feb. 1956), pp. 78–9.

Kaldor-condition can be fulfilled, in addition to the Scitovsky, then we know that $\Sigma p_1 q_2$ can*not* be $< \Sigma p_1 q_1$ and that the contradiction we have just mentioned does not occur. Although $\Sigma p_1 q_2 > p_1 q_1$ may not suffice to demonstrate that Kaldorian compensation is possible, at any rate it excludes its opposite: it shows that $\Sigma p_1 q_2$ is not $< \Sigma p_1 q_1$ and that the Scitovsky criterion does not contradict itself. But it remains true that either of the two versions of the Compensation Principle, when taken alone, may result in contradiction, and fails accordingly to qualify as a satisfactory criterion or definition.

Before considering the later stages of the discussion of this principle, we may conveniently look a little deeper into the significance of this difficulty. For this purpose let us take again a simplified 2-good and 2-person case, and along the axes of a graph let us represent the total quantities of the two goods x and y (which we can think of, if we like, as bread and wine). Any point in the plane, such as P will represent a certain quantity of x and y, distributed between the two persons A and B 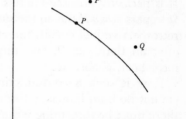 in a certain way; points to the north-east of it such as P' will represent more of *both* goods than at P; but movements in either a south-easterly or a north-westerly direction from P will represent more of one good and less of the other. Suppose that, as we consider a move in either of these directions, we ask the question: how much more of x would be just sufficient to compensate both parties, A and B, for a given loss of y (or conversely)—compensate in the sense of yielding equivalent satisfaction to what they had together lost of y, or leaving each of them on the same indifference-curve as they were at P? In answering this question we could draw through P a line (or curve) to which the name of a 'compensation-line' might be given.*

---

* This is one way of drawing a so-called community indifference-curve. It has to be noted, incidentally, that, if P is an equilibrium position, both A and B will be at points on their respective indifference-curves at which these are tangential to the prevailing price-line. This defines the proportions in which y is withdrawn from A and B respectively as one moves from P along the curve, and correspondingly

Such a compensation-line could be used in the following way. With its aid one could look at any other point such as Q (representing a certain combination of x and y), and see whether it lay above the line through P or below it. If Q lay above it, one could make the judgement (it would seem) that, measured in terms of utility or satisfaction, Q represented *more* of both x and y than P, and could accordingly be defined (like P' relatively to P) as representing a greater real income. A converse statement could be made of points lying below the compensation-line through P. This is, indeed, what the Kaldorian principle is suggesting.

Let us further suppose that by virtue of this judgement it was decided to move from P to Q, and that having done so one were to look back at P along a new compensation-line through Q. It is perfectly possible for this new compensation-line through Q to pass *below* P (*i.e.* to the south-west of it). According to this retrospective judgement, therefore, P had a larger real income after all than has Q, and the move to Q could be deemed to have been a mistake.

How is such a contradiction possible? Real income at Q cannot be both larger and smaller than real income at P, and there must be something wrong with a principle that can yield both answers simultaneously. The contradiction arises because any compensation line such as we have drawn *presupposes a certain distribution of the x's and y's between A and B, and is entirely relative to this distribution.** The contradiction in question would

the amounts of x to be supplied to them in compensation. In other words, P is assumed to be a Pareto-optimum, and the same must be true for all other positions on the line (they are all points on an Edgeworthian Contract-curve). If at all positions on the line both A and B are kept on the same indifference-curves as at P, this is equivalent to saying that the distribution of real income between them has not changed with movement along the line, although the constituents of real income have changed. Thus it could also be called a line of constant real-income distribution.

* It is for this reason that one cannot simply aggregate individual indifference-curves into a collective one, and hence transfer Professor Hicks's conclusions about index-numbers which were summarised above to the level of the group or the community as a whole, as was pointed out in the Note to chapter 3. To aggregate individual curves into a collective one implies a certain *weighting* of the individual curves in arriving at the summation, and the 'weighting' assigned is that given by the distribution of income. (If one were to postulate equality between individuals, then of course one could derive a collective indifference curve directly from individual ones: correspondingly 'compensation' would then have a unique meaning.)

not be possible if distribution at Q were identical with that at P (if 'identical' can be given a clear meaning when A and B are severally on different indifference-curves at the two points). But if in the course of moving from P to Q the distribution of income between A and B has changed, the relevant compensation-line through Q will belong (as it were) to a different family of curves from the original one through P. It is in this case, when comparisons between the two points are made in terms of compensation-lines belonging to different families that the possibility of contradiction arises. Once we allow for different income-distributions between A and B we need to amend our diagram. It becomes obvious that there is, indeed, not one compensation-line through P but a whole set of them, and similarly for lines through Q and other points. The method of ordering all points in one x-y plane by means of compensation-lines through a series of points breaks down. The set of lines

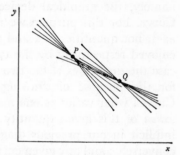

through any point such as P will be fan-shaped.* About points outside the range of any fan, or between certain broad zones, one can make judgements about real income relative to the reference-point in question (*e.g.* points within the north-east quadrant hinging on P). But within the extent of the fan judgements about comparative real income must necessarily remain ambiguous and distribution-relative.

This relativity of social income as a magnitude to its distribution—it may be worth underlining—is because measurement is in terms of 'utility', or individual satisfaction; whence it follows that one cannot avoid the question, '*whose* utility?'. The measure, from its nature, will itself be affected by the manner in which income is divided among, and enjoyed by, various consumers (consumers who not only have different tastes but have their wants satiated in differing degrees). The same

* It may be noted that the two sides of each fan are in effect the tangents to the indifference-curves of A and B at the extreme ends of the Contract-curve (representing extremes of distribution in favour of either A or B); hence the spread of the fan depends on the *curvature* of the Contract-curve.

would not apply to another type of measure, such as a productivity-measure in terms of labour as a cost-unit. While this would yield a different comparison of magnitudes, and one that had no direct relevance to comparisons of welfare (and it would not be, of course, without its own type of index-number problem), it would seem not to be subject to this particular problem of distribution-relativity.

Once we introduce income-distribution as an explicit factor in our diagram, it may be preferable to adopt an alternative mode of representation, and one that has become familiar by use in most writings on the subject over the past two decades: namely, the graphical device known as a Utility-Possibility Curve. For this purpose we need to represent along the two axes, not quantities of x and y, but the satisfaction or utility* enjoyed respectively by the two individuals, A and B. In this case the quantities of the two products are treated as constant for the purpose of drawing a particular Utility-Possibility Curve: what varies as one moves along the curve is the *distribution* of this given quantity between A and B. (What was implicit in our previous diagram now becomes explicit, and conversely; and any given curve can be thought of as representing all the possible distributions at any given point on the previous diagram, such as point P.) Expressed more precisely, each point on a Utility-Possibility Curve shows the maximum satisfaction or utility† that can be enjoyed by B consistently with a given level of satisfaction or utility for A, and conversely (in face of a *given* quantity of the two commodities, say bread and wine). For other product-combinations, such as those represented by P' and Q on our previous diagram, there will be other Utility-Possibility Curves—a different one, indeed, for each different product-combination.

How, then, will these different Utility-Possibility Curves be related to one another? Can their relationship throw any light on what constitutes an increase of social income independently of distribution?

Here, again, we have one piece of firm ground beneath our

---

* This can be regarded, if need be, as strictly ordinal in character, and not as a cardinal magnitude.

† This again implies that all points on the Utility-Possibility Curve are on the Contract-curve.

feet. Any change involving an increase in *both* commodities (like a move from P to P' in the north-east quadrant in our previous diagram) *must* be represented by an outward extension of the Utility-Possibility Curve throughout its length. For example, if curve P'–P' represents more of both bread and wine than does P–P, a redistribution of bread sufficiently in favour of B can hardly fail to improve B's position and hence to extend the curve near to the U^B axis, even if B is not a consumer of wine at all—and even if wine has been increased much by the change and bread very little. The same applies, *mutatis mutandis*, for a distribution of bread and wine very favourable to A, and hence for the position of the curves close to the U^A axis. But in 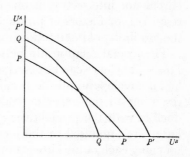 all cases other than this there is nothing to guarantee that the curves may not intersect (as with curves P–P and Q–Q in the diagram); one being outside the other for some distributions and inside it for others. Thus suppose that the new situation Q–Q is one of more wine and less bread than the original situation P–P; and that A has a strong taste for wine while B has little or no use for wine and lives on bread and can indeed show a gargantuan appetite for it. Near the U^B axis B is almost bound to be less well off with Q than he was at P; since although the distribution is very favourable to him, no amount of extra wine will compensate him for deficiency of bread (of which in the old situation he had presumably consumed most of the larger supply of it that there then was). It follows that the Q–Q curve must here be *inside* the P–P curve; and this despite the fact that when distribution is very favourable to A, A can enjoy much more wine than before and be better off, even if he gives up most of the bread there is to B (so that the Q–Q curve is above and outside the other curve close to the U^A axis).

A Utility-Possibility Curve, with the properties that we have described, can be drawn, however, on the assumption, not of a given *product*-combination, but of given productive resources (or factor-combination)—productive resources which can be turned to producing *either* the product-combination most preferred by A (and in demand if income-distribution is in A's favour) *or* that which is most preferred by B. This definition has the advantage of giving the resulting curve greater generality, and of giving it, perhaps, more relevance to problems concerned with the allocation of productive resources. It would seem likely to decrease the chance of such curves intersecting; but without banishing this possibility. One could be sure of two curves not intersecting if one of them represented more of *all* resources, or factors of production, than the other: otherwise the possibility of intersection is not excluded.

The formal relationship between these two types of Utility-Possibility Curve can be described by saying that the second will be an envelope to all the possible curves of the first type, representing all the possible product-combinations that are producible with the productive resources in question when these latter are organised in the most efficient manner; the former touching each of the latter at one point. Being 'organised in the most efficient manner' to produce a given product combination implies that both halves of our Production Condition (as described in chapter 4 above) are fulfilled.* We have said that every point on our first type of Utility-Possibility Curve must be on an Edgeworthian Contract-curve (where the Consumers' Condition is satisfied). It follows that at all those points where curves of this type touch the envelope-curve both sets of Optimum Conditions are satisfied.

How much can Index-Number data tell us about the relative positions of Utility-Possibility Curves and their intersection or non-intersection? And what is the precise relation between such curves and the compensation criteria that we are discussing? The first part of this question is equivalent to asking what information, if any, it is possible for Index-Numbers to give us at the level of the *group*, analogous to the kind of indications about differences of utility that we considered in an earlier chapter at the level of the single individual. The latter is, of course, preliminary to the former enquiry, since what Index-

* The first half must be fulfilled as a condition of being efficiently organised, and hence of being on the so-called 'production frontier' or 'production-possibility curve'; the second half follows as being simply a definition of the *slope* of the production-possibility curve at a particular point when the demanded product-combination is being produced.

Number data can tell us about the individual sets the *limit* to what can be deduced about the group. One would expect to be able to deduce much *less* in the case of the group because of the tiresome possibility of shifts in distribution. Only if (like Pigou) one were comparing positions between which distribution had not changed, could one expect complete parallelism between what such data can tell us in the two cases. There are certain analogies, however, between the deductions that can be made about the individual and those that can be made about the group; and accordingly it may be worthwhile to set these out in detail before attempting to sum up the results of the Compensation debate.

Let us make clear at the outset that *no* Index-Number data can tell us that a given change shifts a Utility-Possibility Curve outwards throughout its whole length. This can only be deduced from knowledge that *all* output-changes have the same sign: *i.e.* if any products have increased in supply, all others have increased or remained unchanged, and none have decreased. The most that Index-Number data can do is to afford information about shifts in the curve along particular stretches of it close to the situation in the prices of which the price × quantity comparison is made.

We may take a look, firstly, at the so-called Paasche Product-Index, the inequality $\Sigma p_2 \, q_2 > \Sigma p_2 \, q_1$, which we have said above implies fulfilment of the Scitovsky criterion for an 'increase in social income'. What can it tell us about the 2-person Utility-Possibility Curve and how this is shifted between Situations 1 and 2? Reflection will show that it implies that there is some conceivable distribution of the quantities available in Situation 1 (*i.e.*, some point on the Utility-Possibility Curve) at which this inequality holds for both individuals composing our 2-person group. (If it holds for the group, there must evidently be *some* way of distributing the q's between A and B that will make it hold for both of them severally and simultaneously.) If the difference expressed by the inequality is sufficiently small, this must be substantially the same distribution as exists in the second of the two situations, in the prices of which the quantity-comparison is being made. Let us denote this position on a graph as point Q *sans* suffix: a point on the Utility-Possibility Curve passing through Q_1. We have already seen* that if the inequality holds for an individual, this must mean that he is on a *lower* indifference-curve in the first situation than the second. It follows that our point Q must stand to the south-west of Q_2: *i.e.* in the vicinity of Q_2 the Utility-Possibility Curve of Q_1 is *below* Q_2, since both A and B are worse-off at that distribution (in the sense of being on lower indifference-curves). This can be seen to be equivalent to the statement that it would not be possible by redistributing the goods available in the Q_1 situation to reach a situation as good for both A and B simultaneously as is Q_2;† which we have seen is essentially the Scitovsky-criterion of 'losers unable to bribe gainers'.

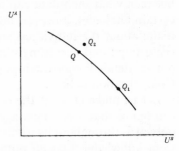

What does the Paasche Product-Index with the inequality reversed, namely $\Sigma p_2\, q_2 < \Sigma p_2\, q_1$, tell us for the group? For comparable reasons to the above, it implies that by redistributing the Q_1's one could make the inequality hold for each individual. But we have seen that for this inequality to hold for each individual is *not* sufficient to prove that they are severally better-off than at Q_2 (in the sense of being on a higher indifference-curve). Accordingly it does not follow that in this case the Utility-Possibility Curve of Situation 1 passes north-east of Q_2. The inequality in this form is consistent with the curve passing *either* to the north-east *or* to the south-west of Q_2.

What, then, does the Laspeyres Product-Index tell us? Again this depends on its form. Let us take it first in the form $\Sigma p_1\, q_2 < \Sigma p_1\, q_1$. This is capable of telling us that one could *not* by redistributing the q_2's make both A and B as well off as they were at Q_1: *e.g.* you could not give both of them as much bread and wine, valued at p_1, as they had in Situation 1. This is equivalent to saying that the Utility-Possibility Curve passing through Q_2 lies south-west of (or below) Q_1 in the neighbourhood of Q_1.

---

* Above Note to chapter 3, pp. 44–5.

† *N.B.* this is *not* the same as saying: "as good for the *sum* of A and B" (although if utilities are assumed to be additive, the latter is of course implied by the above statement for *this particular distribution*—and for this distribution alone).

The proof of this is analogous to that in our first, Paasche, case. The Index-Number inequality of which we are speaking implies that there is in Situation 2 some conceivable distribution of the quantities at which the inequality could be made to hold for both individuals A and B. Let us denote this on the graph as Q'. We have already seen that if it holds for an individual, this must mean that he is on a lower indifference-curve in Situation 2 than in Situation 1. It follows, accordingly, that Q' on the Utility-Possibility Curve passing through Q_2 is south-west of Q_1, thus representing less utility for both individuals than at Q_1.

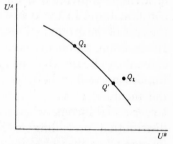

The Laspeyres inequality with the reverse sign is unable to tell us anything for the group since we have seen that it cannot do so for the individual. Even if by redistributing the q_2's one reached a point on the Utility-Possibility Curve where this inequality held for both individuals, this would not be sufficient to show that they were here on higher indifference-curves than at Q_1. This form of inequality is accordingly consistent with the Utility-Possibility Curve through Q_2 passing either above or below Q_1.

In summary, the same generalisation holds at the social level as at the individual, that, if they are to afford a decisive answer, Index-Number inequalities must have the general form, $\Sigma p_x\, q_x > \Sigma p_x\, q_y$: i.e. they must compare the outputs of the two situations in terms of the prices of the situation in which the social income (measured in terms of utility) is the greater.

Each of the two types of Product-Index can tell us about the relationship of Utility-Possibility Curves of two situations under comparison in the immediate neighbourhood of *one* particular point, or at *one* income-distribution. Thus the Paasche can tell us that in the neighbourhood of Q_2 the Q_1-curve is below it. But they cannot tell us about more than one point on each curve; and accordingly they cannot provide evidence, severally or jointly, that the two curves do *not* intersect between the two points Q_1 and Q_2. Such non-intersection would be the equivalent of Scitovsky's *double* criterion (*i.e.* the fulfilment *both* of his own 'losers unable to bribe potential gainers' *and* of Kaldor's compensation criterion).

But while Index-Number data are powerless to demonstrate *non*-intersection, they are quite capable of demonstrating the certainty of intersection. This is the (apparently) contradictory case where *both* $\Sigma p_2\, q_2 > \Sigma p_2\, q_1$ *and* $\Sigma p_1\, q_2 < \Sigma p_1\, q_1$. We have seen that such a contradiction would be impossible in the case of a single individual if he were a consistent individual with constant tastes in the two situations. But it is quite possible in the case of the group as a result of shifts in income-distribution.*
Intersection, and hence contradiction, is not just a hypothetical case : it can be shown to be an actual possibility. The possibility implies a conflict between different scales of measurement; the meaning of such intersection being that Q_2 represents a larger social income when measured in terms of the prices and distribution prevailing in Situation 2, but a smaller social income when measured in terms of the prices and distribution prevailing in Situation 1.

As an example of what an 'intersecting' case of this sort would look like, we can take (and adapt) one that was advanced by Professor Kuznets, in answer to Professor Hicks (who had sponsored a compensation-principle which was in effect what we have called the Scitovsky criterion).† In an article in *Economica* for February 1948, Kuznets cited an example where the poor consumed only necessities and considered luxuries no substitute for deficiency of the former, while the rich consumed some of both, but relatively little of the former, for which their income-elasticity of demand was very small. Writing q and Q for quantities of necessities and luxuries respectively and p and P for their respective prices, he depicted Situation 1 as follows:

	q	Q	p	P	pq	PQ
Poor	8	0	1	1	8	0
Rich	1	3	1	1	1	3
Total	9	3			9	3

* We have seen that social or community indifference-curves *can* intersect, unlike individual ones.

† 'The Valuation of the Social Income' in *Economica* (May 1940). Professor Hicks coupled this "redistribution of the actual quantities acquired in Situation 1 " with the Paasche Product-Index.

The output of luxuries then increased and income-distribution changed in favour of the rich; prices however remaining the same. In consequence, Situation 2 was as follows:

	q	Q	p	P	pq	PQ
Poor	6	0	1	1	6	0
Rich	1	7	1	1	1	7
Total	7	7			7	7

For this change the Scitovsky-criterion would be fulfilled, thus indicating an increase in social income and in *potential* welfare. (According to the example $\dfrac{\Sigma p_2 \, q_2}{\Sigma p_1 \, q_1} = \dfrac{14}{12}$; and this when divided by *either* the Paasche or the Laspeyres price-index, both of which are equal to unity, yield a product-index greater than unity: *i.e.* $\Sigma p_2 \, q_2 > \Sigma p_2 \, q_1$ and $\Sigma p_1 \, q_2 > \Sigma p_1 \, q_1$.) Yet what Kuznets calls "the reversal test", or the Kaldor-condition of compensating losers, cannot be fulfilled, because however many luxuries the rich were to offer in compensation these could not compensate the poor for the reduction in supply of necessaries in Situation 2. For compensation to be possible, the assumption would be needed that "all individuals reflect in their indifference curves the full variety and quantity of goods included in social income", or that "all goods can be substituted over the full range".*

That compensation is impossible in this example is not demonstrated by the Index-Number data: there is here no overt contradiction between the Paasche and Laspeyres indices, which agree in representing the second situation as superior. To make them demonstrate the kind of contradiction of which we have been speaking, we must adapt Kuznets's example, and in particular assume a change in relative prices between the two situations. Such a price-change is a quite reasonable supposition if we assume that the production of both necessaries

* Professor Hicks was quick to accept the Kuznets-criticism, and wrote in the following number of *Economica*: "Whenever the change which we are considering involves a considerable increase in the output of goods which are only consumed by a section of the community (whether on account of differences in wants or of inequality in incomes) we need to be very careful in our application of index number tests" (*Economica*, Aug. 1948, p. 164).

and luxuries is subject to diminishing returns (or increasing cost), so that the shift in the distribution of money-income and hence in demand will lower the price of the one and raise that of the other. Let us take the following case:

Situation 1

	q	Q	p	P	pq	PQ
Poor	8	0 }	1	1	{ 8	0
Rich	1	3 }			{ 1	3
Total	9	3			9 +	3 = 12

Situation 2

Poor	5	0 }	$\frac{1}{2}$	2	{ $2\frac{1}{2}$	0
Rich	1	5 }			{ $\frac{1}{2}$	10
Total	6	5			3 +	10 = 13

It will be seen that $\dfrac{\Sigma p_2 q_2}{\Sigma p_2 q_1} = \dfrac{13}{10\frac{1}{2}}$, so that the Scitovsky-criterion for an increase between Situation 1 and Situation 2 is fulfilled. But at the same time $\dfrac{\Sigma p_1 q_1}{\Sigma p_1 q_2} = \dfrac{12}{11}$, indicating the impossibility in Situation 2 of compensating the losers from the change, and thereby demonstrating the possibility of applying the Scitovsky-criterion in reverse for a change *back* from Situation 2 to Situation 1. In this case there is certainly an intersection of the Utility-Possibility Curves between the two situations and their appropriate distributions.

Even if such intersection could be excluded, the Compensation Principle would not, however, be free from difficulty. There might still be intersection elsewhere, either to the right or to the left of the two points in question which we denoted above as Q_1 and Q_2. In other words, although a certain change might be justified by both the Kaldor- and the Scitovsky-criterion (the latter's "double condition"), the change might still be unacceptable from the standpoint of some other income-distribution. Consider the case depicted in the attached diagram. A project comes on the agenda involving a move from an original Q_1 to a new situation Q_2. This is a change very favourable to A:

but he can show that it would be quite possible for him to compensate B fully for any loss incurred by him and still retain a substantial gain for himself. What more convincing *prima facie* case could be devised to lay before a Royal Commission or a popular vote? (Even if the B's were in the majority, they might well be persuaded by promise of compensation to vote for it in the higher interests of society.) Yet if B, or some social philosopher on B's behalf, had nurtured hopes of winning the political strength needed to swing the distribution of income in B's favour at some future date, the benefits obtainable from doing so would have been much reduced, and hence

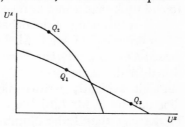

perhaps the chance of ever doing so, by the change to Q_2. If the change from Q_1 to Q_2 were irreversible, the possibility of opting in the future for the favourable position Q_3 would have been entirely lost. In other words, from the standpoint of a welfare-distribution very favourable to B, even a fully compensated change to Q_2 would be undesirable, and would not represent a gain even of potential welfare in view of other possible alternatives foregone.

This was, indeed, the substance of Professor Samuelson's criticism of the Compensation Principle (in any of its interpretations) in an influential article on 'The Measurement of Real Income' in *Oxford Economic Papers* for January 1950. Because of the possibility of intersection of Utility-Possibility Curves, it was insufficient to define an increase of social income as an increase in potential welfare from the standpoint of *some* distributions only. To be consistent and to exclude the possibility of self-contradiction, this must be taken to mean an increase of potential welfare from the standpoint of *all* possible distributions. In the language of Utility-Possibility Curves, an increase of social income must be identified with an outward movement of the curve *along its whole extent*. This is, of course, an unexceptionable definition, but one that is difficult if not impossible to express in a verifiable form. It is not something that is capable of being demonstrated by Index-Number data. The only case in which we can be sure of it on *a priori* grounds is where all changes in output are in the same direction: where there are only increases and no decreases. But this is something that was known *ab initio*: it was derivable by simple commonsense before sophisticated debate started, and is very little help with the more complex changes which generally confront policy-making. One of the baffling things about discussion in this subject is that a new departure setting out with promise seems to end up by returning to the same point.

It is at this point of the debate that what has been called the 'dual criterion' of Mr I. M. D. Little came in: his much discussed *Critique of Welfare Economics* (Oxford, 1950) being published in the same year as Professor Paul Samuelson's article (though evidently written before the latter's appearance). The novelty of Mr Little's approach consists in his acceptance of the fact that Index-Number data of themselves can give no answer as to the wisdom of any proposed change: to do so their verdict must always be coupled with some judgement about the shift in distribution that is involved. As stated in the first edition of his book, the double condition which must be fulfilled for any given change to qualify as an improvement in welfare was: (*a*) that the Scitovsky-criterion was fulfilled, to show that the same result could not be achieved merely by redistributing the quantities of the first situation,* (*b*) that income distribution was at least no 'worse' in the second situation than in the first.

Let us say at once, before examining the matter further, that as a *general* statement this is unexceptionable: indeed, in affirming that no positive statement about welfare can be made at all without taking account of distribution, it can only be applauded. It draws attention, incidentally, to the fact that even a move towards a Pareto-optimum may be undesirable if it involves an adverse shift in distribution (as with derationing of necessities in conditions of shortage, or indeed a shift in relative prices that may seem justified by so-called 'optimising' rules about aligning price-ratios with cost-ratios). In so far as it is open to criticism it is in not reaching as far (within the context of the

* In his 2nd edition (Oxford, 1957) fulfilment of the Kaldor-condition, as an alternative to the Scitovsky, is added—by implication rather than by explicit statement (*cf.* pp. 105, 112–13). He speaks here of the effect on distribution as being generally "a more important part of the criterion" than the Scitovsky-condition (*ibid.* p. 114).

present enquiry) as some people, at least, have hailed it as doing, which may perhaps be a criticism of some Little-disciples and interpreters rather than of Mr Little himself.

What some may possibly fail to notice on a first reading of the book is that in a crucial respect Mr Little shifts, apparently, the subject of discussion. In emphasising (very justly) that no statement about changes in welfare can be made independently of distribution, he seems to abandon the attempt to find a definition of a change in social income as a meaningless enquiry. He is content, instead, with stating the conditions for a change to constitute an "improvement"; an improvement being identified, apparently, with an increase in *actual* welfare (no longer merely potential welfare). Here he parts company with other participants in the Compensation debate, and his own conditions for a desirable change cannot be regarded as affording a solution to the problem as these others had propounded it : namely, to define a change in social income independently of distribution as a basis for optimising principles of the type of Pigou's First Proposition. Thus Mr Little writes :

I have proposed that the phrases 'increase (decrease) of welfare' and 'increase (decrease) of real income' should both be logically subsequent to a judgement about the desirability or otherwise of any change in the distribution of welfare (or real income). To say 'the real income of the community is greater' is not much different from saying 'the income of the community is really greater', which is again not much different from 'the community is better off'. We have therefore treated 'increase of real income' and 'increase of welfare' as synonymous.*

Recognising and accepting this crucial shift in the context of enquiry, we may ask whether Mr Little's method can afford at any rate some answer in cases where those versions of the Compensation Principle that we have discussed, operating without a postulate about distribution, are silent. In interpreting the distribution-half of his double condition there turns out to have been a latent ambiguity ; and although Mr Little has since explained† which of the two meanings he intended, it may be as well to mention both of them, since some had previously

* *Ibid.* (1st edition), p. 219.
† In *The Economic Journal* (Dec. 1963), pp. 778–9.

canvassed the other interpretation.* Personally, the present writer finds this other interpretation more interesting than the one that Mr Little claims as his own; but this may be regarded perhaps as a matter of taste.

First, the distribution-condition (that distribution is no worse in the second situation than in the first) can reasonably be interpreted as an appeal to some *general* judgement about distribution. In observing the direction of any change in distribution in the particular case under consideration, one judges this to be nearer to (or further from) some ideal distribution, or at any rate as being in a better direction or a worse. If, for example, one holds that equality of money-income is superior to inequality, then one can draw the conclusion that, since Situation 2 represents a more equal distribution than Situation 1, it is indeed better and to be preferred; or in an alternative case it is *no more* unequal and accordingly can qualify as an improvement under this half of the condition provided that the other half is fulfilled. But unless both halves of the double condition are fulfilled—both the Scitovsky-criterion and the judgement about the distribution-change (if any)—speaking with the same voice and pointing in the same direction, nothing can be said about the desirability or undesirability of the change.

Interpreted in *this* way, as a truly 'dual criterion', it can presumably give no answer in the cases that we have been discussing, where the Utility-Possibility Curves intersect *between* the two relevant points. No answer seems possible in the case where the Scitovsky-criterion contradicts itself, since the point of employing this is to show that the change of production-potential is such as to enable everyone after the change to be made better off. If this be only true when the change of production-potential is measured in terms of the distribution (and prices) of the second situation, but not when measured in terms of the distribution (and prices) of the first, then it clearly loses its essential meaning.† Analogous considerations apply when

---

* Professor A. K. Sen has named it "the Little-Mishan criterion" (*The Economic Journal*, Dec. 1963, p. 771). Dr Mishan speaks of it as having been sponsored at various times by "most of Little's critics—Arrow, Meade, Robertson, myself and to some extent Dobb" (*The Economic Journal*, Dec. 1964, p. 1014).

† The only escape from this conclusion would seem to be if one were prepared to postulate that, when considering a move to a certain situation, only the distribution prevailing in that situation really matters; and this by virtue of the fact

the Kaldor-criterion contradicts itself. To deny this would seem to be to make the first half of the double condition purely formal; and to allow the answer to then stand in the contradictory case, on one leg as it were, in effect means that the matter is decided in terms of the distribution-effect alone, which is clearly unreasonable.*

If this be accepted, then it follows that the 'dual criterion' can tell one no more than ordinary compensation-criteria can do. It can only yield an answer in cases where Scitovsky's double condition is also fulfilled: namely, when Kaldorian compensation is possible and losers cannot bribe gainers. Even when this is the case, it may fail, indeed, to sanction a change: a fact which may be accounted not a defect but a virtue.

Secondly, we have the alternative interpretation which Mr Little now claims to have been always his intention (and which seems to be plainer in his second edition than it was in the first).† This avoids the difficulty attaching to the other interpretation that we have just mentioned, but only at the expense, unfortunately, of some triviality. According to this an intermediate point on the Utility-Possibility Curve of Q_1 is selected (which may not, it seems, be what is strictly definable as a Utility-Possibility Curve, but rather what Samuelson has called a 'feasibility locus' consisting of positions that are reachable from Q_1, e.g. by whatever redistributive taxes are *practicable*).‡ This intermediate point is judged (by Mr Little presumably, either by intuition or by direct *ad hoc* evidence) to yield more welfare than the pre-existing distribution at Q_1. Let us call this point H. Then if Q_2 stands in the north-east quadrant relative to H (which means that the Index-Number inequality $\Sigma p_2 q_2 > \Sigma p_2 q_1$ is fulfilled for a move from H to Q_2), this shows that Q_2 is a Pareto-optimum relative to H: *i.e.* at least one per-

---

that it is the better distribution. In this way, with the aid of the distribution condition, one could make the Scitovsky-criterion yield more than by itself it was capable of doing.

* It is unreasonable because it could sanction a move when the product-change is such as to cause a much bigger loss to one of the parties than there is gain to the other (so far as one is allowed to compare them): that is, there is a sharp fall in the national income when valued at the prices of one of the situations.

† This interpretation was apparently adopted at a quite early stage by Dr Graaff (*Theoretical Welfare Economics*, pp. 161–2), though he thought it "not very useful", and by Professor Charles Kennedy.

‡ In *The Economic Journal* (Dec. 1963), p. 779.

son can be made better off at Q_2 without anyone being worse-off than at H. Putting these two judgements together, we have what Professor Sen calls (approvingly) a transitive-preference argument :

H is preferred to Q_1,
Q_2 is preferred to H,
$\therefore Q_2$ is preferred to Q_1.

It must be noticed, however, that this interpretation of what is a preferred distribution implies a direct judgement in each particular instance that H is more welfare-yielding than Q_1, *all things* taken fully into account. This is what the judgement about distribution apparently boils down to. It does not consist of using any theoretical generalisation about the kind of distribution that is superior from the standpoint of welfare (such as Pigouvian Proposition 2). It requires a particular *ad hoc* judgement on each occasion : which is why we have called the end-result of this interpretation trivial and uninteresting. It turns out that Mr Little is not offering us any special principle that we can use for ourselves on any occasion when the problem crops up. It does not provide what Dr Mishan has called an "inter-subjective apparatus" as basis for discussion and analysis :[*] one has simply to take Mr Little's word for it (or someone else's) that a point H in the appropriate neighbourhood is more welfare-yielding than Q_1, or else to conduct the appropriate investigation oneself to find out whether this is so. This is, surely, bye-passing all the difficult problems involved in making such comparisons, instead of providing analytical machinery to aid them : assuming the problem already solved by intuition instead of affording reasons on which an answer can rest.

Professor Kennedy once raised the very pertinent query:[†] why, if H and Q_1 can be compared in this way, by direct inspection, cannot Q_2 be directly compared with Q_1 in like manner? What need is there for introducing the intermediate point H, and what place has the Scitovsky-criterion in the judgement? If Q_2 can be compared with Q_1 directly, we are confronted simply with the proposition : "Any point that is to be judged more welfare-yielding than Q_1 is an 'improvement'

---

[*] 'The Welfare Criteria that Aren't' in *The Economic Journal* (Dec. 1964), p. 1016.
[†] In *Review of Economic Studies*, no. 52 (1952–3), pp. 137–42. So also did Dr Graaff, *op. cit.* p. 162.

on Q_1 and is socially preferable." Compensation-tests and evidence from Index Numbers then fade from the picture and cease to have a place.

To this query of Professor Kennedy Mr Little has merely offered what has not unfairly, perhaps, been termed* the "lame reply" that one may find it easier on many occasions first to compare Q_2 with some intermediate point like H instead of making the comparison with Q_2 directly.

One should perhaps add—if only to preclude excessive scepticism as to whether anything at all useful can ever be said about welfare—that this approach, if regarded as providing empirical guidance or a 'practical test' of a gain in welfare applicable to many, but not necessarily to all, situations, would have much more to be said for it than our argument has implied (at any rate if the possibility of comparing individual utilities were not denied). The same applies to the notion of compensation more generally as well as to either interpretation of the Little-condition.† But in this chapter we have been concerned with principles and definitions as a basis for an optimising theorem, and as such a definition must have both generality and logical consistency—it cannot stand if it involves a contradiction and it cannot rest on *ad hoc* judgement in particular cases.‡

There is an incidental consideration to be noted about the Little-condition, that unless some restriction is placed on H so as to give it the same distribution as Q_2 (*e.g.* that it should be on the same radial line from the origin on a Utility-Possibility

---

* Sir Dennis H. Robertson in *The Economic Journal* (March 1962), p. 228. Professor Sen, however, deems it a quite important consideration that the use of an intermediate point may make such judgements much easier (*The Economic Journal*, Dec. 1963, pp. 773, 775–6).

† It is no doubt with this in mind that Professor Scitovsky comforts us with the statement that the contradictory intersecting case is "not very important" (*Papers on Welfare and Growth*, p. 183)—by which he presumably means important in practice (as estimated, *e.g.* by the number of times it is likely to confront practical judgements). This is all right if one's concern is to be able to detect, in a fairly wide range of practical situations, what is a probable improvement. But it does *not* suffice as a basis for establishing a rigorously defined efficiency principle of general applicability.

‡ *Cf.* Professor Charles Kennedy on a "criterion" and a "test" in *The Economic Journal* (June 1963), p. 341: "it is a *criterion* to which even the remotest possibility of contradiction is fatal", whereas "there is no reason why a test should be a perfect one for its use to be justified".

Curve diagram) there is a possibility of its contradicting itself, even when interpreted as a 'transitive-preference argument'.* This it can do if the ideal, or most welfare-yielding, distribution (*e.g.* equality) stands between Q_1 and Q_2. Then a point H, to which Q_2 is superior on Scitovsky-grounds (*i.e.* Q_2 is inside the north-east quadrant pivoted on H), can be more welfare-

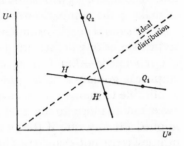

yielding than Q_1 because nearer to the ideal distribution, while at the same time another point H' to which Q_1 is superior on Scitovsky-grounds, can be more welfare-yielding than Q_2 (because nearer to the ideal distribution than is Q_2).

One more general comment is pertinent before we leave the present subject. If there is an essential relativity of size of national income to its distribution (as of space and time in Einsteinian cosmology), this relativity must manifestly operate in both directions. In other words, any characterisation of a certain income-distribution, with respect to its effects on welfare, must be relative to the particular goods-total that one is distributing. What may be ideal in the case of one goods-total may be far from ideal with another collection of goods, quite differently assorted or consisting of different things. This is very relevant to the kind of judgement about distribution that was implied in the first interpretation of the Little-criterion that we have considered; and it is certainly not irrelevant even to the second. What at first sight could have seemed to be more impeccable logic than the proposition we have discussed, to the effect that if Q_1 be redistributed in the direction of what on general grounds is judged to be a preferable distribution, and the Index-Number data demonstrate that everyone can be made better off at Q_2 because $\Sigma p_2\, q_2 > \Sigma p_2\, q_1$, Q_2 must necessarily be superior in welfare-content to Q_1? Yet we have seen that it is dubious if not fallacious; and the fallacy of this type of proposition

* This was pointed out by Dr S. K. Nath in *The Economic Journal* (Sept. 1964), p. 553. Dr Mishan has defined an appropriate condition that would exclude this possibility (in *Oxford Economic Papers*, July 1965, p. 230; *The Economic Journal*, March 1962, pp. 242–3).

consists as much in supposing that what may be a more welfare-
yielding distribution with a goods-total Q_2 must also be the
more welfare-yielding distribution with a different goods-
total Q_1, as in supposing that what is a superior magnitude
measured in one set of prices is necessarily superior when
measured in another set. In other words, definition of a favourable or unfavourable change in distribution may well be
different according to the Utility-Possibility Curve one happens
to be moving along; and one cannot state *in general terms* a
preference between the distribution at Q_2 and the distribution
at Q_1 independently of the particular Utility-Possibility Curves
that are involved. This should become obvious as soon as one
considers the meaning of the differing *slopes* that Utility-
Possibility Curves may have. If a curve slopes either very steeply
or very flatly over the relevant range, this means that one party
loses (or gains) a *lot* of utility while the other party gains (or
loses) relatively *little* from a given redistribution of the goods-
total in question. Since this cannot fail to be relevant to the
welfare-effect of redistribution (except possibly to someone
entirely blind to interpersonal comparison), it follows that
not only the relative positions of the points compared (as
estimated, for example, according to radial lines from the
origin) but also the *slopes* of the Utility-Possibility Curves
involved must be taken into account in any comparison of
distributions.

Take the Kaldor-contradict-
ing case. Suppose that from past
experience with Q_1 it has become
a firmly established principle
that shifts in distribution in a
north-westerly direction are
more favourable to welfare than
their opposite because they yield

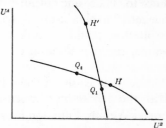

large gains in utility to A for relatively small losses to B. The
chance then arises of a shift to Q_2, which is accepted, since it
seems to yield the double advantage of an apparently favourable shift of distribution and the possibility of more-than-
compensating losers. But with the new goods total Q_2 the new
position is *not* the preferable distribution: moves back in the
reverse direction bring more gain to B than they bring loss to A.

Even if, on these grounds, it is decided to pay compensation and to move to H, this may be no more than a second-best, since the possibility of moving to the more welfare-yielding position H' will have been jettisoned by abandoning Q_1.

This consideration would not, of course, be of material importance if human tastes were uniform. Utility-Possibility Curves, representing different goods-bundles would not then have different slopes : we could suppose them all to be roughly parallel and there would be no problem (and no possibility of their intersecting). In the degree that human tastes vary, what we have said acquires importance. In a community composed of two ethnic groups, one traditionally subsisting on rice and the other traditionally subsisting on wheat (or—to vary the illustration—composed of meat-eaters and vegetarians) equality of money-income would be far from yielding equality of welfare if the cost of providing a certain rice-diet were several times in excess of providing an equivalent wheat-diet (or *vice versa*).

This is merely to repeat what was said in a more elementary form in an earlier chapter : that it is idle to suppose that an 'ideal distribution' can be defined in terms of money-income alone, and output (and prices) then be left to adapt themselves to the resulting demand-structure in some optimum manner. Output-policy cannot be treated as distribution-neutral in this way. It cannot be divorced from considerations of distribution since to choose one output-assortment in preference to another is *ipso facto** to choose one distribution of real income in preference to another; and given the structure of (varying) individual wants, the two things are but opposite sides of the same coin.

Although it is only incidentally, and not logically, associated with the debate on compensation principles, a word about the Social Welfare Function may not be out of place before we close the present chapter and our survey of welfare-theory. This concept owes its origin to Professor Abram Bergson in a famous article of 1938,† and the importance it has acquired is as a

* *I.e.* given a certain pattern of money-incomes, or else such a shift in distribution of money incomes as would enable the changed output-assortment to be sold without a change of prices.

† *Quarterly Journal of Economics*, vol. LII, no. 4 (Feb. 1938), pp. 310 (the article is under the name of Birk) ; reprinted in A. Bergson, *Essays in Normative Economics* (Cambridge, Mass., 1966), pp. 3–26.

formal device for positing something like a community indifference curve, or set of social preferences and orderings,
which will enable a general optimum, akin to Pigouvian Proposition 1, to be formulated. (On the familiar diagram, for
example, this can be defined as the point of tangency of the
Production-Possibility Curve and a Community-Indifference
Curve so derived). The notion of what we referred to earlier as
a 'top-level optimum', or unique optimum governing output
and the allocation of resources, is thereby rehabilitated. The
difficulties we have surveyed are resolved, it would seem, by reintroducing, in the guise of a general value-judgement, all those
things like interpersonal comparisons which the New Welfare
Economics had previously banished in the interests of a
'positive' *wertfrei* language-system. The welcome accorded to so
convenient a *deus ex machina* is scarcely to be wondered at.

With so much to its credit, one might be deemed ungrateful
to question its credentials. Yet its reception has not been an
unmixed one. On the one hand there is the voice of Professor
Scitovsky, apparently half-approving: 'This social function is
completely general. It can take into account external economies
and diseconomies as well as the dependence of one person's
satisfaction on other people's welfare . . . It is a kind of collective
utility function which expresses everybody's preferences
relating not only to his personal satisfaction but also to the
state of the entire community and to the distribution of welfare
among the members of the community." To which he adds,
perhaps a little sadly: "in fact the social welfare function, as
Bergson defines it, is so completely general that it is impossible
to tell, on the basis of internal evidence alone, what use
Bergson wanted to make of it"* (to which one is tempted to
add the words: "or could ever possibly have made of it").
On the other hand, it has been less reverently called by others a
large but empty portmanteau, a capacious "hold-all for all
valuations, set out in a definite order, a device which is supposed
to purify economic investigation of all vestiges of unscientific
matter" (Mr Paul Streeten),† and a "a many-coloured um-

* T. Scitovsky, *Papers on Welfare and Growth* (London, 1964), p. 184 (originally
in *American Economic Review*, June 1951). He speaks of it as having been "hailed as a
major contribution to welfare economics".

† In *Quarterly Journal of Economics*, vol. LXVIII (Aug. 1954), p. 358.

brella" and a "vast parti-coloured mathematical balloon" (Sir Dennis Robertson).* More temperately Professor Baumol judges it to be, though "right, not very helpful".†

In face of so considerable an amount of conflicting opinion, one's own judgement of the matter can be stated, perhaps, quite shortly and dogmatically. The Social Welfare Function (if one has understood it correctly) is an elegant example of the kind of formalism, so much in vogue today, which greatly facilitates analysis by supposing crucial problems to be solved by some ingenious (but undisclosed) device, without providing any actual means for their solution. A formal solution solves nothing if the real problems remain untouched and their solution is only posited in terms of the formalism. Attention then comes to be focused upon a simplified technique of analysis to which exaggerated importance comes to be attached—exaggerated since corollaries are derived with an implied economic content which any corollary must lack if this content is lacking in the main proposition. In this respect it has a cousinly resemblance to Mr Little's supposition that you can intuitively know in each case, or rely on someone to tell you, which is the more welfare-yielding distribution among any given set of alternatives. If one can, that is the end of the matter. There is little place left for Index Number data, little need for any theory and scarcely any point in writing books about it.

Not only this, but the over-simplified technique of analysis that is enthroned by this piece of formalism comes to be applied instrumentally (on the assumption of 'given ends') to situations in which the ends are themselves involved in the choice of means.‡ Thus distribution is assumed to be somehow known and postulated as ideal independently of prices and output (by a procedure that remains discreetly veiled); and applying an optimum is then conceived as being the operation of a certain price-and-output policy, when indeed output-composi-

---

* *Utility and All That and Other Essays* (London, 1952), pp. 39, 41.

† W. J. Baumol, *Economic Theory and Operations Analysis* (2nd edition, New Jersey, 1965), p. 380.

‡ On means and ends and the inadmissibility of treating the former as purely instrumental *cf.* Paul Streeten in *Quarterly Journal of Economics*, vol. LXVIII (Aug. 1954), esp. pp. 359–67; also in the *Quarterly Review of the Banca Nazionale del Lavoro*, no. 69 (June 1964), pp. 11, 16–17, where it is pointed out that the Social Welfare Function may be itself a function of "the policies employed to maximise it".

tion and prices are themselves involved in (since they affect) the positing of an ideal distribution of (real) income, as we have repeatedly shown.

Two particular criticisms of the Bergsonian Social Welfare Function have been made and given some currency; and one may throw these in here for good measure. The first of these, advanced by Mr Little, need not detain us very long. It is that such a device involves a complex ordering of all social states, and hence presupposes knowledge of an ideal social state in all its dimensions before anything can be said. This Mr Little thinks is a counsel of perfection, which can give no guidance in an imperfect and uncertain world as to the direction in which to move at a particular moment. "If economists have to wait for someone to come along and give them a consistent set of value premises they would wait for ever."* "The maximum", he thinks, "is a concept without any possible empirical significance, and therefore it seems preferable not to use it. It is more meaningful to derive the 'optimum' conditions as sufficient conditions for an improvement without attempting to define a maximum position."† In other words, one can often know which is the better without knowing what is the best. In the context of Mr Little's desire to find practical precepts and tests of an improvement this criticism is understandable and to the point. But its relevance seems more doubtful if the Bergsonian notion is viewed in the light of those more ambitious intentions with which we have endowed it: namely, to furnish the basis for a unique set of optimising theorems in face of the prevailing scepticism about interpersonal comparisons of utility on the part of 'new welfare economists'.

A more crucial objection is that made by Professor Arrow in the shape of the famous Impossibility Theorem.‡ Professor Arrow seems to have assumed, not unnaturally, that to form the basis for a system of general welfare-theorems such a set of social judgements and valuations as the Bergsonian function represents must be capable of being derived in some objective manner: if not exclusively from individual market-preferences (suitably weighted), at any rate by some kind of opinion-

* I. M. D. Little, *Critique of Welfare Economics* (Oxford, 1950), p. 83.
† *Ibid.* pp. 115–16.
‡ Kenneth J. Arrow, *Social Choice and Individual Values* (New York, 1951).

DWE

taking or voting-procedure devised to ascertain the sum-total of individual preferences when speaking as members of a community. According to such an interpretation, a Social Welfare Function would embody some 'general will' or common social convention or set of valuations. The possibility of deriving a consistent set of social valuations by this kind of method is accordingly of fairly crucial importance for its postulation.

Professor Arrow's critique, in brief, consists in saying that such a derivation is only possible if the individual preferences or orderings of which it is constituted have a special character, marked by an underlying unity of the system of orderings. This character is that of a so-called 'single-peaked preference system'. Anything other than this would mean that decision was only possible by methods of what he terms "dictatorship", which his rules for an acceptable solution explicitly disallow. Doubt is at once cast upon whether anything so complex as the decisions supposedly embodied in a Social Welfare Function can have this property, even if more simple sets of economic choice have.* If the scale of orderings lacks this basic unity, we are confronted with the familiar 'voting paradox' where the result may be different according to the order in which the chairman puts the choices to a vote.†

* *Cf.* J. Rothenberg, *The Measurement of Social Welfare* (New Jersey, 1961), p. 298, on such a property being unlikely to characterise "preference orderings in welfare economics where the alternatives of choice are complex, multi-dimensional entities".

† This is best illustrated, perhaps, by a very simple political example, with three voters, 1, 2 and 3, and three parties or policies, which we may write as Left, Right and Centre. The condition for a unique solution (independent, that is, of the order in which the vote is taken) is that all voters must agree, whatever their particular preferences, on at least one thing: that the basic structure of alternatives is such that Centre comes *between* Left and Right.

Take first the case where this condition is fulfilled and the preferences of the three voters is expressed in this way:

$$1. \ L \leftarrow C \leftarrow R.$$
$$2. \ R \leftarrow C \leftarrow L.$$
$$3. \ C \leftarrow R \leftarrow L.$$

This, it can be seen, is unambiguous. There are majorities of 2 : 1 for $C \leftarrow L$ and $C \leftarrow R$ and for $R \leftarrow L$; and there is no contradiction.

But suppose a second case where voters' preferences have this character:

$$1. \ L \leftarrow C \leftarrow R.$$
$$2. \ C \leftarrow R \leftarrow L.$$
$$3. \ R \leftarrow L \leftarrow C.$$

Professor Bergson's reply to this is that it misses the mark if applied in criticism of a Social Welfare Function as he himself conceives it, since its function as he sees it is that of giving advice or of "counselling".* As an individual's own moral judgement about what is best or most valuable, or as the policy-element in any social policy or economic plan, it need not coincide with, or be dependent upon, a majority verdict of the community. Even if, in arriving at such a judgement, weight is attached to public opinion and to the probable verdict of a popular poll, it will not be limited thereby and can be made—indeed *should* be made—even where there is no consensus of opinion on the matter.†

But then one is on the other horn of the dilemma. Conceived in this manner, such a conception may be immune to Professor Arrow's difficulty but only at the expense of losing an objective basis. We are left with a mere affirmation, lacking economic content and of uncertain provenance: a subjective judgement incapable of being argued about, defended or disputed—a mere formal device, as we have called it, for enabling an optimising theorem to retain an appearance of verisimilitude. Be it noted that in this respect it is very much less substantial and viable than the now *démodé* Pigouvian Welfare Economics. This postulated the maximising of something called 'utility' as its norm (which at least had a pedigree), and rested its theorems

Then one would get majorities of 2 :1 for $L \leftarrow C$ and for $C \leftarrow R$. This should imply $L \leftarrow R$. But in fact one gets a 2 :1 majority for $R \leftarrow L$, which is a contradiction. Consequently there is no unique result: this can vary with the order in which the vote is taken (*e.g.* if one votes first between R and L, R wins, and then between R and C, C wins; but if one starts by voting between L and C, L wins, and then between L and R, R finally wins.)

The contradiction is evidently introduced by voter no. 3, who is that un-orthodox kind of extremist who prefers *either* extreme to a moderate. Hence his social philosophy lacks an element of basic agreement with the others as to the way alternatives are ordered. What our first case has and our second case lacks is, apparently, agreement that the scale of ordering is governed by some uni-dimensional attribute, capable of being represented in terms of 'more or less' or 'nearer to or further away', along a scale.

* *Essays in Normative Economics*, pp. 35–9, 74.

† This is the view, if I understand it rightly, of Professor J. Rothenberg, although his emphasis is on the fact that one frequently *can* identify a set of "values prevailing in the community" according to certain criteria and that "a particular individual may on this view himself prefer B to A and simultaneously recognise that the judgement 'A is preferred to B' has been socially validated" (*op. cit.* p. 317).

on this comparatively simple and recognisable aim. This could be reasoned about; politicians could be persuaded of it or could reject it (*e.g.* on the ground that 'defence is better than utility'); there was no mystery or dissimulation about the methods by which the objective could be pursued if one wanted to. The theory stated: if it is thought to be a good thing to augment utility as defined, or economic welfare, this can be done in certain ways by applying certain general principles. It was not averse to telling one what it was doing. Various tests could be appealed to in order to indicate whether utility was greater or less. Even so, it could not surmount the size-distribution relativity which dogged attempts to establish a sufficient efficiency-criterion for maximising national income; and it was left, as we have seen, with indicator-lines as to the general direction of improvement rather than with a consistent optimising theorem about equalising marginal net products. Yet this new normative approach, which claims to banish all such difficulties, is much inferior to the old alike in explicitness and definition. What is the precise logical status of this new all-embracing value-judgement? How can we be sure that when we come to apply the corollaries derived from it objectives will not stand in conflict? We are told nothing of the real implications of applying the norm; we are left ignorant as to how and by what means it can be implemented, or even why the corollaries that we are enjoined to adopt should necessarily follow. For this apparently we must await the conjuror's act. Since the norm is curiously undefined (apart from the assurance that it will tell us all we want to know) and is not something to be objectively determined, we seem left to derive it, if not by seeking counsel of Professor Bergson on each occasion, either from divine inspiration or from some system of social philosophy that has yet to be revealed. This may be unavoidably true of a lot of moral imperatives. But if it can be any of these things, one may reasonably ask what kind of basis for a theory of welfare economics, that lays claim to rigour and exactitude, this can possibly be.

NOTE TO CHAPTER 6: TABULATION OF CASES

The following tabulation may prove helpful, in summary of the results of analysis in this chapter of the bearing of Index-Number data on the relative positions of Utility-Possibility Curves and on the fulfilment of compensation-criteria

Index-Number data	Implication by Pigou's method	Implication for an individual by Hicks's Method	Implication for a Group	
			Implicit modus probandi	Information about Utility-Possibility Curves in Situations 1 and 2
(P.) $\Sigma P_2 Q_2 > \Sigma P_2 Q_1$	Decisive for increase	On higher i-curve at Q_2	Redistributing Q_1's	Curve 1 runs south-west of point Q_2
(L.) $\Sigma P_1 Q_2 < \Sigma P_1 Q_1$	Decisive for decrease	On higher i-curve at Q_1	Redistributing Q_2's	Curve 2 runs south-west of point Q_1
(P.) $\Sigma P_2 Q_2 < \Sigma P_2 Q_1$	Not decisive (*may* be + or −)	Indecisive	Redistributing Q_1's	Curve 1 may or may not run north-east of point Q_2
(L.) $\Sigma P_1 Q_2 > \Sigma P_1 Q_1$	Not decisive (*may* be + or −)	Indecisive	Redistributing Q_2's	Curve 2 may or may not run north-east of point Q_1

I.e. $\Sigma P_2 Q_2 > \Sigma P_2 Q_1$ implies the Scitovsky-criterion.

$\Sigma P_1 Q_2 < \Sigma P_1 Q_1$ implies the impossibility of fulfilling the Kaldor-criterion.

$\Sigma P_2 Q_2 < \Sigma P_2 Q_1$ does *not* necessarily imply the impossibility of fulfilling the Scitovsky-criterion.

$\Sigma P_1 Q_2 > \Sigma P_1 Q_1$ does *not* necessarily imply the possibility of fulfilling the Kaldor-criterion.

The Possible Situations   Definable

                                    either as :   *or* as :

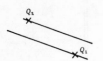

Scitovsky fulfilled for $Q_1 \to Q_2$,   Kaldor fulfilled for $Q_1 \to Q_2$,
   but *not* for $Q_2 \to Q_1$ *not* for $Q_2 \to Q_1$

Scitovsky *not* fulfilled for $Q_1 \to Q_2$,   Kaldor *not* fulfilled for $Q_1 \to$
   but fulfilled for $Q_2 \to Q_1$ but fulfilled for $Q_2 \to Q_1$

Scitovsky *not* fulfilled *either* for   Kaldor fulfilled *both* for $Q_1 -$
   $Q_1 \to Q_2$ *or* for $Q_2 \to Q_1$ and for $Q_2 \to Q_1$

Scitovsky fulfilled *both* for $Q_1 \to Q_2$ Kaldor *not* fulfilled *either*
   and for $Q_2 \to Q_1$ $Q_1 \to Q_2$ *or* for $Q_2 \to Q_1$

PART II

A SOCIALIST ECONOMY

CHAPTER 7

A SOCIALIST
ECONOMY: SOME PRELIMINARY
REMARKS

It is becoming fairly clear that some traditional habits of thought, slow to be surmounted, have specially handicapped economists' thinking about a socialist economy. These have had the effect, in particular, of obscuring certain crucial features of such an economy and of assigning exaggerated weight to elements common to different economic systems (at any rate, to elements common to a capitalist and a socialist system). Of such habits of thought one may single out two in particular, with their attendant consequences, which though familiar are easily overlooked or forgotten.

First, the notion that valuation of the national income (or alternatively total consumable output) can be measured independently of the way in which income is distributed has yielded (as we have seen) an oversimplified, indeed misleading, definition of maximising wealth or welfare, and hence an exaggeration of the degree of precision with which optimum conditions for the efficiency of any given set of economic arrangements can be formulated. One could go further, indeed, and say that it has led to a fallacious formulation of such optimum conditions so as to identify them virtually with the equilibrium position reached by a free market system under conditions of perfect competition; by implication establishing accordingly a stricter test than any planned economy seems likely in practice to attain. This has encouraged a myopic concentration on problems of marginal adjustment as though it were the only type of efficiency problem (encouraging such concentration if only because this problem seemed alone capable of elegant formal presentation). As a word for it one may find it convenient to refer to this below as the Perfectibility Fallacy. True, the relativity of size of total income to its distribution has frequently been mentioned in the discussions of recent years. None the less, corollaries derived from treating it as a simple and independent magnitude have shown themselves to die surprisingly hard.

Secondly, the habit of concentrating attention upon problems of stationary equilibrium has resulted in deficient attention being paid to the quintessential functions of planning : functions associated with the abolition or reduction of what Professor Koopmans has termed 'secondary uncertainty' and with the choice and maintenance of long-term paths of movement. Analysis of the conditions of stationary equilibrium is pre-occupied with the situation that is finally reached after a given change or displacement has occurred rather than with the path by which it is reached (reached, that is, provided that shifts in interdependent elements of the situation can be shown to be convergent, and not divergent, in their mutual interaction). Often, indeed, the notion is accepted implicitly that equilibrium is always reached effortlessly and quickly ; and situations where it may only be reached after a considerable period of oscillation, and hence of *dis*equilibrium, and considerable social cost, are conveniently ignored. Consequently, any function for planning, as distinct from decentralised market processes, is limited to the correction of departures of this equilibrium situation from the optimum (due, for example, to so-called 'external effects' in production or in consumption)—corrections which could supposedly be made by fiscal measures such as taxes or subsidies as well as by direct control over physical quantities. The conclusion is accordingly not surprising that, with a few exceptions everything could be as well arranged (if not better) by a decentralised market system, which would allegedly reproduce in a socialist economy all the supposed virtues of perfect competition.*

Once, however, the context of discussion is shifted to displacement, change and movement, the factor of uncertainty is immediately introduced as something that can affect the process of adjustment and may indeed thwart it so far as attainment of any particular equilibrium is concerned. It becomes apparent

* *Cf.* the remark of Professor Hicks : "In statics there is no planning ; mere repetition of what has been done before does not need to be planned" (J. R. Hicks, *Capital and Growth*, Oxford, 1965, p. 32).

that dynamic growth-paths may be highly unstable; that so-called adjustment processes may involve fluctuations which can even be cumulative, or at least self-perpetuating; and even when fluctuations are of the self-dampening kind, the process of convergence may occupy quite a long stretch of time. In cases such as this no optimal quality attaches to the solutions achieved by a decentralised market system however competitive it may be. The latter is as likely to get bogged down in a state of chronic stagnation as to be straining after growth-rates which are thwarted by a chronic condition of inflationary pressure. There is not even a major probability that a von Neumann maximum (and balanced) growth-path will be attained; and even the prevalence of high growth-rates is dependent on the postulation of an adventurous and pioneering race of *entrepreneurs* in the style of Schumpeter, or (what comes to the same thing) the existence in the economy of an exceptional degree of 'technical dynamism', combined with a compliant labour force.* Sustained growth, in other words, can be the result of a free market system *plus* some *deus ex machina*. It is in all such situations that planning, in the sense of coordinated control and intervention from the centre, has at least potential superiority.

Before turning to problems connected with the determination of output, investment and methods of production, it seems advisable to say something about the definition of a socialist economy. Since opinions about its appropriate definition may well vary, it is perhaps better to speak of what is a reasonable definition to adopt for the purpose of our present discussion.

Some modern discourses on socialism have tended to shift the focus of definition away from ownership towards social equality. Yet a treatment of the essence of a socialist economy as being other than the social ownership of means of production would represent a definite breach with the tradition of socialist thought as this was inherited from the past century and as it has inspired attempts to construct a socialist society characteristic of the present century. Emphasis on social ownership, indeed, was

* Necessary to the acceptance of a level of real wages consistent with a high rate of investment and level of profits, and hence to the absence of what Professor Joan Robinson has called "the inflation barrier".

not only characteristic of nineteenth-century founding-fathers of socialism as a doctrine and a social movement, in particular Marx and Engels,* but it has been the most commonly accepted emphasis of subsequent historians of the creed. We find Professor Carl Landauer, for example, opening his copious two-volume work on *European Socialism* with the statement, "We shall not find a more satisfactory definition than this: Socialism is a system of communal (or social) ownership of the means of production, established for the purpose of making (or keeping) the distribution of income, wealth, opportunity and economic power as nearly equal as possible."† (Equality, or approximate equality, it may be noted, is here designated as the *rationale* or purpose, but the system itself judged conducive to this end is defined in terms of ownership.) Even Sombart, who sought a wider type of definition of socialism as a "social movement" and "a living organism", recognised that "all Socialist writers agree that in the new order there will be no private ownership of property; or if it does exist, will exist only to a very limited degree. Private ownership as it exists to-day will, in the Socialist State, be transformed into common or communistic ownership (without a class of private Capitalist undertakers)."‡ In similar vein Sir Alexander Gray, in concluding his survey of *The Socialist Tradition*, says: "Socialism, in short, beyond indignation and reform, demands the abolition of the private ownership of much (if not all) wealth, and requires that the wealth so transferred should in some way be vested in, and operated by the community as a whole."§ Although more sparing of

---

* *Cf.* Marx's reference to "common ownership of the means of production" as characteristic of the socialist mode of production in his *Critique of the Gotha Programme* (English translation ed. by C. P. Dutt, n.d.), p. 11. It is true, of course, that ownership *per se* does not exhaust Marx's category of 'social relations of production' (there are other aspects of the latter, as we shall see); but ownership does constitute their fulcrum. This is not to deny that these other aspects (*e.g.* the relation of the individual worker to the productive unit of which he is a member and to the social productive process as a whole) have considerable importance in certain contexts, such as the problem of overcoming the 'alienation' of labour.

† *European Socialism: a History of Ideas and Movements*, by Carl A. Landauer (Berkeley and Los Angeles: University of California Press, 1959), vol. I, p. 5. This author adds: 'When we speak of socialism in this sense, we mean socialism as an economic order, that is, as a body of institutions.'

‡ *Socialism and the Social Movement*, by Werner Sombart, translated by M. Epstein (London and New York, 1909), p. 28.

§ Alexander Gray, *The Socialist Tradition* (London, 1946), p. 491.

definition, the original *Fabian Essays in Socialism* of 1889 made it clear that they regarded Socialism as essentially the antithesis of Private Property; while the statement of principles of the Fabian Society spoke of "emancipation of land and industrial capital from individual and class ownership, and the vesting of them in the community for the general benefit".*

Evidently we shall be doing nothing arbitrary if we treat a socialist economy as one in which the non-human factors of production (or means of production, including land) are in social or collective ownership in some form. Whether this means ownership by the State or by cooperative groups of workers or consumers (or some compromise between the two as with the Soviet *kolkhoz* or Yugoslav 'working collective') there is no need at present to specify, since it has little direct bearing on the problems we are to discuss. Sufficient to say that together with ultimate ownership of land or fixed capital vested in the State (with right of reversion) it is perfectly possible to have various degrees and forms of user-right, either temporary or permanent, (and hence limited and conditional ownership) granted to groups of working producers, like the industrial 'trusts' of the Soviet 1920s and the handicraft or agricultural *artel*.

We shall have more to say below about organisational forms and about equality or inequality. But one thing may be said immediately as arising directly from what has been said on the matter of definition. It seems fairly clear that such a definition is capable of embracing both a highly centralised, bureaucratic form of socialism and a more democratic, even ultra-democratic, type. Associated with these there may be varying degrees of inequality of wage- and salary-income: doubtless much smaller in the latter case than in the former, although they will share the common feature of having no class of income from property, with the specific (and pronounced) inequalities that this usually entails. Both of these extreme forms—of bureaucratic centralisation, (probably accompanied by some element of '*élitisme*') and of what the Webbs once called 'primitive democracy'†—

* *Cf.* M. Beer, *A History of British Socialism* (one-volume edition, London, 1940), p. 286.

† In relation to trade unions, in their *Industrial Democracy* (London, 1902), ch. 1. The limitations of such 'primitive democracy' as stressed by the Webbs

will remain socialism, even if both may involve contradictions with what could be regarded as the 'ideal essence' of socialism : in the former case a conflict of interests between the bureaucratic stratum and the rank and file of working producers, and the latter holding the danger of a possible negation of social coherence and planning in a welter of sectional interests. Both in their different ways may prove to be obstacles to a progressive development from what Marx termed the 'lower' to a 'higher' stage of socialism, or communism. But to see no distinction between these variants, on the one hand, and capitalism on the other (the latter being characterised by individual ownership of the means of production and by personal income derived from such ownership) would seem to be at best a slipshod mixing of categories (if our above definition is accepted) and at worst an emotive use of language.*

A matter on which there is greater disagreement than on the question of definition is whether a socialist economy must necessarily be a planned economy, in the sense that major economic decisions (such as would be entrepreneurial decisions in a capitalist economy) are taken by some central governmental body, and embodied in a general complex of decisions, or conspectus, coordinated *ex ante* for a defined planning period. It seems natural to suppose that this must be so, since it is difficult to envisage any other coordinating mechanism to replace the rule of market forces in an atomistic system of individual ownership ; and it is hard to envisage a State that has socialised production immediately dissolving it again into a plurality of independent sovereignties and entirely relinquishing control once more to the market. Yet among economists, at least, who have written upon the subject, many (if not most

were that it "leads straight either to inefficiency and disintegration, or to the uncontrolled dominance of a personal dictator or an expert bureaucracy" (*ibid.* p. 36). Experience of 'syndicalist' developments in the early days of the Russian Revolution suggests that forms of 'direct democracy' in industry, with reference to industrial policy, are limited fairly severely by the requirements of modern 'social production' and of modern technique.

* *Per contra*, 'State Capitalism', it may be noted, was used, for example, by Lenin, to refer to control and regulation by the State of *private* enterprise. The statement, *e.g.* by H. Marcuse (*Soviet Marxism*, New York and London, 1958, pp. 81–2), that socialism requires not only abolition of private property in means of production, but also "initiative and control 'from below'" at once invites the question, how much and in what form?

among 'western' economists) have advocated that something like this should be done. Of this we shall have more to say later. Even if we were to postulate forthwith that a socialist economy must *ipso facto* be a planned economy, this would be open to various interpretations, until we had specified the precise categories of decision that were centrally planned and the relation in which these stood to the operational functioning of lower units of command. The experience of actual socialist economies to-date, and change and experiment recently undertaken or in process of introduction, suggest that no clear-cut, logically defined frontier-line can be drawn between the province of centralised and of decentralised decision, and that concerning the expedient extent of the one and of the other there remain many problems for experience still to decide. In the terminology of contemporary discussion in those countries, the precise relation between plan and market remains undetermined.

Two things, however, it seems safe to postulate about market-relations in a socialist economy; drawing again both upon socialist tradition and upon the practice of socialist countries to-date. In the first place, the retail market for consumers' goods, whereby the products of economic activity that are destined for personal consumption pass into the possession of individual consumers, must normally be a market in the full sense: namely, that individual buyers are free to distribute their expenditure as they please between the supplies available, to purchase severally as much of any commodity as each pleases, and to substitute one purchase for another if this is judged to augment the utility derivable from a given money-expenditure. This we shall see has certain implications for price-policy in this market and indirectly for output-policy as well.

At the other end of the economic process there are some analogous characteristics in the manner in which labour is engaged and wage-differentials for various occupations are formed. To speak of a market for labour, or even a quasi-market, would be to invite strong disagreement from many, who would expect income-differences to be determined by other considerations than market-scarcities and transitory conditions of demand and would deem it incongruous if a socialist society failed to give ethical considerations a place in its incomes-policy.* The fact remains, however, that if direction of labour and restriction of free choice of occupation are to be avoided,† differences of wages between different types of work and different industries and localities must largely if not mainly be influenced by supply-conditions and by the need to attract labour in the directions in which the production plan requires that it should go. Some such differences are required, of course, by considerations of equity, in order to compensate those engaged in work that is more arduous, disagreeable or risky, or involves the individual workers in some special cost, initially or subsequently. Differences in income will to this extent be necessary to achieve Adam Smith's 'equality of *net* advantages' as between different occupations. But the need to move labour quickly, and to attract labour into rapidly expanding industries or grades at the same rate as their expansion, may necessitate the creation of still larger differentials, even if such differentials are temporary and not permanent and will in the fullness of time be revised.‡ They arise as inducements to incur once-for-all costs of movement and to overcome reluctance to move; and for obvious reasons these generally have to be paid in an occupation not only to newcomers but also to those who were in the occupation previously. Perhaps a combination of moral inducement and propaganda might reduce the need for such additional differentials, designed as *ad hoc* incentives; but this is hardly likely to dispense with them entirely. To the extent that the need for them remains, the pattern of wage-differences will be influenced, even if not

* One may recall the words of G. D. H. Cole: "The cry for the 'abolition of the wage-system' is a cry for the destruction of the whole idea that labour is a commodity to be bought and sold like any other commodity, that labour has its market price, settled by supply and demand . . . and not by any idea of human need or social justice, or even of service rendered . . . But essentially labour differs in nature from commodities . . . because it is human, and the value of humanity is not a market value" (*World of Labour*, London, 1917 edition, pp. 416–17).

† Indeed, those who reject reliance on so-called 'material incentives' under socialism as unethical, and hold that 'moral incentives' should suffice, seem bound in logic to admit that for those who fail to respond sufficiently to moral incentives compulsory measures of some kind must be resorted to.

‡ *Cf.* above, p. 66. The widening of wage- and salary-differentials in the Soviet Union in the 1930's, for example, was largely a result of a high growth-rate, with consequential shifts between industries and in the demand for labour (especially skilled and trained labour). Thus the extent of this widening was in large degree 'abnormal' (and also temporary).

regulated, by quasi-market forces concerned with the conditions of demand for and supply of various types of labour.*

The existence of such inequalities is fully consonant with the distinction that Marx made in a famous passage in his *Critique of the Gotha Programme* of 1875 between the two stages of socialism (now generally referred to respectively as socialism and communism). In the former of these differences of income would continue to exist according to the amount and nature of the work done. The individual worker "receives back from society ... exactly what he gives to it ... his individual amount of labour"—after necessary deductions for investment, for "non-productive services" like health and education and administration, for pensions and for a "reserve or insurance fund against misadventures". Only at a higher stage "after labour, from a mere means of life, has itself become the prime necessity of life; after the productive forces have also increased with the all-round development of the individual and all the springs of cooperative wealth flow more abundantly", will the superior equity of distribution according to need (and contribution according to ability) be realised.†

It can readily be seen that such differences in money income would lose much of their force as incentives if their recipients were not free to spend them as they pleased. We have seen that the utility to be derived from a given money-income is increased if consumers are free to adjust their patterns of consumption to their individual tastes. This is equivalent to saying that the real value of a given money income, and accordingly of income-

* *Cf.* the statement of Professor Ota Šik: "Under socialism, with its highly developed social division of labour ... labour cannot yet be man's prime want ... At the socialist stage of development *labour is still relatively onerous* (long hours) *and intensive*. There is a *relative lack of variety*, work is monotonous and, for most people, offers little creative scope. There is still a *fairly rigid division of labour*, binding the majority to *one occupation for life*. Consequently as a general rule people expend their labour for others primarily because labour is the condition for acquiring from others the use values needed for themselves" ('Socialist Market Relations' in C. H. Feinstein, ed., *Socialism, Capitalism and Economic Growth: Essays presented to Maurice Dobb*, Cambridge, 1967, p. 139).

† *Critique of the Gotha Programme*, pp. 11–14. Perhaps it might be said that Marx's statements only refer to wage-differences due to different amounts of effort expended (including that involved in training for an occupation) and different disutilities involved in various occupations, but not to wage-differences due to temporary scarcities. The Soviet Union and other socialist countries to-date, however, have apparently found it necessary and have not hesitated to utilise the latter.

differences or of marginal additions of income (to compensate, for example, for additional work), would be much reduced if consumption goods were extensively rationed. Thus the existence of a free retail market for consumers' goods can be said to be logically consequent upon the use of wage-differentials as production-incentives in a socialist economy (as well as being desirable *per se* from the standpoint of individual welfare to the extent that individual tastes differ).

In what follows we shall accordingly assume that the socialist economy of which we are speaking is characterised *both* by a free market for what in the next chapter will be called 'end products' *and* by free choice of occupation and mobility of labour, with wage-policy regarding the structure of wage-differentials as the main regulator of labour supply.

In addition to individual work-incentives it is quite possible, even probable, that there will also be collective incentives: collective in the sense that they are related to the results achieved by a working group, a production unit or by a whole industry or sector. The economic *raison d'être* of these is that without them the individual worker would feel interested in nothing beyond his own individual job. His horizon would be unduly narrowed, and his attitude to production might be little different from what it was under capitalism when he sold his labour-power as a commodity and concern of each for his own individual betterment was the sole consideration. In these circumstances the individual interest might well conflict with the interests of production in general, since production is a collective or social process: for example, in connection with technical innovation and restrictive practices. This would be the more serious, the greater the influence which workers had in industrial policy, whether through direct participation in control and management or indirectly through their trade unions. At any rate, there would be little or no inducement to initiative from below in pioneering improvements and rationalisation in productive methods or in industrial organisation.

On the other hand, the larger the size of the unit to which such collective payments were related, the more remote would the payment be, *qua* incentive-payment, from the individual and from any direct result of his actions; consequently the weaker would be its probable effect. It is possible to imagine the payment to all earners of a social dividend related, for example, to the size or to the rate of increase of the total national income. But this would be sufficiently remote to render any effect it had symbolic or psychological rather than economic in the strict sense. As a compromise that avoided undue remoteness on the one hand and insufficient 'collectivity' on the other, some kind of dividend or bonus scheme related to the productive achievements of the plant or enterprise (as the managerial unit combining perhaps a number of plants) would seem to be the most reasonable. Its basis could be total production measured in some physical unit or in value, or net value produced after deducting the cost of inputs, or again balance-sheet net income or profit. We shall see later that the use of some of these measures tends to introduce a distorting bias into decisions about output and productive methods; in which respect some are to be accounted superior to others (especially those which generalise or synthesise various aspects of productive work and economic decision-taking). Whatever the basis, however, such collective payments are almost bound to conflict in some degree with purely individual ones. Some would say that they conflict in principle by introducing some other criterion for income-differences than difference in amount or nature of work done. To most socialists, for example, the very terminology of 'dividends' and 'profit-sharing' is apt to have an alien sound. Putting it in the language of Welfare Economics, objectors might say that income-variations are other than would equate the marginal utilities of individual incomes to the marginal disutilities involved in earning those incomes; thus introducing an undesirable degree (or form) of income-inequality. Others might stress the purely production-incentive effect: namely that the payment of collective incentives of this kind, however based, would tend to conflict with the income-differentials geared to differences of work performed, generally in the direction of reducing these differentials as a proportion of total income. In the limit where collective payments composed the major proportion of total income, they might so submerge payment-differentials based on individual work-performance as to render the influence of these nugatory.*

* The same, be it noted, would apply to the lump-sum 'social dividend' favoured by Professor Bergson and Professor Lerner (and mentioned approvingly

Socialism, however, if it is to mean anything in terms of human psychology and relations, presumably must imply the supersession of purely individualistic motivation and the modification (if not subordination) of individual actions and interests in some degree by the influence of the group. Hence *some* merging of individual and collective interests and incentives is surely to be expected; and the most suitable level for this to take place would seem to be that of the productive unit or working group.

Fortunately we are absolved from the need to pronounce at all specifically about such collective income payments, since our concern here is with general problems of a socialist economy and the general form of their solution, rather than with specific prescription. Some degree of payments of this kind seems to be necessary to the smooth functioning of a socialist economy: to supply it with motivation at the operational level. As such, the case for it would be held to be only partly economic, and in major degree to belong to the category of what Marx termed the 'social relations of production'—the relation in which men stand to one another, and in this instance the relation in which workers in one production unit or industry stand to those in others and to the economy as a collective whole (with the economic plan as its expression). One has to recognise, at least, that a problem of complex motivation exists here, if the 'alienation' of the individual, *qua* producer, is to be fully overcome and a socialist economy is to steer successfully between an undemocratic and impersonal bureaucratisation, on the one hand, and atomistic disintegration of the collective economy, on the other hand. It could be called a problem in the fusing of individual interests with larger group or collective interests: a fusion which needs to occur in the sphere of economic or material incentives as a *basis* for the eventual subordination of these to moral incentives and to 'social consciousness' (this rather than setting 'material' and 'moral' motives against one another as *opposites*). The need for something of this kind seems to be one of the lessons (as we shall see in a moment) that actual

by Professor Lange). Curiously, Professor Bergson mentions this effect with reference to expansion of free social services (*Essays in Normative Economics*, Cambridge, Mass., 1966, p. 185), but is silent on the analogous effect of a 'social dividend' in monetary form.

experience to-date has yielded, and of which account must be taken in any attempt to grapple with the political economy of socialism.

Regarding the actual organisational forms in which the operations of a planned economy are embodied we shall, again, make no hard and fast assumption. This is a question that we shall leave open, at any rate for the moment, although what is said later about the nature of the economic problems involved will carry certain implications affecting it. The existence of a planned economy, even if planning embraces a multitude of detail, does not preclude the necessity for operational commands at various levels concerned with execution and with the complex of particular decisions associated therewith; any more than in military operations the existence of a general staff and a high command precludes the existence of a chain of lower commands down to the level of the company and the platoon. Indeed, the spheres of planning and of operational implementation are qualitatively distinct even if they overlap—just as strategy and tactics have always been recognised as being. Thus autonomy regarding the latter, within the framework of planned directives and targets, must necessarily rest with these 'local' executive units. But since planning can scarcely provide for every eventuality, even with the most perfect information at its disposal, the question of principle turns on the kind and type of decision that should be embraced by planning commands or indicators and the degree of detail specified within each category. These highest-level decisions will be made in the light of maximum vision (within the limits of available information and the possibility of digesting it) of the situation as a whole, and will be characterised (at least potentially) by scientific unity and consistency, given the policy objectives* that form the cornerstones of the plan.† Decisions at lower levels, by contrast, whether falling within the category of plan-making or implementation, will inevitably lack the advantage of global vision. Sectional perspectives, even sectional

* Or 'welfare criteria' as economists might say.

† Professor J. Tinbergen has suggested that a consideration relevant to the allocation of decisions between various levels is the area over which the 'external effects' of any given decision are spread : "decisions should be taken at a level high enough to make external effects of such decisions negligible" (C. H. Feinstein, ed., *Socialism, Capitalism and Economic Growth*, p. 130).

interests, are most likely to intrude. It is here that the problem of motivation which we have mentioned can assume crucial importance for the functioning of the system; likewise the problem of compensating for absence of knowledge of the global situation by the provision of some kind of indicators, expressive of the general situation and of planning intentions, as a frame for decision-taking. Market-indicators, or prices, are one form that such indicators can take.

It would be surprising, indeed, if theory could postulate *a priori* what in this field were the necessary requirements for efficient functioning of a system of this type. Moreover, viewed in the perspective of development, the requirements at one stage and in one type of economic structure or environment may well prove to be different from those of another stage and context.* Here the verdict of actual experience could reasonably be expected to be our only sure guide. Possibly the experience of functioning of socialist economies in anything approaching 'normal' or 'typical' conditions is still too short† for the political economy of socialism to be able to formulate more than a tentative pronouncement on such matters. Possibly such experience as there has been to-date requires further sifting and analysis before anything at all interesting, still less final, can be postulated. Yet there has now been experience over several decades, and experience affording opportunity for some comparative analysis that should be sufficient for a provisional listing of some lessons or conclusions. Even those unwilling to endorse the conclusions as we are about to formulate them would probably agree that at least they realistically describe a problem, or an aspect of a problem, that experience to-date has thrown into relief. If so, it seems

* The hypothesis suggests itself, for example, that when large structural changes are on the agenda and a high rate of capital accumulation, a fairly high degree of centralisation will be necessary in planning and administration (and *a fortiori* when development takes place against a previously low level of development). Centralised methods, again, seem more appropriate to phases of 'extensive' development, with reserves of labour to be drawn upon, than to phases of 'intensive' development when the accent is on higher productivity and technical innovation.

† It is often forgotten how much of the time during which the Soviet economy has operated (prior to 1950 at any rate) was in conditions of war economy or semi-war economy—in conditions of reconstruction from the effects of war (as in 1920–5 and 1945–50) or of accelerated rearmament if not of war itself.

incumbent on us to take account of them in our thinking about a socialist economy.

The first and most general conclusion to emerge from experience to-date concerns the function and rôle of prices. In the past economists have been inclined (perhaps by reason of their pre-occupation with conditions of stationary equilibrium) virtually to identify the economic problem with the price-problem; failing to recognise that prices perform a number of distinct functions in a socialist economy and not a unique one. In the theory of equilibrium price performs a unique function as the equilibrator between quantity demanded and quantity supplied (these being normally expressed as functions of price). Price has, indeed, come to be conceived virtually as a point of intersection of two curves (or by the mathematically minded as a mere 'dual' of an optimal arrangement of quantities). Complete price-flexibility has accordingly been regarded as a necessary condition of the *tâtonnement* (or 'trial and error') process whereby equilibrium is reached, and the attainment of equilibrium as almost inconceivable in the absence of a free price-mechanism. For many persons this association of price with the notion of an actual equilibrium has apparently become so ingrained as to exclude from their minds the possibility that equilibrium might be reached by another instrument than that of continually fluctuating market-prices. The movement of stocks, for example, commonly takes the brunt of very short-period demand-fluctuations, and is often used in a market economy as a demand-indicator for adjusting output and supply (*e.g.* in the case of rigid or 'maintained' prices). It seems natural to conclude that indices of stock-movements could be used as an instrument of short-run adjustment of supply in a socialist economy.* Yet one finds a tendency among economists to treat any price-system that does not provide for complete, almost day-to-day, flexibility (like an organised stock or produce market) as *ipso facto* irrational.† So much is our reason captive of particular and habitual modes of thought.

* *Cf.* the present writer's *Essay on Economic Growth and Planning* (London, 1960), pp. 84–5.

† *E.g.* Professor Alec Nove, writing on 'The Reforms behind Russia's New Price System' in *The Times*, 27 June 1967 (p. 21), speaks of the Price Reform as "conceptually incorrect" because the new prices are mainly "based on 'cost-plus'",

Experience has shown, however, what should perhaps have been obvious before : that the position is by no means so simple ; that there are several different *kinds* of price ; and that when dealing with a planned economy it is necessary in each case to ask what kind of price it is according to the function it performs. True, economists have always recognised in the past that to different types of postulated equilibrium (*e.g.* long-period or short-period) different sorts of price were appropriate. But little if any attention was paid to the possibility of conflict between prices of different types,* in the sense of the reactions evoked by the one standing in conflict with the requirements of another type of equilibrium.†

Thus it is clear that in a socialist economy there can be, first, accounting prices used as a basis for planning or for administrative decisions either at the centre or at some lower level. Secondly, there are also accounting prices that are used purely for recording and accounting purposes, but without having any direct influence upon planning decisions or any other type of decision (although they may, of course, influence decisions indirectly) For example, these may be used simply as a unit of account and as a medium for generalising information, providing the 'weighting' in any summation or aggregation of detail expressed in diverse physical terms into a more general form (*e.g.* for handling by an input-output balance, or matrix).‡

whereas "prices must in some way reflect need, scarcity and abundance, supply and demand". *Cf.* the same writer's *Soviet Economy* (London, 1961), pp. 282–3. Whether the fixed prices in question could with advantage be revised at more frequent intervals is a different question, to be answered according to empirical considerations and not in terms of conceptual 'correctness' or incorrectness.

* *Cf.* S. Ganczer in *Acta Oeconomica* (Budapest), vol. I, no. 1–2 (1966), p. 55 : "Prices may be called upon to perform a variety of functions which, however, can be met only in a contradictory way." On different prices relating to decisions affecting periods of different lengths of time *cf.* also J. Lipiński in *Price Formation in Various Economies*, ed. D. C. Hague (London and New York, 1967), esp. p. 124.

† The exception to this is the so-called 'cobweb theorem' dealing with the special case of unstable equilibrium due to delayed response of supply to price changes, with consequential over-shooting of the supply-response at a later date.

‡ These are called "programming prices" by Dr J. G. Zielinski, who emphasises the variety of uses that prices have to perform in a planned economy (in yet unpublished lectures on *The Theory of Socialist Planning* at the Nigerian Institute of Social and Economic Research, Lecture 4). He also points out that different methods of aggregation may be appropriate to different purposes : *e.g.* calorific value is appropriate in the case of coal when constructing the fuel and power balance, but weight in connection with the transport balance.

Akin to them are, thirdly, prices that perform the function of summarising information in the different sense of providing some kind of evaluation of a complex situation, and which may or may not be the basis for decisions. 'Shadow prices' as the 'dual' of linear programming solutions, or Kantorovitch's *otsenki*, perform this function.* But these latter have the further peculiarity that they can only be derived when the optimum production-pattern is known, and are entirely relative to this optimum : in this sense they are by nature 'ideal prices' rather than actual, since in the real world no more than some degree of approximation to an ideal production-pattern is ever likely to be realised. Fourthly, there are prices, whether purely notional or representing actual payments made, that are used primarily as a standard or term of comparison with which prices of some other type are compared, and certain decisions taken (*e.g.* about the pattern of relative outputs or about methods of production) on the basis of this comparison. The special cost-prices of inputs considered in the next chapter are of this kind. Fifthly, there are prices which have the function of governing incentive-payments made to individuals or a collective of individuals (such as an enterprise). Normally such prices are the actual prices, or transactions-prices, in which transactions are actually conducted and upon which the incomes of individuals or enterprises depend. But they need not be so, and can diverge from the price paid by the purchaser of the product in question. In this connection it may be noted that wages will not be a market price in the usual and full sense (as we have seen) even if differentials strongly reflect differences in the demand-supply relationship in different occupations : for example, wages will not fall to zero if there is a surplus of labour. Finally, we have the retail prices of consumers' goods, which must be true market prices, equilibrating demand with current supply, if rationing is to be avoided (whether official rationing or casual rationing by shop-shortages and queues). This price-level and its pattern of relative prices, as we have seen, is of crucial significance in governing the real value that any money wage or wage-differential will have;

---

* Kantorovich wisely emphasised the difference between his *otsenki* and Marxian 'value'. Unfortunately this did not prevent some of his critics (*e.g.* Boiarski) declaring that he wished to *substitute* them for the Marxian category of value.

and no policy with regard to incomes or incentive-payments can be considered in isolation from it. A policy relating to money wage-rates (a policy that is, moreover, likely to be influenced by both social and efficiency reasons as well as by attention to the current supply-demand situation) cannot even have a clear meaning unless it is related to some particular retail price policy, and in turn to an output policy for consumers' goods industries. By contrast, transactions between organisations and the prices at which these are conducted lack this direct impact upon the real value of incomes and income-differentials; and there may be less need for such prices to perform an equilibrating function to the extent that planning includes an allocation system for inputs as well as the setting of output targets. It may also be noted in this connection that the prices paid to producing units and suppliers need not always be identical with those charged to users.*

It would look as though any unique system of 'ideal prices', whether accounting-prices, shadow prices or actual prices, is unlikely to prove successful in reconciling and performing simultaneously the multiform functions required of it. In practice it would seem that there must be either some compromise between different functions or else some combination of different kinds of price (such as accounting prices for certain types of calculation or certain categories of planning decisions combined with actual prices as the basis for incentives and as governors of decentralised decision at lower levels).

Secondly, it would appear that a crucial limiting factor upon what planning can do is the supply of information : its character, its 'objectivity', its extent and its suitability for easy and fairly rapid systematisation and digestion. This more than anything else seems to determine the feasible extent of centralised decision, and hence the volume and nature of the residual decision-making that has necessarily to be decentralised to subordinate

---

* Such a difference may or may not be due to the imposition of a tax (*e.g.* turn-over tax). In Soviet industry it often happens that the buying-price to enterprises is differentiated according as their cost-situation differs for reasons external to the enterprise; such differentiation being a way of dealing with either temporary or permanent 'rent' elements and equalising the situation of various enterprises so far as their profitability-situation is concerned. At the level of the selling organisation (*sbyt*) for the whole industry or branch a uniform price is established, either by averaging or (if selling-price is built up to marginal cost) by averaging combined with a tax-obligation upon the selling organ.

units; and this in turn conditioning the articulation and functioning of the system in the course of plan-implementation, of
which we have already spoken. For easy assimilation and use in
plan-making information has to be quantifiable in the main:
for example, data usable in input-output analysis or in optimal
allocation. At least this is true where anything approaching
precision is required. But most economic information is only
quantifiable subject to a margin of error or of uncertainty,
which sometimes may be too small to matter but also may often
be quite significantly large. This will apply to anything affected
appreciably by the human factor, and *a fortiori* any projection
(explicit or implicit) of recent experience into the future—
a future where innovations and unforeseeable eventualities can
be expected to occur. The door is here opened to the play of
practical judgement, estimating and guesswork, on the basis
of the actual 'feel' of the situation: something which those at
the factory or enterprise level, in close touch with the production-situation, may have, but which planners at the centre
can rarely have. The door is at the same time opened to an
element of bias in the information furnished by those at lower
levels who compile it (because they alone are in possession of
the raw experience from which the generalised information is
derived). Bias arises from the fact that provision of data about
the production-situation is not just an academic exercise. The
information when received is put to practical use, and practical
consequence follow from it (*e.g.* the setting of output-targets and
supply allocations). This, it may be noted, is a bias attaching
peculiarly to the flow of information in one direction—information flowing *towards* those who will take the ultimate decisions
binding on the operations of those supplying the information.
Experience certainly indicates that data supplied (*e.g.* about
production-coefficients and input-requirements) in fact tend
to have such a bias, and one that is apt to be in the direction of
conservatism and caution, underestimating possibilities and
concealing reserves (whether of equipment or of manpower).
In the larger picture such imprecision may not seem seriously
to matter. But the more detailed the planning directives, the
more serious an obstacle it tends to become, if only because of
the rigidity and narrowed scope for operational discretion that
detailed directives introduce, and the premium thereby placed

on the holding of reserves as a means of securing elbow-room and freedom of manoeuvre.

At a comparatively early stage of development this type of problem may remain of minor importance. But as the system grows in complexity, the feasible limits on efficient centralised decision-taking become more evident, and correspondingly the need to decentralise the taking of economic decisions becomes more pressing. A contributory factor may be the approach, in the course of development, to conditions of full employment of the labour force, with population-increase a limiting factor upon economic growth of an 'extensive' kind. In such conditions major emphasis has necessarily to be laid on raising labour productivity by a continuing process of innovation and of rationalisation of working methods: a process requiring constant initiative at the level of production. The approach of such conditions may or may not coincide in time with the arrival of a period in which priority in economic policy for the requirements of growth yields place to greater attention to consumption and to the needs of a rising standard of life.* If it does, the need for decentralisation of economic decision seems likely to be reinforced, in the light of greater attention to the demand-pattern of consumption, with increased variability and complexity of this pattern as average income rises.

An obvious line of demarcation for any horizontal division of responsibility in decision-making would be between decisions regarding investment in durable plant and equipment and decisions about current output. Such a demarcation acquires plausibility because it corresponds to the conventional economists' distinction between the long period and the short period. If decisions concerning investment in plant and equipment were to be centralised, this would set the long-period framework within which the autonomy of production units (firms or enterprises) would operate; the latter having discretion as to what and how much to produce, choice of inputs and sources of supply, problems of employment and personnel on the basis of given plant and equipment. Provided that the pro-

* On transition from a first period of this kind to a second, and the necessarily limited term of the first, cf. the present writer's *Papers on Capitalism, Development and Planning* (London, 1967), pp. 107 *et seq.*

duction-unit has an interest in maintaining full-capacity working and in adapting its output-pattern to demand, auto-nomy is unlikely to have any disorganising effects, save to the extent that a tendency to indulge in hoarding of stocks of materials or of labour may create shortages elsewhere, together with other symptoms of so-called inflationary pressure (a result that experience has shown is by no means always avoided at the peak of centralisation). Central planning would be absolved from the need to fix particular output targets on a short-term basis (as distinct from longer-term 'perspective plans'):* its very control over the creation of new productive equipment, both its kind and its amount, limiting fairly straitly the possible variation of output-pattern and quantity that decentralised output-decision could yield (limiting it the more straitly, the more specialised the equipment in question).

Centralised control over investment has special appeal when we consider the question of overall stability of the economy. Experience has shown that a free market economy, unless it is tethered to a commodity-money system (which itself imposes some drastic costs of its own) is subject to great macro-instabi-lity (*e.g.* as regards inter-sectoral adjustments and the general price-level).† In socialist countries to-date inflationary ten-dencies would seem to have followed any marked degree of decentralisation and to have constituted one of the weaknesses of the latter.‡ Because investment fluctuations are the most patent cause (apart from autonomous wage-increases) of general

* Save for things in particularly short supply, the distribution of which would also require to be controlled by some system of centralised allocation. It may be noted that in Czechoslovakia the economic reforms of 1965–6 left enterprises free to fix their own annual operative plans; centrally fixed output targets being con-fined to the long-term plans.

† *Cf.* Oskar Lange, *Price-Flexibility and Employment* (Bloomington, 1944: Cowles Commission Monograph no. 8).

‡ *Cf.* Svetozar Pejovich, *The Market-Planned Economy of Yugoslavia* (Minneapolis, 1966), p. 62: "The problem of inflation in Yugoslavia appeared as soon as the organisational innovation of 1950–1 had begun to be implemented." In the period 1953–61 "prices rose, on the average, 5·72 per cent a year", and there were two (short-lived) periods of actual "galloping inflation" at the start of 1962 and again in the summer of 1965. *Cf.* also, however, Ota Šik, *Plan and Market under Socialism* (Praha, 1967), pp. 338–9, for the contention that inflationary tendencies may be just as great under a centralised system, where it is apt to take a con-cealed form (*e.g.* extension of the construction period of investment projects owing to material shortages, lowering of quality and shop-shortages of consumers' goods).

fluctuations in demand and activity, centralised co-ordination and control of investment is more likely to promote macro-economic stability than if such investment is decentralised (and controlled only indirectly *via* market instruments like the rate of interest).

The apparent simplicity and logic of such a line of division is disturbed by the familiar difficulty of drawing a distinction between new investment, in the sense of creating additional productive capacity, and the replacement and maintenance of existing equipment. In so far as the latter results in a qualitative improvement, as when equipment of a new and improved type (but of equivalent cost) replaces the old plant that is worn out and due for the scrap-heap, productive capacity in terms of output is *ipso facto* increased. How is this to be distinguished, either in principle or in administrative practice, from an enlargement of productive capacity by installing additional plant alongside existing plant without any scrapping of the latter? It is scarcely conceivable that current repairs and maintenance should not fall within the competence of the operational unit. Where exactly does maintenance end and replacement begin? When does the work of maintenance staff call for invoicing under 'capital expenditure' rather than as part of current operating cost? Such difficulties are not insuperable and should not be exaggerated : somewhere a frontier-line could no doubt be defined (if only in terms of some arbitrary proportion of capital value).* But the division of powers and of jurisdictions would contain an arbitrary element and there exist a large number of possible variants. It might be that in the end central planning would retain such an amount of control over investment and replacement as gave it *de facto* control over the general long-run output-pattern in the desired degree, and that in general terms this is all that can be said of the matter.

We have referred to the need, so far as decisions are decentralised, for 'indicators' to be given to the decision-making unit. These indicators can be either quantities or else prices. As regards the former, output-quantities are manifestly in-

---

* It could, indeed, be argued (and has been) that some latitude to an enterprise for financing innovation and extension is positively desirable in order to encourage it to take an interest in long-term efficiency and not to concentrate exclusively on short-term results.

sufficient unless input-quantities are specified as well. To ensure efficient production, this would need to include labour-inputs as well as material inputs. In its most centralised phase, socialist planning sought to control major inputs quantitatively as well as output, through a system of cost-indices (and cost-reduction indices) combined with supply allocations, with labour-inputs controlled through the instrument of 'wage-limits' (*i.e.* limits on the total wage-bill). These controls could never be entirely comprehensive (for example, in specifying output-assortment in detail), and some of them implied the existence of price-indicators as well (in so far as output-targets or cost-indices were generalised in value terms; just as wage-bill-limits, if they were to control employment and use of labour, implied the existence of wage-rate scales). Price-indicators accordingly always played a complementary rôle, even if at peak-periods of centralisation a subordinate one. On the other hand, in the degree that the area of decentralised decision is widened, price-indicators inevitably play a more important rôle (quantity-indicators becoming *ipso facto* less numerous proportionately to the extent that quantity-decisions are at the discretion of the lower units). It can further be seen to follow that for price-indicators to play the rôle designed for them, an obligation must be laid upon the quasi-autonomous decision-units to be governed in their behaviour by what may be called 'balance sheet' considerations: maximising their receipts at the independently given prices relatively to their expenditures. This is the significance of Soviet *Khozraschot* dating back to the '20s, although given renewed emphasis in the planning and administrative changes of the '60s. This means that the prices used as indicators must be, not merely accounting prices, but *actual* prices, at least to the extent of representing payments credited (or debited) to the account of the decision-making unit in question.*

---

* Oskar Lange's 'accounting prices' for factors (*e.g.* capital) might be held to qualify for this condition, since they would represent debits in the production-accounting balance-sheet of the production unit, even though this were not an actual-income balance-sheet affecting the money income of which the unit collectively and its members could dispose. The difficulty here is of a duality of balance-sheets, as envisaged in the Lange-scheme, involving a contradiction in the motivation towards correct decision-making, of which more will be said below (p. 168).

One of the incidental lessons of socialist experience to-date has been that all quantitative indices, in so far as they have to be defined in terms of some specific dimension (*e.g.* weight, number of items, area or length) inevitably exert a biasing influence upon the type and nature of the product: a bias that only by coincidence will contribute to the utility of the product or of the output-assortment as a whole, and is more likely to do the opposite. Examples of this are sufficiently familiar to need no repetition.* So also, of course, can 'wrong' prices distort the output-pattern; and this very possibility is the reason why any considerable degree of decentralisation immediately brings the question of price-policy to the forefront of discussion. The question of what is the 'right' price-indicator to be used at any particular time in any particular case becomes crucial to the taking of any decisions affecting quantities. Ultimately the answer is, and can only be, the purely empirical one: the right price is that which produces the right result in terms of quantities. But this does not mean that generalisation about rightness and wrongness is not possible. It is certainly desirable, if not essential. In so far as only some, and not all, quantities are stipulated in the central plan, there will be no easy indicator to appeal to of what the right or socially desirable quantity is. (It is no use saying "the quantity demanded" since this will probably vary with the price.) Even if there were, the problem of price-policy would decompose into thousands (even millions) of special cases; and the cumbrous procedure of assigning quantity targets to each enterprise for all products would merely be replaced in the decentralised case by that of fixing economically correct prices *ad hoc* for every product.† Some degree of generalisation becomes essential as basis for the framing of readily applicable rules.

* When expressed in terms of value, there are also difficulties: those associated with gross value targets are numerous and familiar, and even net-value targets have their negative features. A neat (as well as original) example of the distortions resulting from quantitative plan-indices is cited by Mr Michael Ellman (R. Miliband and J. Saville (eds.), *The Socialist Register 1968*, London, 1968, p. 25) from an *Izvestia* article: optimal programmes for goods transport have remained on paper because the plans supplied to transport organisations have been expressed in ton-kilometres (which an optimal programme minimises).

† "We cannot administer from one governing centre the prices of huge masses of specific types of goods produced in our economy with any real knowledge of the matter" (O. Šik in *Czechoslovak Economic Papers*, no. 5, 1965, p. 28).

One can include also as one of the lessons of experience that, so far as what we have called 'balance-sheet considerations' are to be the motivation for decentralised decision-taking, all economic activities covered by these decisions must be reflected in the balance-sheet. This is obvious as soon as it is stated; but its implications have not always been grasped. It means that any consequence of productive activity that involves a social cost, such as the using-up of either material or human resources, should be made to impinge upon the decision-making unit in some form as a money charge or cost. (Ideally this ought to include every kind of social cost, such as urban congestion, river pollution or smoke nuisance, which can be covered by an *ad hoc* tax; but in many cases social effects are not easy to estimate in precise quantitative terms.) We have mentioned the difficulty of drawing any sharp line between short-period and long-period decisions because of the difficulty of separating current maintenance of durable equipment from its initial creation or its replacement. An analogous difficulty applies to any attempt to draw a corresponding distinction between categories of cost. Experience has shown that current maintenance of equipment can scarcely be separated from *use* of equipment, which is in turn dependent on operative decisions about current output; and that unless the use of durable equipment is made to impinge financially upon the production unit as a cost such equipment will tend to be uneconomically used (in some cases subjected to over-use, in others held as a reserve against contingencies and under-used) as well as inadequately maintained. It is not enough, in other words, to include only what economists have termed short-period costs in what is debited to the operational unit.* (The fact that such units may be able to influence the amount and kind of equipment assigned to them, if only by the data which they supply to support or justify assignment, is *a fortiori* to this argument.)

A final conclusion from experience that seems to be worth

---

* There is no known method of costing wear-and-tear of plant in the degree to which this is occasioned by use, save indirectly (*e.g.* of a motor-vehicle according to its loading and the speed at which it is driven). Accordingly, the only feasible way of levying a charge is in proportion to the amount of it and the frequency of replacement (in whole or in part); holding of stocks and goods-in-process can similarly be charged according to the amount of funds (or bank-credits) locked up in these.

listing is that a logical consequence of assigning discretion with regard to output-policy to financially autonomous units is that they should have discretion also as regards the sources from which they draw their supplies of inputs. The connection is a fairly obvious one : the autonomy allowed on paper regarding output may evidently be more nominal than real *unless* there is also freedom (within limits) to choose between suppliers and to vary both the amounts and the quality of the supplies. This implies some degree, at least, of free contractual relations between using and supplying production units.* The degree of freedom is capable of some variation. It could be contained within broad allocation-quotas, for some categories of goods at least ; these operating as permits to purchase and as maximum limits to demand without specifying (as was the former Soviet practice) the source of supply. Such quotas could apply to whole industries, or to groups of enterprises (associations) within an industry, without being broken down in detail to individual enterprises, and in this form be made consistent with some swapping of shares between enterprises, and hence with greater flexibility and greater scope for contractual variation and direct bargaining.† Again, prices might be an item in the contracts (possibly only within certain 'price-limits')‡ as well as quantities and delivery-dates. To the extent that such decentralised contractual relations existed, there would be a market, or at least a quasi-market, *within* socialist industry

---

* This implication was recognised (if still somewhat cautiously) by Mr Kosygin in the course of announcing the new economic changes (in the direction of greater autonomy of enterprises) of 27 September 1965 : "In the future direct ties between producing and consuming enterprises should be more widely developed . . . It is necessary to shift gradually to wholesale trade in individual types of materials and equipment through the regional supply and sales-depots." *Cf.* also Y. Koldomasov in *Voprosi Ekonomiki* (1965), no. 11, pp. 14–25, with its reference to "expansion of direct economic ties" as a "decisive condition for decentralisation in the planning of industrial production" (p. 15).

† The preservation of such quotas might be justified as a means of preventing excess demand for things in short-supply, and as an alternative to price-raising (which might seem the preferable method if the shortage was likely to be more than temporary) ; or alternatively by the need to check spontaneous cumulative movements developing (increased output at one point creating a chain-reaction of either shortages or increased outputs throughout a whole series of industries that would be disruptive of the general intentions and priorities of the plan).

‡ As it provided for in Czechoslovakia and Hungary for a fairly large category of products. A substantial category, in addition, largely consisting of consumers' goods, is not subject to any limits.

itself for producers' goods: this as well as a retail market for consumers' goods sold to individual citizens, about which we have already spoken. It is in this sense that there has been much talk in recent years about a compromise between, or some organic fusion of, planning with market-relations and the emergence of what a leading Czech economist has called "a specific type of market—a market of socialist enterprises".*

There are other lessons or implications of socialist experience to-date that are relevant to such questions as the structure of production in relation to growth, and of its changing pattern with changing growth-rates and in transition from one growth-path to another; just as there are also more particular conclusions to be drawn as regards the use and methodology of particular planning techniques (*e.g.* input-output methods and coefficients of investment effectiveness). But the discussion of these would probably take us outside our immediate context, which is that of optimising problems as traditionally viewed. No doubt there are also other lessons germane to our present theme than those we have mentioned which experience could be said to have already yielded, but of which one is at present unaware, or at best uncertain, perhaps because of insufficient generalisation as yet of the basic raw material of economic experience. As a rule one is only aware at any time of what has been formulated as problems and become the occasion of discussion as such. In view of the existence of possible *lacunae* of this sort, what has been said in this chapter must be taken as no more than provisional. In the chapters that follow we shall be primarily concerned with the problems of efficient choice of methods of production and of adjusting the output-pattern of consumers' goods in accordance with the wants of consumers, and in these two connections with the rôle that prices have to play and the requirements of a price-policy.

In conclusion, before passing to more specialised topics, some kind of answer may seem called for to the following summary question. In what ways, if at all, will a mechanism such as we have been indicating differ in its economic results from that of the familiar market mechanism, as depicted, for example, in

* Ota Šik in *World Marxist Review* (English edition of 'Problems of Peace and Socialism') (London, March 1965), vol. 8, no. 3, p. 17.

the economists' abstract model of so-called perfect competition? First, and of most importance, it will differ as regards the long-term path and pattern of development, in so far as major investment decisions at least and hence structural change are centrally planned. Save in conditions of exceptional entrepreneurial optimism, an atomistic market economy will be essentially short-sighted, bounded as decision-making is by the narrow horizon to a firm's vision that is set by uncertainty as to what the macroscopic constellation of the economy is likely to be at future dates (Koopmans' "secondary uncertainty').* Expansion of capacity for producing capital goods will depend upon estimating the trend of total investment in the future (as well as the amount of competing capacity likely to be created in the interim); and since this is subject to a high degree of uncertainty, such expansion is likely to be restricted, *ceteris paribus*, to what seems the probable minimum. Analogously, expansion of capacity for producing consumers' goods will depend upon the estimated trend of employment and *per capita* income over the future, which will itself depend upon the volume of total investment in the interim and upon the precise character of expansion in productive capacity. Expansion of subsidiary industries will tend to wait upon prior expansion of the main industries whose needs they serve; just as the latter in turn may hesitate to expand if the supply of subsidiary products and components necessary for full capacity working are not assured. All this is sufficiently familiar to those who have given consideration to the problems of underdevelopment and to the so-called vicious circle of backwardness. Even when entrepreneurial expectations are buoyant, although an investment boom may be stimulated and high growth-rates result, there is no major probability that the structural pattern of expansion will be just right. In many directions excess capacity (relatively to the resulting demand) may be stimulated, deflating optimism at later dates; while in other directions bottlenecks occur that arrest the momentum of growth. The literature of economic fluctuations is, indeed, full of reasons why self-perpetuating fluctuations, if not cumulatively 'explosive' movements, may in such conditions occur.

* T. C. Koopmans, *Three Essays on the State of Economic Science* (New York, 1967), pp. 154, 163; *cf.* also the present writer's *Essay on Economic Growth and Planning*, p. 8.

Familiar theorems in recent growth-theory have shown that 'warranted growth-rates' may diverge from 'natural'; and such mechanisms of convergence of actual upon 'natural' growth-rates as have been suggested are problematical and at best very long-term in working out their effects. Only myopic concentration upon stationary equilibrium could breed the supposition that there is even a *prima facie* case for regarding long-term investment under free market conditions as optimal.

Another way of expressing the same thing is to say that all long-term, or investment, decisions will be relative to (expected) future prices. Since these prices (with certain rare exceptions)* are not part of the furniture of a market system, they can exist only subjectively as guesswork, or as extrapolations of past trends into the future. Hence there is no means of postulating *a priori*, in terms of simple and familiar theorems about equilibrium, what entrepreneurial actions will result. In this connection Oskar Lange has aptly written: "Planning of long-term economic development as a rule is based on overall considerations of economic policy rather than upon calculations based on current prices ... Actual market equilibrium prices do not suffice here, knowledge of the programmed future shadow prices is needed. Mathematical programming turns out to be an essential instrument of optimal long-term economic planning ... here the electronic computer does not replace the market. It fulfils a function which the market never was able to perform."†

It will only be as regards short-term decisions, mainly within the framework of productive capacities fixed by longer-term decisions, that there will be any resemblance between the functioning of a (competitive) market mechanism and the kind of mechanism of which we have spoken above.

Secondly, the two mechanisms will differ to the extent that planning decisions are capable of embracing those wider social

---

* Even where future prices exist as a market fact, these have little or no objective significance as a picture of what supply or demand conditions will actually be at future dates: they remain the product of guesswork and expectation, if of the most informed (or least uninformed) opinion.

† 'The Computer and the Market' in C. H. Feinstein (ed.), *Socialism, Capitalism and Economic Growth*, pp. 160–1. *Cf.* also Leif Johansen, 'Some Problems of Pricing and Optimal Choice of Factor Proportions in a Dynamic Setting', in *Economica* (May 1967), pp. 141–3, 147, 150–1.

effects of production and consumption that fall outside the balance-sheet calculations of the individual financial unit, and are customarily referred to as 'external economies' (or diseconomies). For reasons that are sufficiently well known, this type of wider repercussion of economic decisions by individual units is more extensive and has much greater significance in a context of development than in that of stationary equilibrium.* It may well be that not all of these wider effects will be taken into account by those who take decisions centrally, and not all of such effects are likely to be easily calculable or known. What is clear, however, is that the wider perspective from which the repercussions of any development are viewed will ensure that a much larger proportion, at least, of such social costs and benefits will be taken into account than in the sectional and self-interested decision-taking of an individual production-unit (an additional reason for investment decisions affecting expansion or contraction of industry being centralised rather than decentralised).

Thirdly, the distribution of income, as we shall emphasise below, will be a constant preoccupation of policy, both from the side of production and price-policy and from the side of money income : for example, policy regarding the comparative rates of expansion of different lines of production of consumers' goods. This will not be left to emerge as the incidental resultant of market forces and market movements.

Fourthly, although the tendency of enterprises to 'act monopolistically' (in the sense of framing output-policy with a view to price-maintenance and price-raising) will not be entirely absent in a socialist economy, and may have to be expressly guarded against especially in a decentralised system, it will evidently be very much weaker than it is under contemporary capitalism. It will be very much weaker (and some might claim almost non-existent), first because of the prevalence of price-fixing from above through standard price-lists, at any rate in the case of all major products and product-groups ; and the fact that such prices are independently controlled will straitly limit the possibility of self-interested price-maintenance even in the interstices of the lattice of controlled prices. True, the enterprise may not be without some influence upon the price fixed through

* *Cf.* the present writer's *Essay on Economic Growth and Planning*, pp. 6–7.

the costing-information that it supplies to higher authorities; and it is clearly utopian to rely upon direct competition exerting a counter-influence in specialised fields where economies of scale dictate the large plant and large managerial unit. It is not utopian, however, to expect comparison of close alternatives or analogous cases to place a fairly narrow restriction upon 'monopoly of information' and to expect planners in a planned economy to possess independent sources of costing data. A second and far from negligible reason is that the *ethos* of the system, instead of affording sanction and approval to price-maintenance as legitimate business-practice, is calculated to weight the scales in favour of price-reduction and of the consumers' interest; while the market-pressure exerted by the large unit will not be one-sided, and in the majority of cases is likely to characterise the buying organisation (e.g. consumers' cooperatives) as much as the seller.

Fifthly, when maladjustments occur, it seems clear that re-adjustment processes can be made to operate more speedily and smoothly than they would in a competitive atomistic system. This is not to say that direct physical controls, or the method of administrative command and directives, can always achieve results more swiftly than can the movement of prices and the self-interested response of individual *entrepreneurs* to market prospects and indicators (although the common adoption of such methods by governments in wartime suggests that this may well be the case). It is to say that, in the kind of mechanism we have depicted, with its blend of planning and market elements, administrative action designed to correct malad-justment has a richer arsenal of weapons: it can utilise alter-natively or in combination both the weapon of direct inter-vention or command (including physical controls and quotas) and market instruments (*e.g.* price-movements, credit opera-tions, market-intervention through central bulk-purchase or sale) which operate indirectly upon production-units as inducements or deterrents. It will further be the case that those undertaking the intervention will have a broader vision of the repercussions of any given course of action, and hence a greater possibility of achieving short-cuts in any corrective or con-vergence-process. This presumption is reinforced by the fact that a large part of any *tâtonnement* process of adjustment or approximation can be conducted 'on paper', within a planning office, instead of as a series of actual market operations, each with its specific time-lag. (Convergence-processes in the real economic world of markets and men are often, as we have said, notoriously slow.) In these days of computer-calculation such a difference may mean a great deal more than is apparent at first sight.

CHAPTER 8

THE STRUCTURE OF PRODUCTION AND CHOICE OF METHODS OF PRODUCTION

One thing that economists, with their preoccupation with marginal conditions, have generally failed to do in discussing the problems of a socialist economy is to undertake an analysis of the structure of production. Yet this must, surely, be a key to the kind of shape that the problem facing economic planning will assume. To say that this was ignored was at any rate true until the recent vogue of input-output analysis; and even today there is some tendency to regard the latter as a specialised, departmentalised study within, or even apart from, the general stream of economic analysis applied to the comparative functioning of economic systems.

In order to indicate the relevance of the productive structure to the problems and the functioning of a socialist economy, as well as to put the issues of the traditional 'marginalist' debate in perspective, we shall first consider a simplified case of structural pattern, with its implications for planning problems, and then successively modify (and complicate) the assumptions from which we start.

Let us begin with a case where all inputs other than labour are *produced*, in the sense in which we used this phrase at an earlier stage.* To this let us also add initially the assumption that all lines of production represent a fairly simple pattern which one can describe as a straight-line series of production-stages, starting from an initial stage through a series of intermediate stages where incomplete products or components are progressively worked-up until they emerge in the form of a final product, yielding what the classical economists would have called a final use-value. At each of these stages in the chain of productive processes there is a unique method of production available, thus yielding fixed 'technical coefficients' relating inputs and

* Above, chapter 4, p. 55 n.

outputs. It follows that the initial stage of each straight-line process must represent essentially an input of labour alone, and that in so far as labour here works upon natural objects, whether collected, cultivated or quarried, these are not bounded by natural scarcity and hence can be treated for economic purposes as 'free goods'. It follows also that all end-products would be 'non-basics' in Mr Sraffa's sense of the term.* The situation we have is that of an economy composed of a collection of independent straight-line processes, of the kind implicitly envisaged by Menger with his graded "first order" and "second order" goods and his notion of "imputation" (*zurechnung*), whereby the values of the latter were derived from those of the former and hence from the marginal utilities of these "first order" goods to the final consumer.† The notion of a "period of production", extending from initial stage to emergence of end-product, would have a simple and unambiguous meaning, as Böhm-Bawerk intended it to have in his theory of capital.‡

With growth imported into the system, the inputs (of labour and of produced material inputs) at earlier stages of each production process would have to be equivalently increased relatively to those at later stages, and for steady growth the size of the former would have to bear a certain relationship to the latter§ (a relationship needing to be maintained along the whole line of intermediate processes to ensure a steady flow). This simple and obvious consideration may be worth underlining, since it will be found to have quite a crucial place in the analysis which follows.

The essentials, indeed, of our simplified case need not be altered to allow for some 'feedback' of outputs as inputs at

* P. Sraffa, *Production of Commodities by Means of Commodities* (Cambridge, 1960), pp. 7–8, also *cf.* p. 51.

† The opposite sequence of derivation was, of course, equally plausible: values of 'first-order' goods derived from those of 'second order', and these in turn from the (total) amount of labour applied at previous stages of production.

‡ That is, as a *time*-dimension it would have this simple meaning. As a weighted sum of dated labour-inputs, with labour of various dates weighted by some interest-rate or time-discount factor, it would lose this simple character; the relative sizes of two totals of given structure being dependent on the level of the interest-rate (and hence on the weighting). *Cf.* P. Sraffa, *op. cit.* p. 38.

§ Of the kind depicted in the equations on pp. 50–1 of the present writer's *Essay on Economic Growth and Planning* (London, 1960).

early stages (including the first stage, *e.g.* as tools and equipment or fuel), provided that the independence of each series of production-stages leading to each given end-product is maintained. To the extent that such feedback-relations occurred one would be substituting a 'circular' for a straight-line pattern of production.* One could, indeed, imagine a completely circular production-process, where part or all of the final outputs became inputs in a von Neumann-type model of production and of growth (examples of such outputs could be fuels or instruments of production or subsistence for workers). This could be thought to constitute the purest example of inputs being exclusively 'produced inputs' in a self-perpetuating production-process.

Our simple case could also be adapted, without change of essentials, to include the confluence of numerous distinct production-streams or input-flows into some later assembly-stage. The effect would be that our simile of a straight-line series of stages would be blurred, or even replaced, by a pattern with the shape of an open and downward-pointing fan; numerous and distinct original (produced) inputs being combined at some stage, as with motor-car manufacture or ship-building, to compose the final product. The main restriction imposed by our present case would be that none of these original inputs were used in any other line of production as well as this one: in this sense the independence of various production lines or processes would be maintained.

As represented in an input-output table, the case we have been considering would correspond to the so-called diagonal (or quasi-diagonal) pattern (with zero quantities to the right and above the diagonal line as well as below it). In so far, however, as this case was extended to allow for outputs becoming inputs at earlier stages in a series of circular feedbacks, the diagonal representation would cease to apply: it would then assume something of a 'triangular' pattern.

Manifestly, the planning problem in these circumstances would be a relatively easy one. Given a decision about the

---

* The notion of a period of production, or a sum of dated labours, would then seem to involve an infinite regress. But, as Mr Sraffa has pointed out, beyond a point the relevant input-quantities diminish to a size where they can be ignored (P. Sraffa, *op. cit.* p. 35). To this matter we shall return.

relative quantities of final outputs, the main concern of planning would be an appropriate adjustment of the various successive stages of each straight-line (or alternatively fan-shaped or else circular) production process so as to ensure an uninterrupted and continuous flow; resembling in this respect an engineering problem on an assembly-line or series of automatic transfer-machines. Given the decisions regarding final outputs and their relative rates of increase, this would constitute the optimising problem *par excellence* and be the main preoccupation of planning. Nor should growth and change introduce any great difficulty *per se*: at least, the dynamic problem would be fairly simple once growth in each line had settled into a steady rhythm since changes would be equi-proportional ones down the line (or round the circle). In the case of changes of direction or of pace (acceleration or deceleration), however, there would arise special questions of prevision and of timing once-for-all input-changes, such as an increase of inputs at appropriate points and appropriate dates in advance of the target-date for an increased rate of flow of end-products; and to achieve this so as to minimise the loss from dislocation and delay, or from possible oscillations in the course of adjustment, would be a principal function of planning (by contrast with the atomistic operation of market forces). But in view of the independence of the various branches of production (which has been for the present assumed), the composition of the total plan would amount to no more than a combining (in the sense of adding together) of various industrial or branch plans. The framers of the several industrial plans would need to know, of course, the crucial technical coefficients at each stage of production, but in the absence of substitution this should not be difficult. There would be no special problems of scale or complexity in the sense of difficulties connected with a multiplication of industries and of the number of end-products.

What of the decision about end-products? This would present an economic problem *par excellence*, even if there were no question of choice of methods of production. It could be, of course, an 'arbitrary' policy-decision taken on social grounds (*e.g.* favouring sections of the community with certain needs) or because certain tastes are held to be ethically more desirable as contributing to the good life than are others. But it could equally well rest on the verdict of a consumers' market, and (as a long-term goal at least) relative outputs could be decided (partly or wholly) by an approximation of market prices to costs. In other words, if the ratio of market-price to cost was relatively high in the case of certain end-products, their production would be expanded by an increased application of inputs into their production-lines. As the supply of these was increased in successive plans, their market prices would fall until they no longer showed an excess over their costs (or no longer an above-average ratio of market price to cost). The converse of this would apply to such end-products as happened to be in sufficiently plentiful supply to cause their market prices to be below the level of costs, or to cause the ratio of market-price to cost to be below the average level. Since all inputs other than labour are produced inputs, the costs relevant to such a calculation (of a long-term optimum pattern of final outputs) would be the sum of labour expenditures at all stages of production, calculated for example in terms of wages as the wage-cost of output. This could be regarded as a sufficient basis for costing in stationary conditions: *i.e.* in the absence of growth.

It may be noted that no question of choice of methods of production will arise in the situation we are at present contemplating, and hence there is no need at this stage to consider the effect upon them either of the system of costing and pricing or of the relative outputs of end-products. In other words, the production-efficiency condition of which we spoke in an earlier chapter does not at present arise.

To the extent that growth was occurring, however, there would necessarily be a permanent excess of the total value (at equilibrium retail prices) of final output over its wage-cost, since as we have seen the labour-input at 'earlier' stages would tend to be larger,* *ceteris paribus*, than at 'later' stages; this excess being a simple function of the rate of growth. If the period of production differed between different industries, the excess

---

* Hence, the total labour employed in a branch of production (and hence the total wage-bill) at any date would always exceed what is embodied in currently-emerging final output. *Cf.* the present writer, *Essay on Economic Growth and Planning*, pp. 91–2. It is being assumed here that there is no saving out of wages: the whole of currently received wages are spent. An example to illustrate this key relationship is given in a special Note appended to this chapter.

of final price over wage-cost should ideally be distributed
between different products, *not* in proportion to wage-cost, but
in proportion to the sum of *dated* wage-costs, with each item
weighted appropriately according to its remoteness in time
from the emergence of final output; the basis for this weighting
being the rate of growth (which we have seen is the ground for
the ratio of final price to total wage cost being greater than
unity).* The *rationale* of this (which will be considered more
fully in the next chapter) is that increase of final output (*i.e.* of
end-products) in any direction involves at some earlier date the
diversion of labour to its production, and this diversion will
represent a social cost in the sense of diminished possibility of
growth elsewhere in the system (given the total available
labour-force): a diminished possibility extending from the
date in question until the emergence of the desired increment of final output (*i.e.* for the period, as it were, over which
the labour in question is 'advanced' in time, or 'locked up'
in the emerging end-product).† Hence the latter should
not, ideally, be increased in supply unless the social value
placed upon it (in this case a use-value to consumers) justifies
the reduction in the general growth-potential that its increase
entails.

It will be clear from what has been said that this weighting
attached to wage-costs incurred at relatively early dates, with

* Thus if g is the annual growth-rate and n the number of years previously (to
the emergence of the end-product) that any item of wage-cost is incurred, the
weight attached to this wage-cost for costing purposes should be $(1+g)^n$. It will be
recalled that in the von Neumann model the rate of interest (or of profit) was equal
to the rate of growth. *Cf.* also J. Kornai, *Mathematical Planning of Structural Decisions* (Amsterdam, 1967), p. 271, and J. Kornai's discussion-intervention in
E. Malinvaud and M. O. L. Bacharach (eds.), *Activity Analysis in the Theory of
Growth and Planning* (London and New York, 1967), p. 327.

It will be apparent that what is being said here is simply an application at the
micro-level of those macro-relations discussed in chapter VI of the present writer's
Essay on Economic Growth and Planning.

† Thus, consider a decision to undertake a (continuing) increase in the output of
a certain end-product, which requires an initial expenditure of labour four years in
advance of the emergence of that product. The expenditure of this labour will only
make its contribution to growth (of end-products) in four years' time; and accordingly, unless the total labour in the system is increased, this must involve a
diminished potential growth-rate during those intervening four years. An analogous decision to increase the output of something requiring labour to be expended
only two years in advance, instead of four, will involve a diminished growth-rate for
no more than two years instead of four.

the consequential bias given against long production-periods, will vary with the general growth-rate; thereby reflecting the fact that the deleterious effect of the withdrawal or diversion of any growth-inducing input will be proportional to the current growth-rate.*

It may be worth emphasising parenthetically at this point, to obviate possible misunderstanding later, that if we hold to the view that labour must always work with produced inputs, the method of reducing everything to 'dated labour' implies an infinite series. In the sequel this is essentially the method we are using. Any one such series can have a definite magnitude and be compared with another series with a different dating-pattern. For some purposes, however, it may be convenient to speak of a production-period of definite length (and of changes or of differences in this period); and to do so obliges one to assume a starting-point with only labour as an input. This is admittedly abstract simplification. In any infinite series, however, there is always a point beyond which further quantities in the series become so small as to be negligible;† and if our series is terminated here, leaving labour as the only input at this 'cut-off point', the effect on the argument of so doing can be regarded as insignificant. But it may be as well to bear in mind that when we speak of a change in the time-dimension of a production-process of finite length (or a comparison of production periods of different lengths), this is intended as a convenient synonym for a change in the dating of all or of some of the labours in an infinite series. No material difference is made by substituting one form of statement for the other.

Nothing essential of the principle we have enunciated will be altered if we allow for some produced inputs consisting of durable means of production whose use extends over more than one act of production or one unit-period of time (instruments of labour instead of objects of labour according to the Marxian distinction). Like any other input, such as a material, a component or a fuel, its cost at the date of its introduction into the process will be debited to the output for which it is (in part) responsible over the period of its economic life. In addition to this, however, allowance must be made for its period of dura-

* *Cf.* further discussion of this below, in chapter 9.
† *Cf.* footnote on p. 155 above.

bility, in the form of debiting output also with an allowance for the length of that period (calculated in an analogous manner to what we have already described in the case of 'dated labour' and spread over the total output of the period in question). This will of course imply some principle of depreciation, governing the proportion of the value of the durable instrument to be debited as an input-cost to the current output of any given year of that instrument's productive lifetime.* But *given* such a depreciation-principle, durable productive equipment as a produced input can also be accommodated to the terms of our simplified case without significantly complicating the nature of the economic problem; and 'stored-up labour' can be assimilated to 'dated labour'.

Nor do we need to adhere too rigorously to our assumption about the absence of natural scarcities. If scarcity of natural endowment takes the form merely of limitation of sources or sites of first-class fertility or ease of access, additional production will need to resort to progressively less favourable sources or sites, and the labour needing to be expended here will alone be relevant to decisions about extending (or alternatively curtailing) production. If follows that what is relevant to calculations concerned with the appropriate level of output is the labour expenditure at the prevailing margin of extended use of the natural resource in question (this and not the average of all expenditures on most fertile and less fertile sites and sources). Where, *per contra*, natural scarcity has the form of an absolute inelasticity beyond a certain point (*e.g.* a fixed number of Marshall's meteoric stones or an exhaustible stock of a mineral), this will impose an absolute limit (in the absence of possibilities of substitution) to any extension of the scale of production.† The question of deciding, and of how to decide, upon extension of output beyond this point accordingly does not arise. It may be remarked incidentally that it will be

---

* *Cf.* P. Sraffa, *op. cit.* pp. 63 *et seq.* Because the outputs of the various years over which the durable instrument is used are joint-products, no direct reduction to a series of dated-labour terms is possible (as explained by Mr Sraffa in his discussion of joint products). But once an appropriate depreciation-principle has been reached by an alternative route, one is enabled to proceed *as if* such a reduction had taken place; although the reduction will be relative to the rate of profit (*i.e.* in our present context to the rate of growth).

† Or, indeed, to *any* further production, if it is an exhaustible *stock*, rather than an inelastic flow that is in question.

indifferent* whether natural limitation in this case is reflected in a rise of price at the stage of production in question, and hence as an element in cost, or at the stage of final output as an excess of price above cost (in the former case appearing as the scarcity price or rent of a natural facility or resource, in the latter case as a surplus profit or as an *ad hoc* sales tax).

It is time for us to take a look at the two assumptions whose removal is likely to make a more serious difference. These two assumptions are those of unique methods of production (and of input-combinations) at each stage and the absence of alternative employments for any produced input in other lines of production. Both of these are manifestly unrealistic, and their retention could only be defended on grounds of heroic simplification. To render such a defence plausible, it would also have to be shown that such simplification did not exclude problems that were of major importance in the practical conduct of a planned economy ; and this, as will emerge, it would be difficult to do.

To remove the first of these assumptions without the second would not in itself change anything very much—although it would add some complexity to planning decisions. At each stage of production in a given industry there would still be one method of production that enabled output to be produced at minimum cost.† Given sufficient time all produced inputs could

* It will be indifferent if there is no choice of methods of production ; if there is such a choice it will not be indifferent, since when entered as a cost it will influence the substitution of labour-inputs and produced inputs (or of one produced input for another) at all stages subsequent to the one where the natural scarcity in question appears. Also if the natural limitation is left to appear as a surplus profit at the end-stage of production (*i.e.* as a difference between price and cost), this must be excluded from consideration when calculating the desirability of expanding the supply of the end-product in question relatively to others.

† The substitution of a method involving the use of more of some input but less labour would not, of course, be desirable if the production of that input itself required more labour than its use displaced. But even where there was a net economy of labour resulting from the substitution, the change might involve a shift from using labour at later stages to using labour at earlier stages that would be detrimental to the general growth-rate (*cf.* below, pp. 192–4). In such a case choice could not be independent of the current growth-rate, and to make the substitution might appear desirable at one growth-rate but not at another.

This consideration makes clear that choice of methods of production cannot be made on a *simpliste* version of minimising labour expenditure (or maximising labour productivity), as some have suggested. Nor can it be made in terms of factor prices,

be increased in supply to any required extent. But within any period of time of limited duration or when growth was occurring, the time involved in augmenting the supply of a produced input would be relevant to a decision. To speak of minimum cost raises the question immediately of what is a correct system of costing, in the sense of yielding a choice of methods of production that gives optimum results from a social point of view. The answer will be different according as growth is occurring or not, and according to the size of the growth-rate: a matter with which we shall deal subsequently in some detail, but with which we need not trouble ourselves at the moment. Once chosen, this least-cost method, with its particular combination of labour and produced inputs, would remain the best choice in the absence of technical innovation and improvement.

But when viewed in conjunction with a removal of the second assumption—*i.e.* in the context of produced inputs having a number of alternative uses—the correct choice between available methods of production becomes less easy to define, and the choice once made may well be affected, for the time-being at least, by shifts in the relative outputs of end-products. A method of production using relatively much of a particular input may result in minimising cost in its own line of production, but the economising effect of using more of this input may be even greater elsewhere, in other industries, so that preference should be given to employing it in the latter, even to the extent of reducing its employment in the former.

If production processes were timeless, this situation would present no difficulty; and in the sufficiently long term there is no doubt what the correct answer would be. Moreover, it is a simple answer. More of this particular input should be produced until it suffices to meet all the industrial uses in which the substitution of more of it for either labour or for some other input would result in greater productive efficiency (or alternatively in an economy of cost as we have previously defined this). This conclusion follows as much for something that is in demand from numerous industries and has alternative uses as it does for an input that is specific to one line of production

as determined by relative factor scarcities in relation to a given demand-pattern for final consumer goods, as established in the traditional type of static-equilibrium model.

alone. But for the purpose of any plan whose horizon is narrower than the total production-period of the input in question,* so that it is impossible for that plan itself to provide for an increase of supply of the good in question such as can meet all needs, this long-term answer (as we may call it) cannot be applied. For the purpose of planning decisions within this period the available supply of it will have to be taken as a datum of the planning problem. Priority will have to be given to those productive uses for it where its effectiveness is greatest (estimated in terms of increasing output from a given quantum of other inputs, or alternatively of decreasing the unit-cost of output). In consequence, some (less effective) employments for it will have to be sacrificed even when its use would be beneficial and would be sought after by the managements of the industry in question.

The task of achieving a proper allocation in all such cases severely qualifies what was said earlier about the comparative simplicity of the task of planning as a mere combining together of various sectional or industrial plans severally conceived. But the task of working out centrally a series of allocations of scarce inputs according to scales of comparative effectiveness is far from an impossible one. Its complexity, of course, will increase with the number of alternative uses and the range of possible substitutions, each with its specific coefficient of effectiveness. Beyond a certain point it may well be that this complexity passes the limits of possible handling within a given planning time-table,† even when aided by modern computing techniques. A more important limit to centralised solution of such allocation problems, however, lies as we have seen in the field of information. Knowledge of the possible substitution-

---

* This is a *minimum* requirement for its being impossible. If there were only one scarce input in question, it would be a sufficient requirement. But when many scarce inputs are in question, it may not be possible to increase any one of them to the requisite extent because of insufficiency of labour and of other produced inputs to augment the output of all of them simultaneously except at a relatively slow rate. To some extent, however, this consideration will be reciprocally connected with the determination of a practicable growth rate (and hence with the weighting of dated labour). In other words, the overcoming of specific scarcities will compete with, and at the same time these scarcities will be dissolved by, growth in the system at large.

† *Cf.* the present writer's *Soviet Economic Development since 1917*, (Revised 6th edition, London, 1966), pp. 358–9, footnote 3.

alternatives will be fully known only at the level of the in-dividual industry or individual plant. These data can be transmitted, of course, to the higher planning authorities in suitably quantified form for the necessary calculations to be made at a single centre. But while this may be easy to do, and with a fair degree of precision, as regards data relating to past experience and the immediate present, it becomes much less easy when it is a matter of estimating future trends and future possibilities, which may diverge appreciably from past experi-ence where innovation and technical change are at all rapid. Here there is bound to be a margin of guesswork and un-certainty. Yet it will be with future potentiality rather than with a photograph of today's or yesterday's situation that perspective planning will be mainly concerned. And we saw in the last chapter that where guesswork and uncertainty blur precision, information transmitted from lower to higher levels can hardly fail to be influenced in some degree by the local and sectional biases of particular industries or production-units. If planning targets and supply-allocations are likely to depend on the information provided, this information will scarcely remain uninfluenced by the hopes and intentions of those who furnish it.* Experience of planning to-date indicates that this may be a factor of quite a high order of importance and by no means a trivial consideration.

Whether or not this is a sufficient reason for an explicit decentralisation of such decisions to lower levels, it is clear that decisions will be *de facto* influenced in considerable degree by lower levels; and when it is a matter of initiating some novel substitution and method which has not been practised before, the inclinations and preoccupations of those close to day-to-day experience in the industry in question will inevitably exert a paramount influence. It is here that we meet a crucial con-sideration about prices, which at first sight may seem to be an anomaly. Prices will evidently be an important factor in shap-ing the result whether decisions about allocation are centralised or decentralised: in the former case because they will be the

---

* Thus if a particular production-plant or industry has set its heart on being allotted a certain scarce material or component instead of a second-best sub-stitute, the data it provides in relation to its production-possibilities are likely to lean in the direction of 'making a case' for this claim.

medium in which comparative effectiveness-ratios are expressed and calculated, in the latter case because the relative prices of inputs will affect the comparative costs of alternative combinations of inputs and hence the least-cost method of producing a given output. Yet the input-prices appropriate to centralised decision about what we have called the long-term answer will be *different* from those required to evoke economically correct decentralised decisions within a short-term horizon within which the available supplies of a large number (at least) of important inputs have to be treated as fixed, and hence as data of the allocation problem. It suffices for the former as we have seen, if prices of alternative inputs reflect their production-costs at all stages (including, when growth is occurring, an appropriate allowance for the datings of labour-inputs). But in the case of the latter this no longer suffices. An individual industry or production plant will have no way of knowing the alternative uses for a scarce input, and hence of assessing the *social* cost of diverting it from those uses, unless its productive effectiveness in the latter is reflected in its price. And the industry in question will certainly have no inducement to place the social interest in this matter above its own sectional interest unless through the price system the social cost of depriving other industries is debited to it if it secures this input for itself at the expense of others. It is here that we can see the importance of the kind of pricing principle suggested by Kantorovitch or Novozhilov (the former in the context of optimal linear programming solutions, and derived from or implied in these under the designation of *obiektivno obuslovlennie otsenki*; the latter in the guise of a measure, not of labour-expenditures actually incurred, but of potential labour expenditures that would be imposed elsewhere if the input in question were to be put to a sub-marginal use).* This type of price can be conceived of as a device for conveying to decentralised decision-takers, and imposing upon their calculations, a quantitative indication of the wider social repercussions of decisions made by them.

* L. V. Kantorovitch, *Ekonomicheskii Raschot Nailushego Ispolzovania Resursov* (Moscow, 1959 and 1960, p. 32 and *passim*); V. V. Novozhilov, 'Izmerenie Zatrat i ikh Resultatov v Sotsialisticheskom Khoziaistve' in V. S. Nemchinov (ed.) *Primenenie Matematiki v Ekonomicheskikh Issledovaniakh*, vol. 1 (Moscow, 1959), pp. 130–83, and V. V. Novozhilov, *Izmerenie Zatrat i Resultatov* (Moscow, 1967), pp. 117 *et seq.* See below, p. 205.

It is thus a distinct category of price, performing a special function.

What is here involved is the assigning to each scarce input, whether it be some metal or building material or high-quality fuel, a special (and temporary) price of its scarcity, constituting a sort of differential rent (or quasi-rent) akin to that which would attach more permanently to a natural object that was incapable of being reproduced (for which prices of an analogous kind would need to be set for all natural factors having alternative industrial uses). As such this type of price implies of course the previous attainment of an equilibrium (optimum or near-optimum) allocation of each scarce good in question, and has little or no meaning apart from the latter. It will be clear that a crucial factor in determining this equilibrium-allocation will be the relative output-quantities of the various end-products; so that every change in these output-quantities will result in a change in the prices (or rents) of scarce-inputs, which will in turn cause some adjustment in the uses to which these inputs are put. It is in this sense (as noted in an earlier chapter) that (given) supplies of scarce factors in relation to the relative output-quantities of end-products will determine the optimum choice of methods of production. Only when all inputs are produced inputs the supply of which can be speedily adjusted to the requisite extent can an optimum method of production in an industry be independently and uniquely defined.

In so far, however, as decisions are being taken decentrally about matters which concern the longer-term perspective—decisions, that is, about allocation of a certain input or inputs over a period of time sufficiently long to give an opportunity for production of them to be undertaken, and their supply to be augmented, in the requisite degree—such a (short-period) pricing principle will cease to be appropriate. In this sense the two *kinds* of prices (those related to cost in the way that we first talked of and those constructed on the principle we have just described) will stand in conflict. In the case of centralised decision this conflict will not matter, provided it is clearly recognised and its implications seized; since centralised planning can rest its calculations on *accounting* prices, and if these have no balance-sheet or income-creating significance there is no obstacle to using a different kind or system of accounting-prices for one category of decisions from what is used for other categories. Such a multiplication of accounting-prices may complicate calculation, but it does not obstruct or prevent it by introducing a contradiction. *Actual* prices, however, that operate at the level of an industry or an industrial enterprise necessarily affect the balance-sheet and the actual income of an individual unit (possibly of the workers in it also) : at least, they do so if anything akin to the operational and financial practice of Soviet *Khozraschot* applies. In these circumstances it is difficult if not impossible to see how two sets of prices for the same commodities can apply : *i.e.* in the sense of prices that are paid, or are guaranteed to be paid (or alternatively charged), to the production-unit in question. Even if some structure of 'spot' and 'future' prices graded over time were practicable to devise, the price-differences over time might well have effects that stood in contradiction with the assumptions on which this price-structure had been based. If, for example, the future price of a certain scarce commodity was set at a substantially lower level than its present price, this would presumably be because the planning authorities intended to augment its supply fairly rapidly so that by some target-date in the future planned supplies of it would be brought into balance with anticipated demand. But the very fact that it was known to have a lower price in future years than today might put a premium on actions at lower levels which tended to frustrate this intention : industrial enterprises might be discouraged, for example, from expanding their output of the thing in question in future years and others who could use it with advantage today be tempted to postpone their use of it until the future.* How much damage would in this way result, and whether it would be greater than that involved in long-period decisions being adversely influenced by prices that uniquely reflected transitory scarcities, could only be judged from actual experience.

But, it may be asked, why should not industrial units base

* *Cf.* A. K. Bagchi, 'Shadow Prices, Controls and Tariff Protection in India' in *The Indian Economic Review*, vol. 1 (N.S.), no. 1 (April 1966), p. 30. Dr Bagchi adds the comment : "There is nothing paradoxical about this result ; the shadow prices are associated with an optimal or efficient programme and there is nothing in the market mechanism to ensure that no switch of activities between periods should take place."

their decisions on *accounting* prices if central planners can do so? There have been, it is true, some decentralised models for a socialist economy that have provided for decisions to be taken in this way.* This would mean presumably that each industrial unit or enterprise was concerned with two sets of prices: one of these being accounting-prices in terms of which it would be supposed to make the relevant calculations and to take its economic decisions; the other being the actual prices at which it was credited and debited in its financial accounts for the results of its activity. It would be the latter and not the former that influenced the income of this unit or enterprise (whether or not the incomes of individuals working in it depending on the incentive-system in use). The difficulty here is one of supposing that in practice managers or industrial executives could remain uninfluenced by what was happening in terms of *actual* prices, even though in principle accounting-prices were accepted as basis for their production-decisions and however conscientious they tried to be. Let us suppose that the relation of accounting-prices was such as to indicate the choice of a combination of inputs that would be appreciably more costly in terms of actual prices. The choice of this method might accordingly involve the industrial unit in a loss of income in actual money terms, which in turn would involve a depletion of its working capital, perhaps an inability to purchase sufficient of the dearer input that accounting-price valuation was encouraging it to use and hence an inability to maintain production at a normal level. Is it not almost inevitable that in these circumstances the managers would pay attention to valuation in actual prices, and not only to accounting-prices as the letter of their instructions constrained them to do? Some might even say that they would be fools if they did not do so.

The complexity of central determination of prices of all scarce inputs, and their periodic revision to keep them in line with changing circumstances and to give the price-structure sufficient flexibility, might seem perhaps to be almost as great as that of central determination of output quantities and of supply allocations. This is why the reduction of price-determination to some fairly simple principle that can be embodied in a

* The best known example of this being the scheme proposed by Professor Oskar Lange in 1938 in his *On the Economic Theory of Socialism* (Minnesota, 1938).

simplified set of rules (as we saw can be done in the case of long-term pricing) is preferable from the standpoint of feasibility; with special and *ad hoc* treatment of special cases reserved for a relatively few exceptions to the general rule. We shall see, however, in the next chapter that the taking of decentralised decisions on the basis of centrally determined prices is not the only method by which decentralised decision-taking could operate. Instead of operating on the basis of assigned prices (with these prices adjusted, presumably, through time, by means of some kind of trial and error process), decentralised decision could operate within the framework of centrally assigned *quantities* (as regards output targets and supply-allocations), and a mutual adjustment of these quantities in the light of decentrally indicated prices could be operated under a system called 'two-level planning'. *Prima facie*, at least, such a division of labour between higher and lower levels would seem to have fairly strong claims as a practicable solution.

The importance of distinguishing inputs that can and inputs that cannot be reproduced (and hence increased in supply) within any given planning-period is thrown into relief by those structural models of the productive system which provide for a separate sector, or group of processes, concerned with the production of durable productive equipment, or capital goods, as instruments of production. It is true that the parent of such two-sector models, the famous reproduction-schema of Marx, does not separate out durable equipment from other produced inputs ('instruments' from 'objects' of labour) in its department concerned with producers' goods (*i.e.* goods destined for productive consumption as distinct from individual or personal consumption). But most of the subsequent uses to which this type of model has been put, and certainly adaptations of it such as Feldman's,* have stressed the character of this sector as producing durable capital goods for the purpose of extended production either in this sector itself or in the sector producing consumers' goods (some again preferring a three- or even four-sector division, in which raw materials are separated from machinery, and the latter possibly distinguished according to its

* On whom *cf.* the present writer's *Papers on Capitalism, Development and Planning*, pp. 109–12.

destination and purpose).* The conceptual picture thereby
created was of durable objects which not only continued to
serve a function as productive inputs for a considerable length
of time (for decades in the case of some kinds of structure and
equipment), but the rate of augmentation of which as a class
was subject to a strict upper limit: namely, an upper limit set
at any one time by the size of the relevant sector as measured
by its output capacity.† Feldman, indeed, spoke of the relation between the output-capacity of this sector and of the productive system as a whole as being a measure of the level of
industrialisation of a country, and hence of its capacity for
economic growth. Development thus becomes an example, *par
excellence*, of that circular process of which we have spoken—
of machines to make machines to make machines within Marx's
Department I. As the experience of socialist countries has well
illustrated, the development of productive power up to or
beyond any given level depends in a crucial sense upon the level
of capital goods production, if not in any single country, at any
rate within the whole area of socialist exchange. There is
reason to treat this, accordingly, as the historical limiting
factor at any given period upon the degree to which the stock
of durable instruments of production as a whole can be changed.
In the course of time this stock changes and the limiting factor
itself changes; but this is a relatively slow rather than a quick
process—a matter of decades rather than of years.‡ It follows
that for any given period, in analysing its problems and framing
its essential mechanisms, this limiting factor has to be taken as
an historical datum; and the same is true also (with no more
than minor modification) of the stock of capital instruments in

---

* *E.g.* K. N. Raj and A. K. Sen in *Oxford Economic Papers*, vol. 13 (N.S.), no. 1
(Feb. 1961), pp. 43 *et seq*. It is to be noted that Marx in his *Grundrisse der Kritik der
Politischen Oekonomie* of 1857-8 put production of raw materials and of machines into
separate sub-sectors of a general production department of means of production.

† This applies as an upper limit to the production of capital goods both for
replacement of existing ones and for additions to the stock of capital equipment. If
one is speaking of the potential rate of increase of supply of instruments of production as a class, then the limit on this is, of course, narrower than our statement
implies.

‡ One is reminded, however, of the remark of Lord Keynes about "a properly
run community equipped with modern technical resources, of which the population is not increasing rapidly" being able to reduce "the marginal efficiency of
capital to zero within a single generation" (*General Theory of Employment, Interest
and Money*, London, 1936, p. 220).

the productive system as a whole. While scarcities of particular capital goods (a type of machine tool, a special metal, a fuel or source of power), if they stood alone, could be resolved fairly quickly, these particular scarcities merge into and share a common element attaching to the whole *genus*, and below this minimal scarcity they cannot as a rule be severally reduced for a whole generation or more.

Clearly such an emphasis is encouraging to the idea of representing capital as an original factor of production, on a par with labour and land, rather than as a category of what we have termed 'produced inputs'; although there is no logical necessity for this notion of capital as an original factor to be implied by the kind of schematisation we have just been depicting. But the notion of productive instruments or equipment as a *genus* (and of their historically conditioned scarcity and hence 'rentability' as such) is obviously associated with an emphasis on them as a pre-determined and enduring stock, the size of which can be modified only relatively slowly through the investment-process. In discussions of pricing and costing (and connected therewith the choice of methods of production) it has become habitual to regard the valuation of durable instruments of production as dependent on the degree to which they partake of a common substance called 'capital'—a substance or original factor which is itself priced in terms of its scarcity. This price is a rate of yield (or of profit or interest) constituting an *agio* in the price of all capital goods—as indeed of all other goods. According to the well-known 'Austrian' theory, this yield or *agio* is derived by a process of "imputation" (*zurechnung*) from the prices (and utilities) of Menger's "goods of first order". When the technical (input-output) coefficients are not fixed but variable, this rate of yield and the input-combinations, or methods of production, in the various industries will mutually determine one another.

The difficulties associated with this view are now sufficiently familiar. In a capitalist economy the view that there is a common substance ("ectoplasm" it has been dubbed by Professor Joan Robinson) in all durable instruments of production has some plausibility, since all such durable assets (including intangible assets asociated with them like business goodwill, as well as working capital) acquire a market valuation on a special type of market. But when looked at in the context of a socialist economy such a common element can scarcely fail to appear as a metaphysical entity. At any rate, attempts to pin it down to an independently definable magnitude such as a 'period of production' have hitherto proved unsuccessful;* while attempts to derive the values of heterogeneous capital goods from their *yields* provides no basis for calculating a uniform *rate* of yield.† In view of such difficulties, there is evident advantage, both of formal simplicity and of realism, in replacing (as we have done) the notion of 'capital' as a third original factor by the notion of variously dated labours embodied in produced inputs.

None the less, in all long-term planning decisions, concerned as these mainly are with the distribution of investment, there is an initial convenience and practical appeal in thinking of the potential output of capital goods, or durable instruments of production, as a composite entity of given magnitude. Moreover in all macro-decisions it is tempting to think of this investment-total available for allocation as a value-total that can be both added together, despite its heterogeneous composition, and divided up. This is indeed implicit in the use of an instrument of decision such as an effectiveness-ratio in choosing methods of production; and the value adopted as the standard ratio (below which investment-projects will not qualify for inclusion on the agenda) will *ipso facto* represent a measure of the general 'scarcity' (*deficitnost*) of available investment-potential compared with all the demands upon it, or with the (currently known) social uses for it in developing productive power. The alternative of treating each type of capital good as *sui generis* (each metal, even each *grade* of that metal, each machine-tool or type of building material) and deciding separately on its allocation between alternative uses (moreover, simultaneously organising its allocation as a material input at various stages

* *I.e.* as a magnitude independent of and prior to a rate of return (*cf.* P. Sraffa, *Production of Commodities by Means of Commodities*, pp. 35–8). *Given* the rate of profit (or in our case, as above, the rate of growth) different patterns of dated labours, or production periods, *can* be arranged in an order of magnitude. But they cannot independently of the rate of profit, since with a change in the latter their order of magnitude will change.

† *Cf.* P. Garegnani, *Il Capitale nelle Teorie della Distribuzione* (Milano, 1960), pp. 183–5; and his 'Switching of Techniques' in *Quarterly Journal of Economics*, vol. LXXX (Nov. 1966), pp. 562–5.

and in various branches of the capital goods sector *as well as*
its allocation for constructional purposes in the economy at
large)—this, as we have seen, enormously enhances the complexity of the decisions that have to be taken, possibly in a
developed economy to an unbearable degree. It makes decentralised decision-taking much more difficult than it would
otherwise be, because for the purpose prices have to be worked
out and fixed *ad hoc* for each of the various goods as a basis for
the choices of decentralised decision-takers: a process which
may be no less difficult to achieve (in the absence of appeal to
any rule of thumb) than working out centrally the actual
allocations themselves.*

Since for practical purposes all capital goods must be assigned
some price (accounting or actual), even if they are exclusively
fed back as inputs somewhere in the same sector where they
have been produced, the task of assessment would be greatly
facilitated by adopting the kind of principle indicated earlier
in the present chapter (and further discussed in the next).
Such an assessment would then be on the basis of a uniform
costing system (given the planned growth-rate) ; cases of relative
scarcity likely to endure throughout the planning period in
question, such as those of which we have been speaking, being
treated as special cases for *ad hoc* determination, and carrying
some kind of mark-up on the standard price, expressive of the
estimated degree of differential scarcity. If approximation
rather than ideal precision (in the sense in which we have used
the contrast) be the *desideratum*, there seems to be no reason why
a practicable system of costing and pricing capital goods should
not be devised, and with it a method of calculating an investment fund, such that its allocation and the choice of methods of
production resulting from this calculation was sufficiently
optimal. To do otherwise would be to cause price-fixing to
decompose into a vast array of special cases : moreover special
cases subject to review at monthly or even weekly intervals if
the logic of so-called short-period prices were to be fully seized.

Manifestly implicit in such a system of costing is the existence

* Professor Ota Šik refers to a million and a half specific prices in Czechoslovakia : a number that could be reduced to "about 25,000 price groups" if
central price control were confined (as he suggests it should be) to adjusting "the
macroeconomic price relationships" (*Plan and Market under Socialism*, Praha, 1967,
p. 262).

of a uniform ratio, or profit-rate, in all lines of production towards which current investment is being directed, and the inclusion of such a ratio (*i.e.* as an equal ratio to productive funds or assets) in all prices. If this be not uniform, but differentiated, methods of production in low profit-rate industries will be encouraged that yield an investment-effectiveness that is lower than elsewhere (and lower than existing limitation on the investment fund warrants when this limitation is related to all its potential uses or effects). The converse will be true of high profit-rate industries. Accordingly, a shift in methods of production (and in investment) between industries (in the direction of lower capital-intensity in some and higher capital-intensity in others) would be capable of augmenting output in some industries, at least, without any loss of output in others : a possibility which we have seen characterises the initial position as non-optimal. This is the *rationale* of so-called 'prices of production', which has been sponsored by one school of opinion in the Soviet price-debate, or akin to it of Novozhilov's *narodnokhoziaistvennie stoimost*.*

Such a principle is entirely reasonable if we can ignore the possibility of specific (and relatively greater) shortages within the larger category, and assume that within the planning period in question any relative scarcity of this or that capital good can be overcome by switching resources from producing one kind of output to producing another kind in the required degree. Only the general constraint (imposed by the historically given size of this sector) on the potential supply of this whole class of goods is recognised. This contrast between limitation of the *genus* and elasticity of the supply of each species within it may not, as we have seen, be always realistic. It is possible that over the relevant period aluminium (say) may remain a scarce metal relative to other metals, or possibly some plastic, re-

---

* *Cf.* below, chapter 9. The objection levelled by some against the application of anything like a 'prices of production' principle to a socialist economy has been the alleged impossibility of finding any basis for the 'true' rate of profit (*cf.* the references on p. 206 below to Professors C. Bettelheim and B. Minc ; on one occasion the present writer was so incautious as to give expression himself to this view, in *Soviet Studies* (Oct. 1957), p. 136, reproduced in *Papers on Capitalism, Development and Planning*, London, 1967, p. 172). Under capitalism this is determined by the rate of exploitation : does it, then, under socialism become quite arbitrary? As we have now tried to show, it *only* becomes 'arbitrary' to the extent that the rate of growth must necessarily be treated as a 'planning variable'.

quiring the development of a whole branch of chemical industry, be in short supply, or that the supply of electricity or of oil may be unable to catch up with the growth of demand for it. In this situation some eclectic solution seems inevitable: a departure from an equal profit-rate to the extent of allowing certain differential scarcity-rents and deficit mark-ups (as one might call them), with the object of securing an economy in the use of these scarce goods* as inputs when choosing methods of production. Perhaps in this respect planning for twenty years is distinguishable from (and, apart from uncertainty, simpler than) planning for a single decade. But it may well be that within feasible planning horizons no clear and simple line can be drawn, and that there may always have to be some departure from any uniform rule. Nothing in price-policy, it would seem, is capable of presenting a completely tidy picture. Perhaps the nearest to one is to demand uniformity so far as possible, and to throw the *onus* of justification upon cases that show a good *prima facie* claim to be listed as exceptions. In this way it might be hoped that the category of things requiring *ad hoc* price-fixation as special cases could be kept relatively small.

There is an incidental complication here which brings us back to a difficulty we mentioned earlier about the scrambling together of short period and long period categories. If the planning period is of any considerable length (covering, say, three quinquennia or more), the pricing of some scarce input that may be rational at the start of the period may be irrational by the end. Planning would be lacking in prevision or effectiveness if in the course of a decade it had failed to provide for relaxation of the more acute scarcities that were acting as bottlenecks on development and forcing upon industry substitutions in the input-pattern that would otherwise be unnecessary. In so far as planning had succeeded in doing so, the exceptional prices

---

* It is to be noted that most of the cases complained of by Kantorovich (on the ground of *under*-pricing) are those "in the production of which large specialised and also scarce equipment is being used, namely prices of metals, petrol, coal, cement and railway transport" (L. V. Kantorovitch, *Ekonomicheskii Raschot Nailuchshevo Ispolzovania Resursov*, Moscow, 1959 and 1960, p. 155 (English translation, ed. G. Morton, 1965, p. 135)). On temporary deviations of price from 'prices of production' cf. Ota Šik in *Czechoslovak Economic Papers* (1965), no. 5, pp. 23–6; also his *Plan and Market under Socialism* (Praha, 1967), pp. 265–9, where it is emphasised, however, that "it should not be permitted to increase sales prices in cases where the production of scarce goods can be quickly increased", p. 269.

of the early years could be graded downwards nearer to the standard case. If the degree of this subsequent revision could be foreseen and announced in advance, no harm would result (apart from a possible result that was mentioned above).* In so far as the direction only, but not the amount, of the change was forseeable, some adverse effect upon investment-decisions could result; although this might fall within the 'tolerances' (or degree of approximation) to which any solution must be subject. Here the distinction is of some importance between things that are used as material inputs and those which are used as part of a durable installation (*e.g.* aluminium as a current material input and aluminium embodied in a machine). So far as the latter is concerned, what is relevant is its price at the date when the investment-decision is made; and what this is will always be *known* at the relevant date even if its price is destined to change over time to an unforeseeable degree. But investment-decisions can also be affected by the future price-trend of what will be important current inputs into the production process (objects of labour) when the new investment-project is completed and in operation, since this will affect the degree of economy of current operating costs that the new project will yield (and hence its 'effectiveness ratio', or its 'internal rate of return'). Replacement and repair costs (*e.g.* the prices of spare parts) may also be relevant in this connection. Here the intrusion, with short-period scarcity-prices, of uncertainty about future price-trends may be more serious. Experience alone will suffice to tell how serious, or alternatively how negligible, this consideration will be. The possibility, at any rate, of its exerting some distorting effect may be a reason, again, for keeping this category of prices to a minimum.

NOTE TO CHAPTER 8 ON LABOUR INPUTS AND GROWTH

It has been said above (p. 157) that "the labour-input at 'earlier' stages of production tends to be larger, *ceteris paribus*, than at 'later' stages; this excess being a simple function of the rate of growth".

Let us illustrate this by a simple straight-line production-process

---

* P. 167 above.

in which a given amount of labour has uniformly to be applied in each of five time-periods (which could be regarded as either five months or five years) before the object of this labour can emerge as a final product. Diagrammatically the process could look like this:

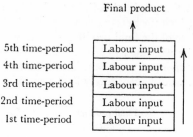

Final product

5th time-period	Labour input
4th time-period	Labour input
3rd time-period	Labour input
2nd time-period	Labour input
1st time-period	Labour input

or alternatively in conventional double-entry table:

Processes of production

		I	2	3	4	5
Produced inputs	I	o	x_1	o	o	o
	2	o	o	x_2	o	o
	3	o	o	o	x_3	o
	4	o	o	o	o	x_4
	5	o	o	o	o	o
Labour input		y	y	y	y	y
		↓	↓	↓	↓	↓
Outputs		x_1	x_2	x_3	x_4	x_5

(It will be noted that x_1, x_2, x_3, x_4 stand for what have been called above 'produced inputs', and x_5 for a so-called 'end product' of the process, emerging annually (if a time-period be taken as one year). The y's represent labour-inputs.)

If we are dealing with stationary conditions, where successive months and years repeat always the previous one, such a representation will suffice to describe what is happening. In each period five units, or 'lots', of labour-inputs will be separately applied to five production-lines, each at a different stage; only one of these being destined to mature into a final product immediately (or before the period is up). Thus each period will have its batch of output, which is product of five lots of labour-input, spread over this and the preceding four periods.

If, however, growth was occurring at a certain rate, say 5 per cent. in each period, then the final product emerging in the next period after this would have to be 5 per cent. greater than it now is, and

5 per cent. greater still in the next period after that. To make these future increases of final product possible, the labour-inputs now being applied to 'earlier' stages in the production-process would have to be equivalently greater; these additional labour-inputs (directed towards future increases of final product) getting larger as one passed down the production-lines to the one that was nearest to its beginning (since the nearer one was to the latter, the more distant the future date of the final product towards which the labour in question would be working: hence the larger both future product and present labour-input must be). The production-line, or set of production-lines, would accordingly look something like this.

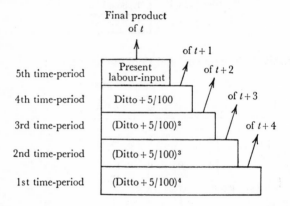

Putting it alternatively in double-entry-table form, one can represent it, by comparison with the representation adopted above (for stationary conditions), as follows (using g for the growth-rate):

Processes of production

		1	2	3	4	5
Produced inputs	1	0	$x_1(1+g)^3$	0	0	0
	2	0	0	$x_2(1+g)^2$	0	0
	3	0	0	0	$x_3(1+g)$	0
	4	0	0	0	0	x_4
	5	0	0	0	0	0
Labour input		$y(1+g)^4$	$y(1+g)^3$	$y(1+g)^2$	$y(1+g)$	y
		↓	↓	↓	↓	↓
Outputs		$x_1(1+g)^4$	$x_2(1+g)^3$	$x_3(1+g)^2$	$x_4(1+g)$	x_5

Let us call the *additional* labour at each and all of the relevant stages (other than the immediate present) that is necessitated by growth 'investment labour'. From our schematic representation this can be seen to consist of $y(1+g)+y(1+g)^2+y(1+g)^3+y(1+g)^4-4y$. It will evidently be larger proportionately (*i.e.* to the labour currently needed to maintain a constant stream of output over time) the higher is the growth-rate; and *given* the growth-rate, the total of this additional or investment labour will be larger the larger the number of stages (or the 'longer' the production-process). Thus it would be substantially larger if we were to lengthen the process from our 5 time-periods to 10 time-periods. Let it be noted that we are speaking here of investment labour that has to be applied *now*—in anticipation of future outputs.

Hence what one may term the 'dating pattern' of labour-inputs at any time will be different with different growth-rates, given the method of production (and given the growth-rate it will be different with different *methods*); while the rate at which *total* current labour-expenditures will change over time will depend upon the growth-rate of final output and will necessarily be equal to it.

What has been said of labour-inputs could be said also, *mutatis mutandis*, of what we have called produced inputs.

It will also be apparent that, in the case of the comparatively simple productive structure that we have depicted, if the structure is modified so that any of the labour-inputs are 'advanced' in time (in the sense of being required at an earlier period or date), the total amount of investment-labour required will be increased by g times the quantity of labour so advanced, per unit period of that advance. Methods of production will not always conform to such a simple structure, and choice between any two methods of diverse structures may involve a comparison of very different patterns of dating of labour-inputs. The same principle, however, will apply to these more complicated comparisons: that the amount of investment labour occasioned by any given labour input will be greater the more 'advanced' its dating (or the more remote in time it is from the emergence of its end-product), and greater by some factor of g.

To choose a method of production with a 'longer' production process, or with an 'earlier' dating of labour-inputs, would have no point unless it yielded a higher productivity of this labour in terms of eventual end-products (without this it would never come onto the agenda for consideration at all). This advantage can be represented alternatively as a larger income of end-products at any date resulting from a given quantum of labour-expenditures, or as an economy of labour-inputs required to maintain a given flow of end-products. Ideal choice between methods of production involves balancing this advantage against the increase in investment labour that the altered dating of labour-inputs involves. Thus a method of production may be optimal in this sense at one growth-rate, but not at another.

It is worth noting, if only as a curiosity, that in comparing two very different patterns of dated labour, it is quite possible to find method A preferred to B at certain (*e.g.* low) growth-rates by reason of economy of investment-labour required by those growth-rates; for B to be preferred to A at higher growth-rates; and then at still higher growth-rates for the preference for method A to re-emerge. This will not seem surprising to those familiar with the

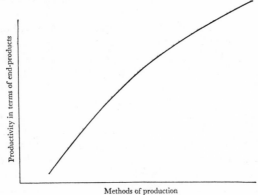

Methods of production
differing in length of period

discussion about 'switching of techniques' in connection with Mr Sraffa's system.* The result is to be attributed here to the differently distributed weight (due to the altered relative influence of the compounding factor) of the proportional additions represented by investment labour (as between labour-inputs of different dates) when the growth-rate changes. But this is no way contradicts the principle enunciated in the present chapter and in the next.†

The main relationship indicated here can be depicted in a series of diagrams. For this purpose we must revert to the assumption that the methods of production under consideration are of a homogeneous structure, differing only in the dating-pattern of their

* *Quarterly Journal of Economics*, vol. LXXX (Nov. 1966) (esp. articles by L. Pasinetti and P. Garegnani). See also below, p. 192, footnote.

† The principle is not contradicted since the method which comes out the cheaper when costed in the manner indicated (dated labour-inputs costed with g as the weighting factor of time) will be that which involves the smaller total of investment labour at the growth-rate in question.

labour-inputs (assumed also to be of uniform total amount in static conditions). First, we may correlate a series of methods of production differing only in the way that we have just mentioned (*i.e.* according to their time dimension or length of production-process) with their productivity in terms of end-products. If we make the familiar and plausible assumption that the latter advantage generally diminishes proportionately with lengthening of period, the methods in question will fall along a curve having the shape shown in the figure on p. 180 opposite.

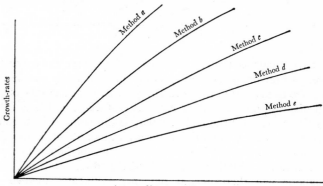

Amount of investment-labour required

Next we may correlate the amount of investment-labour required for a given method of production with different growth-rates. For each method of production, *a, b* . . ., *n*, we should have a different curve (here we depict five such curves, with *a* referring to the method with the shortest period).

These relations can then be combined into an index of what may be called 'effectiveness of invested labour' (defined as the productivity of a given production-process in terms of end-products divided by the total amount of labour, including investment-labour, needed to maintain a certain (rising) flow of income). This effectiveness will be different for different methods of production and different growth-rates (being negatively correlated with the growth-rate *ceteris paribus*) ; so that if one were to represent effectiveness along the ordinate and methods of production along the abscissa (arranged in ascending order according to their length of production-period) and drew a series of curves for various growth-rates, it would be found that these curves reached their peaks of effectiveness at *different methods of production*. Generally the lower the growth-rate the longer the method of production (*ceteris paribus*) corresponding to its peak, and conversely, in some such fashion as this:

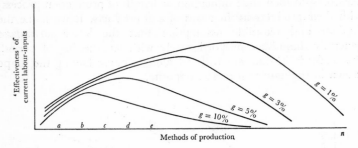

We have spoken of the relationships depicted here as applying to the comparison of methods of production of a fairly simple and homogeneous structure. In more complex cases the curves of our second diagram may lose their regularity of shape and may intersect. This will express the real fact that at the point of intersection both methods will involve the same total amounts of investment-labour, and that beyond it (to the right) the method which previously, at lower growth-rates, involved the lower totals of investment-labour will thereafter at higher growth-rates involve the higher totals. In such cases the curves for different growth-rates in our third diagram may no longer be single-peaked. It follows that the kind of costing system suggested here (based on the use of *g* as an interest-factor applied to time) will have the effect of reaching a relative maximum (compared with neighbouring positions), but the peak so attained will not necessarily be a *maximum maximorum*. This, however, is a limitation on the use of *any* costing or time-discount system, and not only on the one suggested here.

CHAPTER 9

FOOTNOTE TO A DEBATE

The old debate about *wirtschaftsrechnung*, commonly held to have been opened by von Mises,* is nowadays sufficiently familiar to need no summary. The ground of it has been so much traversed, by so many people and in such various ways, for any suggestion of revisiting it to invite disinclination rather than attention. Let us rest content here with making one or two comments only; which may serve to relate the issues of this debate to the analysis of optimum conditions with which we have been concerned hitherto.

In the original form in which von Mises framed his critique of socialism, the alleged impossibility of rational calculation clearly rested on the impossibility of a market for factors of production when the latter (at least non-human factors) were in the ownership and at the disposal of the State ("just because no production good will ever become the object of exchange, it will be impossible to determine its monetary value"; "it is irreconcilable with the nature of the communal ownership of production-goods that it should rely ... upon the economic imputation of the yield to the particular factors of production").† Without such a market costs would lack any economic meaning and there could be no economic calculation. Criteria would be altogether lacking for distinguishing an 'economic' from an uneconomic method of producing a particular commodity or for deciding whether it was being produced on too large or too small a scale.

There can remain scarcely any doubt that the von Mises objection in the form in which he stated it cannot be sustained.

---

* Article, 'Die Wirtschaftsrechnung in sozialistischen Gemeinwesen', in *Archiv für Sozialwissenschaften und Sozialpolitik*, vol. 47 (April 1920) (English translation in F. A. von Hayek (ed.), *Collectivist Economic Planning*, London, 1935); also L. von Mises, *Die Gemeinwirtschaft*, Jena 1922. There were those before von Mises, however, who had taken a similar line of criticism, such as N. G. Pierson in Holland, Georg Halm in Germany and Enrico Barone in Italy.

† L. von Mises in F. A. von Hayek (ed.), *Collectivist Economic Planning*, pp. 90–2.

It may be remembered that in stating the Production Condition in chapter 4 we emphasised that the first half of this Condition (concerning choice of factor-combinations or methods of production) did not need the introduction of factor prices; while its second half (concerning equalisation of factor-yields in all uses) did not require their introduction either, provided one was content with the Lenient (or Proportionality) Version of that condition (with which alone the problem of allocation *per se* is concerned). At a less abstract level there is Oskar Lange's famous retort that "Professor Mises seems to have confused prices in the narrower sense, *i.e.* the exchange ratios of commodities on a market, with prices in the wider sense of 'terms on which alternatives are offered' ... It is only in the latter sense that 'prices' are indispensable for the allocation of resources, and on the basis of the technical possibilities of transformation of one commodity into another they are also given in a socialist economy."*

It is possible, of course, to fall back upon "a second line of defence" (as Oskar Lange called it) by interpreting the von Mises denial as applying, not to the question of theoretical possibility or impossibility, but to the practical *feasibility* of reaching a solution by any of the available or suggested mechanisms. We lose something in definiteness and rigour thereby, and in the dogmatic quality of the original, since arguments about feasibility always involve personal judgements and impressions as to the shape of various situations and the weight to be attached to various factors therein. But this was the interpretation implicit in Professor von Hayek's subsequent summing-up of the "state of the debate" in 1935.† To adopt it is to put the argument, however, on to a very different footing: to involve the argument in a variety of questions about admin-

* Oskar Lange, *On the Economic Theory of Socialism* (University of Minnesota, 1938), p. 61.

† *Collectivist Economic Planning*, p. 207: the solutions advanced by Professor Dickinson and others were "not an impossibility in the sense" of being "logically contradictory"; they were simply "not a possible solution". Reference was made to the "thousands of equations" involved in any hypothetical solution. Pigou's more impartial summing-up was that under socialism "the practical task of securing that the actual allocation of productive resources shall conform to the *chosen* allocation, can, *in principle*, be solved. But ... the task is extraordinarily difficult ... Except in a world of supermen, many and grave lapses are certain to occur" (*Socialism versus Capitalism*, London, 1937, pp. 118–19).

istrative methods in relation to institutional frameworks, about information and control systems and about human motives and incentives. Into such questions we cannot and shall not try to enter here, except for those points which are no longer purely speculative but about which experience in socialist economies has something relevant to say. The fact that by now consider-able experience has been garnered on all such matters; that experimentation is today in train both to formulate what the essential problems are and to find practicable solutions; that modern computing techniques as well as mathematical tools of analysis such as linear programming have brought enrichment (at least potentially) to planning methods since the thirties—all this must incline one increasingly to view the categorical *non possumus* of the Mises–Hayek school as dated and uncon-vincing.

But has not a subtle element of bias been imparted to this question of practicability by the very way in which the per-spective from which it is viewed has been slanted? The start-ing-point (and term of comparison) is a competitive market. Such a market reaches, supposedly, a unique equilibrium—reaches it precisely, 'objectively' and 'automatically', without any of those cumbrous calculations that any conscious solution of an optimising problem would have to go through.* What is automatic in its attaining of an equilibrium is *ipso facto* 'rational'. By contrast with the smooth precision of the one, the clumsy, slow-moving craft of planned calculation inevitably suffers. The latter's image is projected onto the screen as at best a rough approximator, its so-called solutions inevitably bearing numerous marks of non-optimality.† But then has not the qualifying standard been set too rigorously, while our free market image, with all its blemishes, has been left conveniently veiled? Any judgement of feasibility will manifestly depend

---

* *Cf.* "as analysis of the competitive system revealed the complexity of the prob-lem which it solved spontaneously, economists became more and more sceptical about the possibility of solving the same problems by deliberate decision" (F. A. von Hayek, *op. cit.* pp. 25–6).

† In one place Professor von Hayek even cites the alleged impossibility of 'interpersonal comparisons of utility' as a reason why it is an "illusion" to sup-pose that socialism could adjust the relative outputs of consumers' goods according to a "utility calculus". He does not see—or at least does not choose to mention—that if true, this is *no less* damaging to the possible optimality of any competitive equilibrium (*op. cit.* p. 25).

on the 'tolerance' or degree of approximation within which one is content that a solution should lie. We have said above that it would be *simpliste* to suppose that in our present subject the permitted 'tolerances' should be anything but fairly wide; and it is a consideration to which we shall later return. Yet in much of past discussion talk of rational solutions has proceeded as though rigorous micro-economic precision were obtainable and obligatory. We seem to have been beguiled by a Perfectibility Fallacy such as is apt to haunt any application of optimum conditions to real situations, and can least of all be entertained when the argument is explicitly about feasibility.

Our second comment relates to the solutions that were offered in reply to the von Mises challenge: notably, the 'competitive' solution of Professor H. D. Dickinson and the 'quasi-market', or accounting-price, solution (as we may call it) of Oskar Lange. These were explicitly devised as decentralised models of socialism, with decisions about both output and investment taken at the level of individual industries or production-plants (enterprises). According to Professor Dickinson's scheme they would be taken on the basis of prices on actual markets (competitively determined, it was hoped), including a market for loans (*i.e.* for capital). In the Lange model it would be all done on the basis of accounting prices, which would be set by higher economic authority and varied at intervals according as the situation was one of excess demand for the thing in question or of excess supply. What was less stressed, and seems to have been little remarked upon by most people at the time, was that the amount of decentralisation envisaged would be sufficiently great virtually to negative centralised planning such as is customarily associated with a socialist economy.* Professor Dickinson himself had very frankly described his own proposal as "a sort of similacrum of a capitalist economy" being "set

* Professor von Hayek's comment on the competitive scheme was that "it certainly does not involve much more planning than the construction of a rational legal framework for capitalism", and it is questionable "whether it still deserves the designation of planning" (*op. cit.* p. 218). Dr Paul Sweezy later commented that Lange's "Central Planning Board" is "not a *planning* agency at all but rather a price-fixing agency", and criticised the scheme for failing "to take advantage of the constructive possibilities of economic planning" (*Socialism*, New York, 1949, p. 233). Professor Dickinson, as we shall see, still hoped, however, that some place could be found for planning.

up within the socialist community"—"purged from the grosser errors (of capitalism) but, like it, actuated by the blind choice of millions of uncoordinated consumers and producers".*

But if one is to exalt 'market autonomism', one cannot carry over from capitalism the advantages of an automatic decision-making mechanism without importing its principal defects as well. The question immediately arises as to whether these advantages may not be too dearly purchased at the expense of possible fluctuations of the 'cobweb-theorem' type, or at the macro-economic level of the trade cycle variety, along with the uncertainties attendant on atomistic decision-taking. The present writer at one time expressed the view† that the instability at a macro-level of such a decentralised mechanism might possibly be even greater (under the competitive real market scheme)‡ than that of the capitalist market-mechanism with its predisposition to cyclical fluctuation; and this because the multiplier-mechanism of an initial expansion or contraction of the rate of investment would still be in operation, perhaps even in an enhanced degree. *A fortiori* such a decentralised system might have more trouble with dynamic instability—with maintaining a stable growth-path over time—than does a capitalist economy. At best a wholly decentralised system might prove a hesitant and uncertain instrument of growth. If one is to have an automatic equilibrating process, one cannot ignore the possible cost involved in the process whereby equilibrium is attained.

For this reason it is difficult, if not impossible, to believe in the practical existence of a completely decentralised socialist economy in which 'market autonomism' is allowed full rein, and planners refrain from interference in its beneficent opera-

* *Economics of Socialism* (Oxford, 1939), p. 220.

† In *The Economic Journal* (Dec. 1939); reprinted in *On Economic Theory and Socialism: Collected Papers* (London, 1955), pp. 45 *et seq. Cf.* also, commenting on this, the reference to "an Harrodian cumulative tendency" in *Essay on Economic Growth and Planning*, p. 4.

‡ Under the Dickinsonian scheme an increase of demand (arising, for example, from an initial increase of investment and employment) would provide a justification for expansion of investment by industries experiencing the larger demand; and by bringing enhanced profits to industrial enterprises it would provide them with the financial means to finance expanded investment (possibly making them immune to control *via* higher interest-rates). Unless industrial profits were very heavily taxed, the 'multiplier' in this situation might be abnormally large and instability equivalently great.

tions, save perhaps in the sphere of so-called monetary policy and in the manner in which 'indicative planning' lays an occasional gloved hand upon the reins. Professor Dickinson, indeed, regarded planning and his market process as being "not opposed, but complementary, principles of economic regulation", and he himself outlined a number of ways "in which economic planning is required to supplement a system of quasi-individualistic pricing and costing".* Some blend of centralisation and decentralisation is what confronts us as a practical possibility and what we have before our eyes in the countries of Eastern Europe today. How much this qualifies the force of the Dickinson–Lange answer to von Mises will be a matter of varying opinion. But if it should qualify the force of these models as an answer, it also qualifies the objections that can be levelled against them on the score of introducing the Trojan horse of a capitalist market mechanism into the citadel of socialist planning. How far the blend is able to combine the positive elements of centralised and decentralised models without their negative ones is not capable of any quick and easy answer. Into discussion of what is and is not feasible an additional dimension has been imported. But there is nothing in the content of the *wirtschaftsrechnung* debate to demonstrate that it cannot do so. This alone experiment, inspired by invention, can show. Many today would contend that to work out some such feasible synthesis of plan and market is the essential next step.

The third comment upon this old economists' debate (which must be given credit at least for having anticipated some of the contemporary discussion) takes the form of an initial expression of surprise that so little attention was paid to the enunciation of a centralised solution (*i.e.* one consistent with a high degree of centralisation of decision about output and investment). It might seem to many that here one had to-hand a surprisingly simple answer, at any rate so far as allocating the main 'original' factors of production between alternative uses and productive methods was concerned. Economists of the Utility School had always emphasised that demands for productive factors were "derived demands" (Marshall)—derived from the final demands (and ultimately utilities) of the end-products that

---

* H. D. Dickinson, *op. cit.* pp. 220 *et seq.*; *cf.* P. M. Sweezy, *op. cit.* p. 235.

they were used to produce.* The productivity (marginal) of factors in terms of these end-products would be no less known to industrial managers than they are in capitalist industry today; and if there is a free market for consumers' goods, whereby prices of final output are determined, why should not the problem of allocation be solved by directly comparing the productivity of these factors in different uses, and at all levels of allocation pushing factors always towards a more productive use from a lower one? Thus, if not at the first move, through a series of moves, approximations and improvements, could not a maximum position fairly quickly and effectively be attained? Here again the *doctrinaire* deserves to be reminded of the commonplace that to make things equal to one another at the margin of alternative uses does not necessarily require that they be first of all made equal individually to some *tertium quid*.

The apparent simplicity of this solution depends on treating factors as capable of being aggregated into fairly large groups and on the implicit assumption that each factor can be reduced to some unit of itself (*i.e.* a unit which is not a market value of itself) and its allocation handled accordingly. It is a familiar supposition that labour and even land can reasonably be handled in this convenient manner, provided that allowance is made for a certain amount of grading to meet differences of quality (with some kind of equivalence-ratios between units in different grades). At least, results could thereby be obtained with what could not unreasonably be regarded as a sufficient degree of approximation. In the case of capital, however, there is no such unit; since a characteristic of the *genus* Capital is its extraordinary *heter*ogeneity—beyond anything that applies as between different acres of land. For this reason economists have generally conceived of Capital as a sum of values; implying a

---

* This was, indeed, the answer made at the time (if little noticed) by Sir Robert Hall (as he now is) to Halm and von Mises: "Demand for the factors of production . . . is a derived demand . . . There is no theoretical difficulty in the way of calculating costs . . . as long as there is a market in consumers' goods" (*The Economic System in a Socialist State*, London, 1937, pp. 71–2, 74). *Cf.* in a review by the present writer in *The Economical Journal* (Sept. 1935), p. 534: "The data required [for the distribution of productive resources] consist in the physical productivity of resources in different uses (a technical fact), the available resources, and the valuation of the products; and no separate problem apart from this arises." Also *cf.* C. D. Baldwin, *Economic Planning: its aims and implications* (University of Illinois, Urbana, 1942), pp. 122–3.

value-unit for the purpose of quantitative representation of a rate of return : moreover, it is a collection of products of the economic process, which have to be treated, along with other products, as outputs as well as inputs ; and as such their valuation will be affected by every change in relative prices. Such a value-measure, however, involves one in circular reasoning in speaking of the determination of this rate of return, since the latter will affect the very valuation of heterogeneous capital goods that is being used as measure of the *genus* Capital. In the matter of allocating capital goods, in which we are immediately interested, the valuation (it would seem) would be affected by the allocation, and the allocation could not be conducted (save arbitrarily) without valuation, and hence a value-unit. For economists nowadays this is a sufficiently familiar story.

The notion (already mentioned in the previous chapter) that allocation would have to be worked out separately for each specific capital good, and that no generalisation into a wider category is possible, was no doubt responsible for the ready adoption of the axiom that centralised allocation would be much too complex to be feasible, and for acceptance of this conclusion even by those who stood on 'the other side' of the debate. That it would involve the solving of "thousands of equations" (even tens of thousands) was altogether too baffling ; and this type of solution seemed hardly worth discussing.

Is there any release from this dilemma? If there is not, there would seem to be little hope for compromise of decentralised models with centralisation, since the most obvious sphere for the latter, we have seen, is investment-allocation, because this *par excellence* shapes the macro-structure of the economy. Yet, if the dilemma of which we have spoken is unresolved, allocation of capital would seem to be of all things the most unsuitable for centralised decision. Are we then thrown back upon the conclusion that, if there is to be any optimising in the economy at large, the rôle of centralisation must be confined to the sort of 'indicative planning' or 'steering' that has become familiar in capitalist economies, based predominantly on private enterprise and free markets?

There is, however, a way of escape from this dilemma—on condition that one is willing to take the rate of investment and hence (given certain productivity-conditions) the growth-rate as an independent *datum:* given exogeneously, that is, as a policy-decision of the community or the government, and embodied as cornerstone of the plan. At any one date, indeed, one could regard this as historically determined, either by the existing productive capacity of a capital goods sector of industry, or alternatively by some 'consumption fund' setting a limit (at any given level of real wages) to the possible size of employment on investment-projects. Further into the future, however, both these historical limits are modifiable by the shape of investment-policy itself.

We have indicated in chapter 8 that a positive rate of growth (if this rate is to be uninterrupted) will impose the necessity for relatively larger quantities of labour-inputs to be applied at 'earlier' stages of production than at 'later' stages (the reason being that the earlier stages are already producing with an eye to the larger output of final products tomorrow or the day after or the day after that). One can regard all these *additional* labour-inputs at earlier stages (*i.e.* the difference between the labour required there with any given positive growth-rate and what *would* be required if the growth-rate were zero) as a measure of the amount of investment being undertaken; and this as a ratio to total labour-input can be taken as a measure in labour of the rate of investment.* We also saw that an appropriate way of weighting labour of various dates (in the sense of remoteness in time from the emergence of an end-product) was to use the growth-rate as a weighting-factor for this purpose. In other words, if the rate of growth of output in the system at large per unit of time be represented by g, then g would be the appropriate weighting-factor to apply per unit of time to labour of earlier dates compared with labour of later dates in the

---

* If one abstracts from the time-factor (as was implicitly done in the writer's *Essay on Economic Growth and Planning*, chapter IV), then the matter can be expressed as a ratio of labour needing to be employed in an investment sector to labour in the consumption sector: in the notation used in that *Essay* this was $(L_i + L_{m1+2})/L_c$. This ratio will be relative to the growth-rate; and *ceteris paribus* the larger the productivity (per unit of time) of this investment labour the smaller the amount of investment labour needed to sustain a given growth rate. (*Cf.* the relevant equations expressing this relationship, *ibid.* pp. 50–2.) Our present analysis is an alternative (in one sense, perhaps, simpler) way of presenting the argument of that chapter IV; but with the additional consideration of a (variable) time-factor to the structure of production.

sequence of production-stages and production-flows. Thus production-processes differing in the patterns of their dated labour
could be appropriately costed and compared.

What, then, is the justification of this in terms of social costing
and pricing: of using, for example, this growth-factor as a basis
for the pricing of all capital goods? It is, in brief, that if we
change the method of production in any line of production in
such a way as to lengthen the period of production* (or to
advance in time the use of a unit of labour-input) by a unit-
period of time, this will necessitate an increase in the amount
of investment (measured in labour in the manner just described) by a marginal amount equal to g—if the existing
growth-rate is to be maintained. Alternatively, if the total
amount of labour devoted to investment is fixed, the change
will mean a transfer of that amount of investment-labour from
other industries and a fall in the growth-rate there by an
equivalent amount.†

In case this is not immediately clear, we may illustrate it by a
simplified example, which can be taken as representing the
situation in one line of industry alone or in the economy at large.
Let us suppose that inputs of labour have to be applied over a
period of 10 unit-periods of time before the product emerges
as final output. (It will make no difference to the result whether

* An incidental consideration is relevant here. Once we have taken the growth-
rate as a *datum*, this has the advantage of enabling us to give an unambiguous
meaning to a 'period of production' or a 'weighted sum of dated labours' for any
given growth-rate (it will be like postulating a given rate of profit in Mr Sraffa's
system). It remains true, however, that of two totals, representing different input-
patterns, one may be greater than the other under one growth-rate and the converse be the case under another growth-rate—which is the crucial objection to
using the notion of a period of production as an *independent* measure of quantity of
capital (*cf.* P. Sraffa, *Production of Commodities by Means of Commodities*, p. 38). But
this objection is conveniently by-passed in our present treatment.

† A. Lurie, in *Voprosi Ekonomiki* (1966), no. 7, p. 63, rightly emphasises that the
need for time-discount arises from the fact that "an increase in quantity of any kind
of resources will make possible the obtaining of a larger increase in social productive power, and hence a higher satisfaction of social needs, the earlier in time
this increase occurs". In stating, however, that the size of this discount must be
such as to equalise the existing size of the planned investment fund with current
demands upon it, he asserts that the larger the fund, the *lower* should be this discount, and hence the ratio of effectiveness (*ibid.* p. 70). But this conclusion ignores
the fact that an increase in investment if accompanied by an increase in the growth-
rate will raise the demand upon investible resources as well as their supply (and
raise the former in *greater* proportion relatively to *total* available productive
resources).

we assume that labour-inputs continue to be applied successively in each of the 10 periods, or that the labour-input is applied once-for-all in the initial period and matures, like wine, into final output over the whole period.) In stationary conditions the application of this amount of labour in each successive period will suffice to maintain a steady stream of final output; and the same will be true (after an initial adaptation-period) if the methods of production are so changed as to involve an extension of the total period over which labour-inputs have to be applied from 10 unit-periods to 11. But if growth is occurring, the position is different. If the growth-rate is g then, as we have seen, the labour-input currently being applied to 'early' stages of the production-process will have to be increased by some function of g, since additional labour will have to be invested here and now in preparing for the larger output of future years. (We have emphasised that the amount of this additional labour will be a function, *ceteris paribus*, *both* of the growth-rate, g, *and* of the period over which labour-inputs have to be advanced.) If in these circumstances the method of production is changed so as to involve an extension of the total period over which (given) labour-inputs have to be advanced from 10 unit-periods to 11, the amount of investment-labour (*i.e.* labour additional to what is involved in maintaining a steady rate of present output) will have to be raised both absolutely and relatively. Let us suppose that the labour previously applied uniformly during each of periods 1 to 10 is now applied during periods 2 to 11 (one period earlier,* that is, in each case); but that no labour need now be applied during period 1.†
Reflection will show that the amount by which labour currently

* It is here convenient to reverse the order of numbering adopted in the Note to chapter 8, and to use the highest number for the 'earliest' period and the lowest for the 'latest' in order of production-sequence. (There we were regarding the matter from the standpoint of a *given* production-sequence, here from that of *changing* the sequence in the direction of lengthening the total time-dimension.)

† This is the right way of putting the matter if we wish to isolate the effect of a change in the time-period, or in the *dating* (merely), of labour-inputs. If we were to assume that labour was still being applied in period 1 as well as in periods 2-11, we should be combining a rise of *total* labour-inputs with a lengthening of the production-process. What we have to imagine is that in this last period of maturing production (period 1) we now have *only* produced inputs (*e.g.* maturing wine or a completely automated process) which are the product of the preceding periods; the net effect of the change from a 10-period to an 11-period process being an overall substitution of produced inputs for labour-inputs.

applied each year (including investment labour) has to be increased as a result of this change (if growth is not to be adversely affected) will equal g.*

The factor g will, then, represent in an important sense the social cost of so altering productive methods as to extend the time-dimension, or the dating of labour, at the margin of industry. With a given total investment labour-force, an extension in one direction must involve a contraction of it in some other direction. It will presumably be the case (unless technical possibilities of doing so are already exhausted) that every such extension of this time-dimension can enhance the productivity of labour in terms of final output (both of what we called in the previous chapter end-products and of produced inputs). We are confronted accordingly with two contrary effects of a change in methods of production, to be balanced one against the other. On the one hand we have an increase, *ceteris paribus*, in the investment labour-force needed to sustain a given growth-rate when methods are changed in the direction of lengthening productive processes; on the other hand, we have a 'labour-saving' effect of raised productivity, such that less current labour will be required each year to sustain a given rate of output (and hence immediately a given rate of increase from a given output-level). It can be seen to be a condition of maximising the growth-rate attainable with a given amount of investment-labour (or alternatively of minimising the amount of investment-labour needed to maintain a given growth-rate) that extension of the time-dimension of the productive process should not occur in any industry beyond the point where the

* Since all the labour previously applied is now applied one period earlier, *current* applications of it will have to be uniformly increased by a factor equal to g, since all labour-expenditures are now directed towards the final output of *one year later*. An alternative supposition that we might have made is that *only* the labour-input of period 10 is put back to period 11, leaving period 10 with zero labour-input. In this case, since only the two latter periods are changed, all other periods 1–9 remaining the same, comparison is equivalent to that of a 1-period process with a 2-period. One is, in effect, substituting in period 10 produced inputs (produced by the labour now applied in period 11) for labour-inputs; and since the labour in question has always to be expended one period earlier the amount of it being applied must be increased by g. This accordingly represents the social cost of the change to be taken into account when assessing whether such a substitution is worthwhile. Analogous comparisons could be made in other cases: *e.g.* where the labour-inputs of periods 5–10 are 'put back' by one period, but those of periods 1–4 remain as before.

increment of productivity (resulting from a marginal extension) is equal to g (*i.e.* to the growth-rate per unit-period).* If costing were to be based on wage-cost alone, irrespective of dating, there would be no limit to such extension so long as *any* gain in productivity, however small, resulted therefrom. Such productivity-gains would raise the level of output of end-products, but at the cost of reducing the growth-rate towards zero.

If this be a correct way of representing the social cost of using more 'capital intensive' methods of production, then an important conclusion seems to follow. This is that all produced inputs should be priced in an analogous way; and the appropriate interest-rate per unit-period to be used for this purpose should be equal to g. If this and the time-pattern of inputs are known, the appropriate pricing of all produced inputs can in principle be derived; and in practice a sufficiently close approximation should not be too difficult to achieve by an iterative process of successive adjustments. Costed in this way, the most socially beneficial method of producing a given output will come out as the least-cost method.

Given the average length of the period of production (and the pattern of dated labour within it), the ratio of what we have termed investment-labour to labour involved in maintaining the present rate of output will be also given. According to what is now a familiar piece of economic reasoning, this will be equal to the ratio of total profit (or surplus) to wage-cost in current (final) output of consumers' goods—on the assumption that the price of the latter is a supply-demand market-equilibrium price, and that all wages are spent.† Thus the price-system of which we are speaking has the convenient property of being in this sense self-balancing at the macro-level. If all production-processes were sufficiently similar to make the period of production (the value of n)‡ uniform throughout the system, then this would be the correct mark-up on wage-cost to be applied

---

* This can be put in the form of $dx/dt = d(x/l)$, where x stands for output and l for labour, and $d(x/l)$ is the increased productivity (a given amount of) labour from a lengthened production-process. If the marginal cost in labour of improved productivity is equal to dx/dt $(= g)$, this can be seen to be the condition for maximising the average productivity of invested labour.

† *Cf.* the present writer's *Essay on Economic Growth and Planning*, pp. 91–2.

‡ Also the time-pattern of labour-inputs within this period.

in the determination of price; this mark-up applying to the prices of produced inputs as well as of final output of end-products.* Actually the period of production (and also the time-pattern of labour-inputs within the period) is likely to vary between different lines of production; and as a result the appropriate mark-up on wage-cost will vary accordingly, in correspondence with the differing ratio of investment-labour to labour required to maintain present output in various lines of production.

Thus both these ratios—that of profit or surplus to wages-cost (whether in general or in a particular industry) and of investment-labour to labour needed to maintain present output—as well as the rate of interest, will be functions of the growth-rate, rising and falling with the latter. They will only be unity (and the rate of interest zero) when the system is stationary and no growth is occurring.†

An objection, however, may be raised against this analysis. To postulate the growth-rate as a *datum* in this way (or alternatively to postulate a rate of investment) is, surely, to introduce a quite arbitrary condition that can have no relation to maximising welfare. There is no obvious reason why either methods of production or the comparative outputs of different consumers' goods should be affected by the accidental consideration that growth is occurring at a particular rate, whether fast or slow.

---

* For practical purposes this mark-up might be taken accordingly as a starting-point for calculating the appropriate addition to wage-cost; adjustments being made for the degree to which capital-intensity in any line of production diverged from that applying to the consumer goods sector as a whole.

† If only to avoid a charge of implicit definition, this may be the place to clarify what one means by growth (and zero growth) in this context. Our reference here is to a planned-for trend of growth over a period *with given methods of production*. Hence it will necessarily be correlated with a certain proportion of the labour force used as investment-labour (as well as with a certain rate of increase of labour-inputs through time). In the example given above of a shift in methods of production, resulting in higher productivity: this would cause a once-for-all change in output when the shift occurred, including a change in the present level of end-products, but not a continuing one. The quantity of labour needed to produce a certain output in any year would thenceforth be smaller (or alternatively the level of output maintainable by a given quantity of labour would be higher); but the trend growth-rate would remain unaffected. The same would apply to the effect of technical innovation: this exerts an effect on productivity and hence on the *level* of output obtainable from given inputs, but not necessarily upon the trend of change. *Cf.* also below, pp. 200–1.

If consumers' welfare be the objective, should not choice of both comparative outputs and of methods of production be governed exclusively by the availability of certain basic factors of production in relation to consumers' needs, and hence be the same whether growth is occurring or not?

It is quite true that the propositions of welfare economics have been formulated hitherto in what has been essentially a static context, with problems even of saving and investment being treated quasi-statically as a choice between utilities with different dates (or between income at various dates). It is true that to introduce the rate of growth in the way that we have done is to introduce into the centre of the problem a new dimension that was not there before (at any rate explicitly); and this may be responsible for the impression of something unfamiliar, even alien, about the setting. To some, of course, this new dimension might serve to recommend the approach as a way of integrating the requirements of growth with the allocation-problem as traditionally viewed. But this will scarcely recommend it to the confirmed individualist, who believes that saving and investment can only be *optimum* in volume if they are decided by individual preferences expressed in a market; and compared with such a unique rate, a governmental decision about growth will be regarded as arbitrary and irrational.

There are serious objections, however, to this view.* At a fairly early stage of the von Mises debate Sir Robert Hall forthrightly declared that "there is no index by which it can be decided that one rate of saving is better than another, since we are allowing for the future and can only guess about the data required for a decision . . . the decision is a political rather than an economic one. Some arbitrary decision must be made."† Without much doubt this is a view that, on balance, has gained rather than lost ground since that time, whatever reservations there may be about the possibility of defining an optimum rate of saving *a priori*. One can hold, in contrast to the individualist, that the supreme welfare-decision in a socialist economy, dwarfing all others, will be that concerning the rate at which the real

* *Cf.* discussion of it in the present writer's *Essay on Economic Growth and Planning*, chapter II. Professor A. K. Sen's "Isolation Paradox" is highly relevant in this context ('On Optimising the Rate of Saving' in *The Economic Journal*, Sept. 1961, pp. 487–9); and see further below, p. 217.

† R. L. Hall, *op. cit.* p. 125; *cf.* also pp. 200–8.

income, and hence the potential standard of consumption, of the community is intended to rise. This can well be regarded as more significant for the sum of utilities enjoyed over any stretch of time than whether at any given date consumers have just the right number of nailbrushes compared with hairbrushes for their maximum satisfaction.* It would seem perfectly right and proper that in a socialist economy such a crucial decision as this, and one least of all suited to guidance by market-criteria, should be taken by the community in some form. As such it will in practice be treated by planners as a key political constituent of their plan-making, on which most of the latter must necessarily hinge. This decision will thus be *a priori* (and not *a posteriori*) to any costing or pricing process in terms of which methods of production are chosen.

At a more formal level, one could, indeed, carry this point further in counter-attack by saying that when dealing with a process of economic growth the traditional method of deriving costs from prices paid by consumers (and hence from utilities) is bound to break down. This traditional Jevonian-Austrian method of *zurechnung*, or 'imputation', (whereby Menger's 'goods of higher order' derive their values from 'goods of first order') essentially rests on the notion of production as a straight-line process of original inputs emerging as use-values for consumers. But when growth is occurring, part of production must take the form of what we have termed produced inputs, which are fed back into the production-process, as it were in a circular loop. In a pure von Neumann-type circular growth-model, in which all outputs become inputs, utilities do not appear as determinants.† To the extent, therefore, that growth is occurring in the system, one must surely expect the valuation and costing of inputs to be determined by the requirements of the growth-process itself, especially where the time-dimension is involved.

What of the implications of giving the growth-rate so crucial

* *Cf.* P. J. Wiles in *Oxford Economic Papers* (Oct. 1953), pp. 315–16.
† *Cf.* D. G. Champernowne "A Note on J. v. Neumann's Article on 'A Model of Economic Equilibrium'", in *Review of Economic Studies*, vol. XIII, no. 1, p. 17: "One is left with the impression that consumers' tastes play, in fact, a comparatively minor rôle in the determination of equilibrium prices . . . The novelty of the distribution of emphasis which it implies is, from some points of view, an advantage."

a place and deriving from it a price for all produced inputs?
Are these capable of rational interpretation or are they, on
the contrary, to be dismissed as arbitrary and irrational? A
leading result of the method of pricing that we have indicated
will be that, the higher is the postulated growth-rate, the greater
the bias against capital-intensive methods of production (if this
means 'time-consuming') and against augmenting the supply
of things whose production involves relatively high capital-
intensity (in the sense of requiring labour-inputs to be relatively
far advanced in time). Is this an unreasonable result? If the
community places a high premium on increasing the income of
future years, and to this end devotes an unusually large quantity of labour and produced inputs to investment, then it can
the less afford to increase the quantity of these produced inputs
still further by catering so fully as otherwise for the wants of
consumers for commodities whose increases involve a comparatively large amount of investment-labour. Similarly it can
the less afford generally to employ methods of production that
involve a further addition to the amount of investment labour.*
Conversely, where less weight is given in planning-policy to
future increase of income, the natural implication would seem
to be that correspondingly more weight is assigned to a
balanced satisfaction of different consumers' needs and to augmenting the productivity of the labour already in use (both
investment-labour and the labour required to maintain the
present rate of output of end-products). The community, in
other words, can afford to be less parsimonious about satisfying
consumers' demands for things involving a relatively large share
of investment-labour and about buying additional productivity
by extending processes in time. Analogous considerations would
apply (even *a fortiori*) if a low (or possibly zero) rate of growth
was imposed by shortage of labour and by inability or un-
willingness to divert any labour from producing for the needs
of the immediate future. With the possibilities of growth by
means of so-called 'widening' so straitly limited, the balance of
advantage would now be tilted in favour of achieving once-

* Reflection will show that there is implicit here the assumption that a growth-
rate of given magnitude is to be preferred to a once-for-all rise in the *level* of real
income of the same magnitude (such as lengthened processes would yield). But
this is, surely, quite reasonable as a general assumption, and one likely to be widely
accepted.

for-all gains in output (or economies of labour needed to maintain a given output-flow) by improving methods of production. (One way of putting it would be to say that, with a low rate of growth, 'time' would be less costly in terms of investment-labour.)

It follows that *only* if no growth is being planned for (in the sense of allocating labour and other inputs as investment inputs) will there be no obstacle to raising labour productivity progressively towards the highest level afforded by known productive techniques. The quantity of labour-inputs expressed in wage-cost will then (but *only* then) be a sufficient basis for pricing and for allocation-decisions. Even so, this situation will not be reached immediately: it will take some little time to achieve; and in the meantime there will be a transitional situation in which a problem analogous to the one we have been discussing will exist , and with it the need for the type of costing and pricing we have indicated, if only to keep methods of production (in course of their progressive change) 'in step' with one another as between different sectors and industries; thereby making the most effective use of labour at any given date.

This process of advancing towards the highest level of known techniques (and hence of productivity) will be in itself, of course, a process of growth, bearing some analogy with growth as we have treated it hitherto. But it will be growth by a different route or in a different dimension: growth achieved by 'deepening' instead of 'broadening', to use a distinction familiar to economists.* It will likewise need to employ (for the time-being) a rate of interest or discount (and to include this in costing), but in this case a *falling* rate to encourage the 'deepening' (or alternatively 'lengthening') process to continue; the degree of this fall being dependent upon the intended rate of growth. The need for this is reinforced by any tendency there may be for the growth-rate of output to fall, owing to

* It might be thought that growth achieved in this way would not require the use of 'investment labour', since the new produced inputs will simply replace old ones as these are used up (in business-parlance the new methods can be financed out of depreciation funds). But this is not so. In so far as there is a transition to 'longer' methods, investment labour will be involved in the transition: in a given year labour-inputs will be needed to feed the stream of final output of $t+n$ years thence *and* also of $t+(n+1)$ years thence.

diminishing additional productivity from additional 'lengthening'. On the other hand, it will be obviated by the occurrence of technical innovation, which will have the effect of natural *largesse* in conferring output-growth without the obligation to progress from one method of production to another and 'longer' one (*all* methods can be regarded as being benefitted by the innovation and their productivity raised accordingly).

It may have been noticed that there has been no explicit reference hitherto to anything in the nature of an existing 'stock' of capital. Some may regard this as a defect of our analysis and of its corollary: that by devoting its attention exclusively to 'flows' this analysis has ignored the part played by capital 'stocks' in determining the methods of production, and has accordingly reached a fallacious conclusion. At first sight this may look like a more formidable objection than the previous one; and may seem so particularly to anyone well-versed in traditional presentations of the matter.

It is true that in our analysis the existing stock of durable and installed produced inputs has had no place; although it was indicated in chapter 8 that this analysis could accommodate the notion of durable instruments which imparted their services to the productive-process not in a single act but over a stretch of time. But it is also true that there is no need for our analysis to introduce this notion. Reflection will show that so long as capital equipment is increasing, and in step therewith employment of labour, growth being at or within the Harrodian 'natural rate', it is this increase, and not the existing stock, that is relevant to the type of production-process to be used; since if this involves too much investment labour in its creation and renewal, then either the growth-rate or the existing scale of end-products will have to be curtailed. Regarding existing equipment what is relevant is simply current replacement. So long, at least, as the growth-rate is within that of the working population,* nothing is lost by focussing attention on the *expansion* of equipment and of the labour involved in making and using it.

It is quite true that the approach of full (or, rather, over-full)

* *Cf.* the sense in which growth-rate is being used in this context as defined on p. 196n. above. In so far as growth-rate is used so as to include the effect on output of (uniform and continuing) technical progress, it would be necessary to add here the words: "multiplied by productivity-increase resulting from technical progress".

employment *would* be relevant to the choice of methods of production, since the limit would have been reached (or passed) beyond which available labour no longer suffices to meet the expansion of labour-inputs required to sustain the existing rate of growth. But this would be a disequilibrium situation : a symptom of inconsistency in the plan with which it would be beyond the function of any method of costing or discounting principles to deal.* Indeed, this limit could have been anticipated, and some tapering-off of investment and growth been provided for in advance, if investment-planning had been adequately geared to manpower budgeting and forecasting. The consequential fall in the interest-rate (with its weighting of dated labours) would then have encouraged resort to lengthened production-processes as a way of raising the productivity of the existing labour-force. This would be equivalent to substituting produced inputs for labour-inputs, especially in the form of durable mechanical instruments, and by the resulting

---

* This is, of course, the logical consequence of postulating the rate of growth as an exogenously determined variable. If this really is the case, any pricing-process and such variables as are determined thereby must operate strictly within its framework, and this pricing-process must not be expected to modify the planned framework itself.

What remains true is that the implication of thus taking the growth-rate as being exogenously determined by the plan is that any feed-back influence of methods of production upon growth-rate is ignored. If labour-supply is a major constraint upon growth, what is *possible* as a growth-rate cannot be determined without making some assumption about the methods of production that are consistent with various growth-rates at given dates, since these will influence the amount of investment-labour needed to sustain those growth-rates. Hence in practice one may have to expect a preliminary process of mutual adjustment (either in planning calculation or in reality) between methods of production (*via* the interest-rate) and the planned growth-rate, before an equilibrium trend is established.

Perhaps it may be convenient to set out possible antecedents and consequents in this way :

If both the growth-rate and the labour-force (with its rate of change) are given,

> *then* both output-level at any date and methods of production are determined.

If the labour-force (present and future) and present output-level are given,

> *then* there is a method of production that will maximise the possible growth-rate.

If the growth-rate and the present output-level are given,

> *then* there is a method of production that will minimise the labour-inputs needed at any date.

If there is a unique method of production and the labour-force (with its rate of change) is given,

> *then* the relation between present output-level and its growth-rate is uniquely determined.

higher productivity of labour would *ipso facto* make a contribution to sustaining the growth-rate of output (or mitigating its fall). In the absence of technical progress, however, such substitution as we have seen would make a once-for-all contribution only, not a continuing one, so far as the trend of growth is concerned. When its effect was spent, the growth-rate would continue its downward tendency (with a resulting further round of 'substitutions' in the structure of production) until the growth-rate (as a planned trend) was eventually stabilised at a level equal to the rate of growth of the working population; with the ratio of produced inputs to labour-inputs (or the pattern of dated labour) and the resulting size of investment labour and its increase over time adapted thereto.

Admittedly the method of pricing that we have indicated will be unacceptable to those who give priority to maximising employment rather than growth of output as an objective of policy when a reserve of labour exists (as in an underdeveloped economy). Wishing to absorb this reserve as rapidly as possible, they would need to establish a rate of interest that was *higher* than we have indicated in order to rule out all but the most labour-using and capital-saving methods of production. To pursue such an objective, however, either would imply the absence of any constraint upon the volume of employment (in the shape of a 'consumption fund', or surplus of consumers' goods, and a 'floor' to real wages) or else would be to ignore the fact that maximising employment at early dates, if this be at the expense of productivity and of growth, may postpone rather than advance the date when full employment is attained.* And if no such constraint in fact exists, then there is nothing to prevent the planned growth-rate itself from being raised.

An alternative way of deriving a rate of profit for the purpose of price-fixation and costing depends on first postulating a given rate of investment, or quantity of available investment funds, as a policy decision. This is the method suggested by Professor V. V. Novozhilov of Leningrad, which turns upon

---

* *Cf.* the present writer's *Essay on Economic Growth and Planning*, chapter III and pp. 104–8; A. K. Sen, *Choice of Techniques* (Oxford, 1960), pp. 21–36. For the contrary view *cf.* M. Kalecki, *Zarys teorii wzrostu gospodarki socjalistycznej* (Warszawa, 1963).

the use of a coefficient of effectiveness of investment, defined as the saving in prime or operating costs resulting from new investment expressed as a ratio to the investment expenditure in question. The relevant coefficient is arrived at by assuming that the given total of investment funds is allocated between various alternative investment-projects according to a priority scale based on the size of the relevant coefficient : *i.e.* allocation is made to a project with a higher coefficient in preference to one with a lower. Allocation proceeds down the list of projects until the available investment fund is exhausted. At the margin of allocation the coefficient will have a certain value, and this value is taken as the standard coefficient, which in Professor Novozhilov's notation is written as r. Then what is termed 'national economy cost' (*narodnoekonomicheskaia stoimost*) is arrived at in the case of each good by adding to its prime cost (consisting of wages and raw material cost *plus* depreciation of plant and equipment) a quantity rK, where K represents the value of invested capital. In his notation the final cost or 'normal price' is written as $rK + S$.*

This method implies, not only that total investment is given as a datum, but also that the output targets for final products are given (since the number and size of investment-projects will be affected by them) and that K can be given a quantitative meaning. The latter requirement would seem to imply that the problem of measuring capital has not been circumvented; since K can only be expressed as a quantity in terms of the prices of capital goods. It should not be too difficult, however, to arrive at a pricing of all capital goods (along with other products) by this means through an iterative process of successive adjustments, until a reasonably consistent solution was reached. How far such adjustments would, indeed, be convergent (and with a reasonable degree of approximation) upon a single solution, only experience can show.

The *rationale* of this method of pricing is analogous to the one we have already used in connection with our previous case. It is that since investible resources at any one time are strictly limited (within a fairly narrow time-horizon they are always

* V. V. Novozhilov in *Primenenie Matematiki v Ekonomicheskikh Issledovaniakh*, ed. V. S. Nemchinov, vol. 1 (Moscow, 1959), pp. 42 *et seq.*; V. V. Novozhilov, *Izmerenie Zatrat i Resultatov* (Moscow, 1967), pp. 68–113.

limited by decisions taken and by events in the past), they should not be used for any purpose or in any industry unless the contribution that they can make there is at least as great as what they could have contributed in some other use (a use which is deprived of this contribution). 'Contribution' is here treated as the economy in prime cost of producing a given output: in the terminology we have used above, this is the same as an actual economy of labour inputs *plus* produced inputs, and if prime cost consisted entirely of wages, it would be equivalent to an increase in labour productivity. It follows that all inputs into the productive process that compose investible resources should be debited in their prices with a measure of what this contribution, if used elsewhere, would be, in order that this shall find expression in costing. Novozhilov himself has expressed his rK as a measure of 'indirect labour expenditure', in the sense of the additional labour that *would be* required if the K in question were not employed in this line of production (and equivalently of labour that has to be expended additionally elsewhere in uses deprived of it by its presence in the industry to which it has in fact been allocated). To justify itself, any K should enable enough profit or surplus to be produced, over and above the cost of labour and raw material inputs, at least to cover rK; r being the measure of what its effectiveness could have been in some other (marginal) use.

This method has the advantage that it is capable of providing a fairly easy and practicable mechanism whereby decentralised output-decisions could be governed in a compromise between centralisation and decentralisation such as has been indicated above (with investment decisions remaining the province of the centre, in the main, but output-decisions being wholly or largely taken at lower levels). This could be termed the 'normal price' mechanism, and could be applied, first as an actual price for all industrial inputs as the basis for costing, and secondly to all consumers' goods and any other goods the selling-prices for which were market-determined, or adjusted according to market indices (*i.e.* approximated to current supply-demand equilibrium prices). In the latter case the Novozhilov-type cost-price could be used as standard or norm, rather than as an actual transactions-price (in the same way as the costing system described above in chapter 8 and earlier in the present chapter) : whenever the current price was above the standard-price, the rule should be to increase the supply, and conversely. Investment-decisions could also be governed, *ceteris paribus*, by a similar rule : the higher was current price relatively to the standard or normal price, the higher the priority of that product or industry for an increase of productive capacity by new investment.*

There is finally a possible solution along linear programming lines that is consistent with centralised allocation and centralised setting of output-targets. This can be regarded as being, in a sense, a polar opposite (or perhaps the 'dual') to the Lange 'trial and error' method of reaching an equilibrium. In the latter it was prices that were fixed from above and quantities that were decided decentrally at lower levels. In the former, quantities are fixed from above, while prices (in the sense of 'shadow prices' appropriate to linear programming solutions) are settled at lower levels. This has been called, indeed, 'two-level planning' by the two Hungarian economists, J. Kornai and T. Liptak, who have developed it in rigorous detail.† Briefly, and in non-technical language, it can be described in this way. Initially there is some given allocation both of supplies and of output targets among industries, enterprises or localities, which has been drawn up by some central planning body. This allocation will be handed down to the lower levels with the direction that they should prepare an optimal 'local' plan, by use of linear programming methods, for utilising what is assigned to them and for fulfilling the stipulated output-targets. It could thus be regarded as a way of applying linear programming solutions 'from the bottom upwards'. To each such local optimal plan there will be a set of 'shadow prices' (Kan-

---

* Such a mechanism was, indeed, suggested by Professor Charles Bettelheim in the first edition of his *Problèmes Théorique et Pratique de la Planification* (Paris, 1946), pp. 199–202, but withdrawn without explanation in later editions, presumably on the grounds that there was no valid method of deriving a normal or average rate of profit in a socialist economy: a view also sponsored subsequently, as we have seen, by Professor Bronislaw Minc in Falkowski and Lukaszewicz (eds.), *Studies on the Theory of Reproduction and Prices* (Warszawa, 1964), pp. 185–6, citing Bettelheim and Kalecki.

† 'Two-Level Planning' in *Econometrica* (Jan. 1965); also J. Kornai, 'Mathematical Programming in Hungary', in E. Malinvaud and M. O. L. Bacharach (eds.), *Activity Analysis in the Theory of Growth and Planning* (London and New York, 1967), pp. 211–31.

torovitch's *o.o. otsenki*) relative thereto : sets of prices which, on the contrary to being uniform (which they could only be in the first instance by accident), will show divergences from one local plan to another. These prices will be transmitted, in turn, back to the higher planning authorities, who will use them as a basis for subsequent revisions both of supply-allocations and of output-targets : revisions, that is, in the direction of securing greater uniformity as between the local constellations of 'shadow prices'.* The practical utility of this 'two level' method depends on whether the series of successive approximations is convergent with sufficient smoothness and quickness to reach an overall optimum result without too much preliminary oscillation and delay. At least, since the macro-framework is directly under central-planning control, it is unlikely to suffer from the macro-economic instability that we earlier suggested that its polar opposite method of approximation would do.

Our provisional conclusion about centralised solutions (or solutions providing an opportunity for some compromise between centralisation and decentralisation, planning and market) is rather different from that implicit in the pre-war western economists' debate. Indeed it is a contrary conclusion. Instead of a solution being theoretically conceivable but in practice not feasible, as was formerly held, it turns out that a number of fairly simple and feasible methods exist that are quite consistent with central decision and planning. At any rate, they can be regarded as feasible if the degree of approximation to an ideal result with which one is content is not too exacting. If one is a purist who believes in a unique optimum and demands nothing less than its precise attainment, then one will hold the view that such solutions, though feasible, will exhibit serious theoretical deficiencies, and deviations from perfection, from the need to give them an easily-operational form. The result of achieving feasibility will thus be to sacrifice optimality. But if what is optimal is difficult, if not impossible, to define at all precisely, and in an imperfect world even more difficult to reach under any feasible set of arrangements or institutions, does such an objection seriously matter? Commonsense would suggest that it does not.

* *Cf.* also J. E. Meade, *The Stationary Economy* (London, 1965), pp. 212–20.

CHAPTER 10

INDIVIDUAL CONSUMPTION AND CONSUMERS

We have seen in our discussion of *optimum* conditions (in chapter 4) that there is a *prima facie* case on welfare grounds, first for allowing consumers to spend their money incomes freely and without restriction, because in this way individual variations in tastes and in wants will obtain the fullest satisfaction, given the pattern of supply and of prices confronting them; secondly, for choosing methods of production, or input-combinations, in each industry so as to maximise potential output measured in physical terms from a given quantity of inputs. The first of these propositions is fairly obvious, and is indeed sufficiently non-controversial to need no further elaboration; although on occasions it may need some qualification in the light of certain considerations about individual demand that are discussed in what follows. The second requires certain uniform relationships between inputs in different lines of production (as expressed, for example, in uniform ratios of 'effectiveness of capital')* which have not always been observed in the practice of socialist economies to-date. But we have seen in the previous chapter that there are fairly simple mechanisms available to a socialist economy to achieve this result, at any rate if one is content with rough approximation without requiring absolute precision. It is what alone can be called a pure efficiency condition, since without its fulfilment the economy cannot be on its so-called 'production-possibility' frontier, and hence producing the maximum that it could be producing of any given set of output-targets (or given production plan). In this way it bears close analogy with linear programming solutions, as propounded for example by Kantorovitch. The whole matter has received considerable attention above in the context of a socialist economy and it will be referred to again in the concluding chapter.

* Provided that this is expressed in *real* terms in such a way as to refer to the ratio of substitution of different inputs.

To these two theorems we also saw that there is commonly added a third. This, when translated into terms of practical implications for policy, is to the effect that there is a presumption, *ceteris paribus*, in favour of determining (and modifying) the distribution of income between social groups and individuals through the medium of money incomes rather than of prices; the reason for this being that to influence distribution through prices must always involve a failure in *some* degree to adjust supply to individual demands in the most 'perfect' manner. We have, again, seen in the preceding chapters that, if we accept this *desideratum*, there is a fairly simple mechanism for adapting the pattern of supplies of consumers' goods to the pattern of demand (as a long-term goal at least) *via* an adjustment of supplies in such a way as to bring final retail price-ratios into equality with cost-ratios, with the proviso that costs are appropriately defined.

But in this third proposition the qualifying clause of 'other things being equal' covers a number of quite crucial considerations: considerations which may be summed up in the statement that it may well be impossible in practice, or inexpedient, to adjust income-distribution to any desired extent through money-income payments alone; hence it may well be unrealistic to assume (as worshippers at the shrine of so-called lump-sum money transfers* so unthinkingly do) that the instrument of price-adjustments for affecting the distribution of real income between individuals can be abjured altogether. This is the reason why we held that this third welfare theorem should be carefully distinguished from the other two, and in the rigour of its application should be pressed much less hard.

Let us, accordingly, examine a little further what the reasons may be why the instrument of price-adjustments cannot be abjured entirely—even if the degree of precision with which one could conceivably *define* an ideal distribution, with its

---

* The fallacy here, to repeat, is the supposition that such transfers can always be made without having any marginal effects. But even if they do not affect consumers' choice as between retail commodities, they may well have a so-called income-effect, and hence an incentive-effect on the willingness to work and to undertake certain sorts of work compared with others. Only an arbitrary exclusion of certain things from the optimising process (*e.g.* leisure, or disutility of work, or, again, once-for-all costs of movement) can afford an excuse for ignoring this kind of effect.

translation into terms of money income, were much greater than is the case.

First, there is the consideration that in a socialist economy income-payments have to play the rôle of a production incentive, wage-differentials having to be adjusted not only to variations in the *amount* of work performed, but also according to the *kind* of work (*e.g.* as regards the disutility involved in its performance—disagreeableness and arduousness and possible risks to health and expectation of life) and the degree of skill involved, in such a way as to adjust the supplies of various skills to the industrial need for them. We have also seen that in a period of rapid change in technique or in the structure of industry, when the demand for skill in general or for skill of a particular kind changes abruptly (as in the period of Soviet intensive industrialisation during the pre-Second World War Five Year Plans), wage- and salary-differentials may have to be geared to a desired *rate of change in supply* of the more skilled grades of labour rather than to any normal 'maintenance price' of their relative supplies, and hence exhibit an abnormal 'spread'. Apart from the so-called money illusion (the fact that for incentive purposes there is more conscious awareness of differences in money-payments than of differences in *real* income), which may be of substantial importance, there is the consideration that the categories in terms of which such differentials operate are limiting and restrictive and are certainly different from those which apply to any ideal classification according to need. The payment-categories, for example, have to be defined in terms of a certain job or work-grade or work-attainment. All those within the category will necessarily be paid a uniform rate of money earnings, irrespective of whether they all equally require the incentive.* It may well seem desirable in these circumstances to differentiate between different members or groups within the same income-category, if objectively-defined expenditure-differences fit the case, in the only way open by either taxing or subsidising (as the case may be)

---

* A 'Marshallian' case would be where the incentive payment is related to 'supply-price at the margin' and those who are intra-marginally situated enjoy some kind of Marshallian surplus. As Professor A. Bergson comments: "it could not be true of the bulk of the workers who are intramarginal" that wage-differentials correspond to differences in disutility (*Essays in Normative Economics*, Cambridge, Mass., p. 184 n.)

those held to be less or more deserving. An example might be the difference between single men and those with families or the physically strong and the physically weak (whether from age or ill-health). On incentive grounds—and perhaps on grounds of deep-rooted trade union custom—these would have to be paid the same for the same quantity of work and the same job. The difference of need or of ability could be met, it is true, by the payment of family allowances in money in the one case and of an age-graded pension or disability pension in the other. But the degree to which such money-allowances will *in fact* be spent on the object, the need for which is the ground for payment, may vary considerably as between individual recipients. In the former of the two cases mentioned the need-justification for making a supplementary payment is that when received it will in fact be spent for the benefit of children, and failure so to spend it negates the justification. In all such cases, accordingly, it may reasonably be held that real-income variation will be better tailored to need if things of special benefit to children such as milk or children's clothing or schoolbooks and education or additional house-room are subsidised through the price system ; or in the case of those in ill-health or advanced in years by subsidised medical care and free or cheap medical supplies or home-help.

One could generalise this by saying that in all cases where the ground for affecting some shift in the distribution of real income is the degree to which people have a particular expenditure-pattern or are consumers of some commodity (which for social reasons it is desired to encourage or discourage) the only effective means of doing so is by proportioning the subsidy or tax to actual consumption, and this means in effect through a change in the price of the commodity or commodities in question.

Secondly, when speaking of differentials in their aspect as incentives, one cannot easily divorce their effect from non-rational elements : elements which may be connected with custom, a prevailing sense of equity and of social honour or prestige attaching to a given income-differential *per se*. Such considerations are likely at least to colour the attitudes of individuals towards the adequacy of a certain differential as a reward for, or offset to, a difference in disutility of the occupation in question. Such considerations, moreover, are likely to attach themselves to differentials in their *money-form*, partly because it is in this form that recipients, or prospective recipients, are immediately aware of income and of income-differences, and partly because it affords something precise and calculable, on which the mind can fasten, to an extent that *real* income, or the purchasing-power of a given money-income, does not. So far as its attraction for an individual is concerned, a good deal depends upon how long a given income-differential is expected to last (for example, the higher income of a grade requiring education and training to qualify for entry, or of a temporarily labour-short industry). The individual's time-preference, affecting the comparative weighting he attaches to short-run and long-run advantage, may be fairly high, and from a social standpoint irrationally high ; yet a sense of equity* may restrain a government that has widened differentials in order to attract labour into certain occupations from immediately narrowing them again once these have achieved the desired effect. Yet, since the expectation whereby the movement of labour was immediately influenced was of a certain *money* income, the government might not unreasonably feel less compunction about subsequently narrowing the *real*-income differential by manipulating the price-difference between luxuries and necessaries, once the incentive-reason for the income-inequality had disappeared.

Distribution-shifts produced by short-period scarcities (due *e.g.* to harvest deficiency or import difficulties or possibly by the misjudging of demand) present a somewhat different problem. One way of meeting this would be a price-rise, while offsetting the undesirable effect on the lowest income-groups by compensating income adjustments in their case. But it might be thought desirable to meet such situations, not by price-adjustments, but by some form of direct control such as rationing, on the ground that the price-changes requisite to prune demand were likely to have undesirably strong distribution-effects (since higher income-levels would take their fill and leave the whole brunt of shortage to be borne by lower incomes). Enthusiasts for money-transfers would no doubt suggest that the

* Perhaps also the consideration that a trick once played by manipulating income-differences may not be able to be played twice.

effect could be offset by appropriate adjustments in money-income differentials, and that this combined with 'rationing *via* price' would be preferable (because more flexible) to direct rationing of supply. But apart from the possible adverse incentive-effects of such temporary shifts in income-differentials the advocates of them would have to explain the principle on which such income-changes should be made and justify their feasible application. Would such changes be based on a calculation of the proportion of income spent on the scarce commodity in question by an individual or an income-category; and how would they take into account the precise effect of making them on the total price-rise needed for aggregate demand to be equated with diminished supply?

Even more important and far-reaching are perhaps all those cases where for sundry reasons it would be unwise to rely on consumers' sovereignty: where there is ground for dissenting from the generalisation that individuals best know what is good for them, or that there is some positive welfare-component in allowing people to choose for themselves. As Dr Mishan has remarked, it should be "transparent that in many circumstances some measure of constraint on a man's choice can increase his welfare".* To make a judgement of this kind is by no means necessarily to lean on an arbitrary value-judgement. It may well be a factual judgement, capable of proof or disproof, that individual choice fails to achieve what best contributes to human well-being, individually and/or collectively.† Thus one may make the observation that if young children hold out their hands joyfully to the flame and burn themselves, or somewhat older children take to drugs or adopt habits that increase their liability to lung cancer, human desire, at least in the young, is not to be relied upon as an index of what contributes to human welfare. One's doubts may increase in face of evidence that even adults, whom experience is supposed to have taught what contributes to their real as distinct from imagined satisfaction, are manifestly short-sighted in their preferences and

---

* *The Costs of Economic Growth* (London, 1967), p. 118.

† This is conceded by Professor A. Bergson, for example, if rather grudgingly. He writes that whether an individual knows what is good for him "is not solely ethical. Rather is there some basis for empirical enquiry" (*Essays in Normative Economics*, p. 53). *Cf.* also Branko Horvat, *Towards a Theory of Planned Economy* (Beograd, 1964), pp. 31–2, on "individual valuations" and "social valuations".

swayed by mass-suggestibility or sales-talk.* Not all, but perhaps many, choices involve some degree of information and some sophistication in weighing alternatives and adapting means to ends. In consequence, one may not unreasonably hold that to seek to maximise welfare by distributing money-income in some ideal manner and leave its recipients free to spend it as their desires dictate is only wise policy if rather straitly limited and made subject to numerous exceptions. The exceptions will take the form presumably of encouraging some forms of consumption and discouraging others through the medium *inter alia* of prices as the most direct and effective way of achieving a more beneficial consumption-pattern.

True, in a socialist economy there may be less reason to doubt consumers' ability to choose reasonably for themselves, since without the high-pressure salesmanship associated with marketing in a capitalist society there will be less "brain-washing of consumers" (as Alvin Hansen has called it)† or manipulation of their desires by systematic 'depth approach' methods of propaganda. But although one is entitled to assume that specific distorting influences are out of the way, the fact that under their influence consumers have shown themselves such pliable victims must inevitably evoke some doubt as to the rationality of consumers' behaviour and as to the wisdom of always taking it as a reliable indicator of what is good for them. In particular, recent experience of consumer's behaviour has emphasised the extent to which social convention and social custom (Veblenesque factors as they could be called) enter into the determination of most wants above the level of physical necessities: in other words, the large extent to which desires depend, not on any estimate of an individual's *own* intrinsic needs, but on what

* Professor Musgrave, for example, concedes that "situations may arise ... where an informed group is justified in imposing its decision upon others" (*e.g.* drugs and health) and that "the ideal of consumer sovereignty and the reality of consumer choice in high-pressure markets may be quite different things" (Richard A. Musgrave, *The Theory of Public Finance*, New York, 1959, p. 14). *Cf.* also A. Bergson: "Because of logical confusion, ignorance and unthinking prejudice, the individual may not choose in accord with any consistent values" (*op. cit.* p. 47). Professor Bergson makes a double distinction between desires or "overt preferences" and satisfactions, and between the latter and welfare; adding that to satisfy an individual's preferences "may not appear specially favourable to his welfare, if emotionally he is more or less pathological or unintegrated" (*ibid.* p. 54).

† *Cf.* above, p. 6.

and how much is being consumed by others.* In many such cases there might be little or no loss of welfare or utility if the thing is question were not produced at all : the individual would not feel deprived provided that he were deprived in the company of others (less still, perhaps, if he had never set eyes on it in the first place). Indeed, it is when advertising propaganda is joined with conventional influences of this kind that its success is magnified in extraordinary degree.†

In these cases of so-called external effects in consumption, whether economies or diseconomies, it is virtually impossible to separate influence upon the pattern of demand from influence upon the distribution of income. Least of all in such cases could a government handle the situation by altering the distribution of *money*-income payments ; and any direct measures taken to influence demand must affect the real income of persons who consume the commodity or service in question to an above-average degree. Take the topical congestion case, where a social cost or disservice to the community results from the free operation of consumers' choice, since each severally indulges his desire to the point where his own individual pleasure compensates him for any expense incurred, without counting the contribution that his presence makes to the general evil of congestion (and hence to a reduction of amenity and of enjoyment all-round). If the number of persons entitled each to indulge his whim (*e.g.* by motoring in an urban precinct at a peak period or parking in a beauty-spot) is restricted by prohibition or an *ad hoc* license-duty, *some* motorists at least will be excluded from enjoying the right (or have their indulgence reduced), so that to this extent their *real* income will be smaller than before. The same will apply if the reduction of congestion is achieved in the form of a price-rise (*e.g.* some meter-charge or toll-charge equal to the average contribution to congestion made by an individual user)—even if those who *continue* to make

---

* It is to this type of demand, indeed, that the "isolation paradox" (see below, p. 217) most notably applies.

† In a socialist economy it seems quite likely that in some degree propaganda and the purveying of selected information about goods may be used to influence consumers' choice. But this will have the crucial difference of not being *self-interested* propaganda and information (at any rate if undertaken by some public authority that is not the producing enterprise of the product in question), and it will almost certainly be on a much smaller scale, if only because of the absence of an organised advertising profession.

use of the service are compensated (on the average) for what they pay by the reduced congestion that each and all now suffer. This distribution-aspect is even clearer so far as the congestion-costs falling on pedestrians or bicyclists or upon dwellers in the places in question are concerned : here it is a matter of charging motorists for the loss of amenity which they cause to others. (Is there really any difference in principle in saying that income-distribution should be shifted to the disadvantage of motorists as a class because indulgence of their whims has anti-social effects from saying that they should be differentially charged in proportion to these anti-social effects?)* Yet to reduce the money incomes of all motorists by an *ad hoc* poll tax or supplementary income tax† would be unlikely to have the desired effect unless it was related to contribution made by individual motorists to the congestion-evil : in which case the imposition in question would become in effect a charge for use, or a price.

Rather similar considerations would apply, *mutatis mutandis*, in the case of an alternative remedy of subsidising substitute (and less congesting) forms of public transport. This would serve to divert demand by lowering the price of the substitute; and in so far as consumers of this substitute represented a distinct group of persons (non-owners of private motor-cars) the effect would be to shift the distribution of income in their favour. The end could scarcely be achieved satisfactorily, however, by giving them tax-reliefs or a bonus (other than in the form of a lower price).

Another and different case of consumers' fallibility, much commented upon, is the widespread tendency of individuals to

---

* Some have treated this type of case as an example of marginal cost pricing, where marginal cost is above average cost by the amount of the "congestion costs" (*cf.* Gabriel Roth, *Paying for Roads*, London, 1967, esp. pp. 12–14) ; the implication being that to include the latter in price is simply a way of perfecting the price-system and its optimising rôle. If such costs were an easily calculable amount, and it were a matter simply of adding them to the price like other costs by means of a tax (and then leaving demand to adjust itself accordingly) this might be a reasonable and sufficient way of presenting the matter. But in fact this is not so ; and it is apparently a matter rather of deciding first on a level of socially 'bearable' congestion and *then* raising the price to whatever level will restrict road-usage by the required amount. (*I.e.* the price in question is a supply-demand or demand-reducing price, not a cost-price.)

† Or alternatively a tax on motor cars *per se* or on petrol, which would amount to very much the same thing.

discount future satisfactions compared with present satisfaction, whether this be due to what Pigou so aptly called "deficiency of the telescopic faculty"* or to Professor A. K. Sen's "isolation paradox".† This has principally been adduced as a reason why the rate of investment in a socialist economy must be a social, or governmental, decision, bearing no necessary relation to the time-preferences of individuals (as some statements of optimum conditions imply that it should).‡ Perhaps this case has little relevance to the market for consumers' goods. It would seem, however, to afford a possible reason for establishing a price-differential between durable goods and those which perish in the instant of their enjoyment (*i.e.* a differential diverging from their cost-ratio and in favour of the former), if there were signs that myopic concentration on the latter led to underestimation of the former. In so far as there existed any system of dual prices for spot and future delivery of things like dwelling accommodation or consumers' durables (as with an instalment system under which payments were extended over a period *prior* to delivery), this might seem, again, to provide a reason for differentiating the two prices in favour of future purchase. Since there would be a social cost involved in paying to individuals a rate of interest higher than the 'social rate' (which in effect subsidising the *future*-price would amount to), any such price-differential should preferably take the form of raising the *present* price of such things above their cost.

Income-distribution is not only relevant to the actual demand-pattern registered by the market: it may affect also the degree of elasticity of demand; and in doing so may introduce complications into the apparent simplicity of textbook adapta-

* A. C. Pigou, *Economics of Welfare* (London, 1920), p. 25.

† A. K. Sen, 'On Optimising the Rate of Saving', in *The Economic Journal* (Sept. 1961), pp. 487–9. *Cf.* also W. J. Baumol, *Welfare Economics and the Theory of the State* (London, 1952), pp. 12, 92; Michael J. Ellman, 'Individual Preferences and the Market' in *Economics of Planning* (Oslo, 1966), vol. 6, no. 3, pp. 241–50. Both Professor Baumol and Mr Ellman treat this 'isolation paradox' as applying to a whole class of individual preferences, and not only to decisions over time: in the case of all such choices a market system will fail to yield rational results. In the Introduction to the Third Edition (1968) of his *Choice of Techniques* (Oxford, 1960) Professor A. K. Sen writes: "This inoptimality of individualistic action is a standard problem in a class of non-zero-sum games, and we referred to it elsewhere as the 'Isolation Paradox'" (p. xv).

‡ *Cf.* the present writer's *Essay on Economic Growth and Planning* (London, 1960), chapter II, and above, p. 74.

tion of output to a given structure of demand. It is a familiar fact that the extremes of very low or very high elasticity are damaging to any simple notion of market-equilibrium *via* price-changes (and similarly to postulates about the optimal character of such equilibria). One result of any approach to equality of income-distribution (as has been observed on another occasion)* is to make demand highly inelastic both above and below a certain price-range, and highly elastic within that range; giving the market demand-curve (as distinct from that

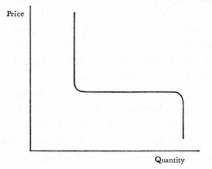

of separate individuals) the shape of the letter L combined with an L-inverted and upside down. There is some evidence that this applies fairly widely to durable consumers' goods such as bicycles (at a lower level of average income), television sets, refrigerators, motor-cars; and it may well apply to other luxury goods and comforts outside this category if they are purchasable only in significantly large units. It is *a fortiori* more likely the more egalitarian is income-distribution. The reason, of course, is that above a certain price very few feel able to afford them; but as their cost falls (or average income rises) the great majority of consumers will wish to buy one, so that a reduction of price to this critical level will evoke an exceptionally large jump in demand. The second 'kink' below which demand becomes again inelastic presupposes an early saturation of demand (*e.g.* one motor-car or refrigerator may have a quite high utility, but a second one have relatively small utility). This in effect means that no market equilibrium exists between zero (or some very low) output and a satiation

* In the present writer's *On Economic Theory and Socialism* (London, 1955), p. 85.

(or near-satiation) output. When indivisibilities exist on the side of production (*i.e.* indivisibilities in productive capacity such that for practical purposes output cannot be changed continuously but only in jumps), the crucial planning decision will be whether to put the item into production at all, and if so whether the community can afford to produce it on a scale sufficient to satiate demand : a decision that can scarcely be a market-guided one, still less decided according to marginal rules. If some intermediate position is decided upon, then this supply-decision will *ipso facto* impose an appropriate distribution-decision. *Either* some priority-system of allocation of the scarce supply will have to be adopted, such as a waiting list (or some rather arbitrary first-come-first-served principle) or a system of premiums in kind (*e.g.* a motor-car as prize for invention or for a good work-record) or a preference-scale according to social category, *or* else an appropriate *in*equality of money income will have to be deliberately created in order to enable the price-mechanism to do the rationing.* It is clearly impossible for choice between these alternatives to be decided *a priori* by applying any simple optimum principle. Yet an increasing number of output decisions facing planners may have this character as the standard of life rises towards levels of so-called affluence.

The type of difficulty to which we have alluded is accentuated to the extent that there is an element of complementarity or joint-demand between products or services; such linkages in demand constituting consumption-patterns or 'ways of life', which are to a large extent mutually exclusive each in relation to others.† This is notoriously true of the motor-car, the expanded use of which requires simultaneous investment on a large scale in roads, road-lighting, road service-stations, roadhouses, motels and the like. The choice for planners will not be between a few more motor cars and a few more washing machines, but between a substantially large increment of all this related group of things and the provision of some other group of goods and services, probably involving indivisibilities

* Be it noted that in this latter case the appropriate price may well *not* be one that is equal (or proportional) to marginal cost.

† Professor Joan Robinson speaks of them as demand "clusters", and suggests that they apply to "goods that represent a rising standard of life" (C. H. Feinstein, ed., *Socialism, Capitalism and Economic Growth*, Cambridge, 1967, p. 187).

(and hence discontinuity) in their production. The problem here will be, *inter alia*, one of how many distinct products to put into production : a matter that optimum conditions are apt to take for granted and not to solve.*

The conclusion is evident that there will be a considerable number of cases where, for good reason, public policy would hold it desirable to *refrain* from bringing relative prices into strict alignment with relative costs. In such cases the second half of our Production Condition as we outlined it in chapter 4 above would not be fulfilled. These would be cases where Dr Mishan's 'top-level optima' would go by the board, or be treated with some measure of indifference, and yet no perceptible loss of welfare be suffered, but possibly considerable gain result. An additional consideration of which it may do no harm to remind ourselves in this and in some other contexts is one that we quoted earlier from Professor Baumol to the effect that, since "desires of the individual are often nebulous", "only extreme deviations from the ideal output are likely to have any substantial importance".†

Perhaps one should hasten to repeat, in order to obviate misunderstanding, that to say this is *not* to contend that such a rule (about equating consumers' price-ratios and cost-ratios) should be lightly jettisoned or disregarded. To suggest that consumers' sovereignty should be a limited one and subject to restriction is not necessarily to call for its dethronement. In many cases, indeed, one might well ask who if not the consumer himself is capable of judging best what best contributes to his own welfare? We have seen that there are numerous cases where such a presumption is not justified : where there is good reason for supposing that his individual verdict is not to be trusted, either because he is insufficiently rational or lacks the experience and sophistication needed to adjust his desires to real satisfactions, because he lacks sufficient information, or because there are effects of his own consumption on others of which he takes no account (or insufficient account). There seems to be no reasonable ground for treating individual desires as an ultimate beyond which there can be no appeal,‡ or consumers'

* *Cf.* below, chapter 11, p. 241.
† See above, p. 65.
‡ It has to be remembered, incidentally, that the line between individual choice

sovereignty as possessing some kind of value *per se* (*i.e.* apart from its estimated consequences for general welfare). To do so would clearly be arbitrary and untenable. But what there *does* seem to be reasonable ground for asserting is that the individual's estimate of his own needs can be taken as presumptive evidence, and as sufficient evidence *in the absence* of sufficient reasons to the contrary. For example, it is surely commonsense to accept the individual consumer's own estimate when there is no ground for presuming a planner's or policy-maker's judgement to be any better. This would place the onus for departing from the principle of adjusting supplies to the prevailing pattern of demand in the manner that is conventionally regarded as optimal upon those who advocate such a departure—and not the other way round. To do so admittedly involves a choice among ends, since one has to decide when a distribution-consideration (which is in *some* degree present in almost every output-decision) is below the critical minimum at which it can be ignored and precedence be given to market-indicators of consumers' demand. But, then, such a choice is only absent in formal systems which conveniently assume 'ends' to be unified in some single magnitude or set of orderings such as utility or a 'social welfare function'; and it is manifestly utopian to suppose that economic theory can really postulate an optimum that is logically prior to all such choices.

In the practice of socialist countries to-date (at the time of writing) the production-pattern has probably been much too sluggish of adaptation to consumers' demand rather than too slavish. If socialism is rightly to be called 'production for consumption' ('for use and not for profit' as the adage goes), this is justification for the emphasis of the last paragraph—even if 'western' economists' talk of so-called consumers' sovereignty has been customarily too slavish and uncritical, and too blind to its necessary qualification.

The kind of exception of which we have been talking, and especially the case of 'external effects', shades off imperceptibly

---

and group (or collective) choice is by no means so clear-cut as is often supposed. In the average household, how much of the choice and decision-making is in fact made by the housewife as part-'dictator', part-representative and interpreter of the desires of the individuals composing the household?

into that of 'public goods', which from Walras onwards has been accepted as one to which the ordinary rules of the market cannot be made to apply. The question that immediately arises is whether the difference here is one of degree only or of kind. Apart from some 'delimitation by type' (parks, museums, public health and education—Jevons added housing for the people), the boundary between these and private goods has seldom been clearly defined, and probably cannot be. Yet the size of such a sector, and hence the degree to which it contributes to social welfare, is crucial for the question of what order of importance ought to be assigned to the kind of pricing rules with which welfare economists have been preoccupied. As Professor Scitovsky has said, "choosing between market and collective goods, deciding whether a given service is better provided through the market or by public spending, determining the best allocation of public funds among their various uses—all these are economic choices no different and no less important than the consumer's choice between two market goods".* In a socialist economy one could expect this category of public goods and services to be larger than under capitalism, in view of the extent to which its boundaries are today confined (most notably in America, to which the Galbraithean adage of "private affluence, public squalor" was applied, and to a smaller extent also in England) by jealousy of its possible competition with and encroachment upon private interests. Where it is financed out of general taxation it is likely to be further obstructed by the unpopularity of its extension at the expense of higher tax-rates—a fear widely cherished by individualist tradition and perhaps most of all by higher income groups who are least likely to be benefitted equivalently to their tax-contribution. Here again the matter of appropriate boundaries, and of the extent of subsidisation of such services, is inseparable from the question of income-distribution, since free education or subsidised milk or medicines or housing will of their very nature affect different families and different social groups and income-levels unequally. They amount to a subsidy to some forms of consumption at the expense of others,

---

* T. Scitovsky, 'On the Principle of Consumers' Sovereignty', in *American Economic Review*, vol. LII, no. 2 (May 1962), p. 262 (reprinted in *Papers on Wealth and Growth*, London, 1964, p. 241).

of a kind and to an extent (as regards incidence upon particular groups and individuals) that scarcely renders feasible any system of distributing the additional tax burden according to any benefit criterion. Moreover, even if the latter were feasible, the prime intention of the provision in many cases (its income-distribution effect) would be negated by such a system of charging.*

If, of course, the cross-elasticity of demand (or degree of potential substitution) was very low between goods and services supplied by this public sector and products sold according to ordinary market principles, the relationship between the two would not matter *per se*. Each would be insulated from the other, and the prices prevailing in the one would have a negligible effect† upon demand in the other. But this seems to be an unsafe assumption to make. For some things, at least, the cross-elasticity may be quite high; and accordingly what happens in the sphere of public goods may have some significant substitution-effects as between the two spheres. When it comes to more long-term influence through the medium of habit and convention, then the effect of the public sphere upon the other may be even greater.

A distinguishing feature (if a neglected one) of Professor H. D. Dickinson's work on socialism is that he has sought to specify and define the main categories of public provision of goods and services in terms of the economic *rationale* that justifies them. In doing so he assigns to them a measure of importance, going beyond that of mere 'exceptions' to the precepts of market-distribution through the price-system, which leads him to speak of a whole Sector or Division of Communal Consumption, standing alongside and in contrast to the Sector or Division of Individual Consumption. To the latter he considers that the conventional pricing rules should apply; to the former, from its very nature and *raison d'être*, they should not. The satisfaction

---

* Professor Bergson's prescription is that expenditures by the State (together with investment-expenditure) should be financed by a lump-sum tax on citizens that bears no relation to their earnings (to avoid marginal effects). But he admits that as such expenditures grew in size, their income-effect would conflict with the influence of wage-differentials on the supply of different kinds of labour to a "self-defeating" extent (*Essays in Normative Economics*, p. 185). So also would his tax have an income-effect (if in an opposite sense) and, incidentally, also his proposed money-dividend.   † *I.e. apart* from any 'income-effect'.

of wants within this communal sphere should be decided out-side the market and on "other grounds than market de-mand"; in many cases distribution could even be free and entirely unpriced.*

The two leading categories of goods and services that qualify for inclusion in this communal sphere are, first, things which satisfy what are essentially collective needs and "are com-munally consumed" from their very nature, and secondly "satisfactions less definite in character than goods and services, which cannot be divided or graduated among individuals, but which must be enjoyed to the same extent by all or none". Both of these "involve preferences which cannot be expressed by any mechanism of individual choice in a market"; the second in particular because this category consists of "prefer-ences for one pattern of social life as against another pattern of social life".†

An alternative way of defining this first category of collective needs and their satisfaction might be to say that it consists of goods and services which either from the nature of their con-sumption and enjoyment cannot be appropriated by an in-dividual and consumed individually, or because of circum-stances connected with their production have to be made available to all (or at least to many) if they are made available to some.‡ For example, in the case of some things the essence of individual enjoyment of them is that they are shared with other persons simultaneously, like a game of football, a banquet or a club. Other things can only be enjoyed jointly (except for the very rich) by reason of their large minimum scale and cost as an efficient collective unit, such as a museum, picture gallery, concert hall, park or police force. Again, the provision of a road or lighthouse, or a drainage or water system, or irrigation and flood-control works—even the laying of telephone cable to a remote village or hamlet§—in being made available to one user

* H. D. Dickinson, *Economics of Socialism* (Oxford, 1939), p. 51.
† *Ibid.* pp. 53–4.
‡ Thus, as Professor Musgrave points out, "social wants", as he terms them, in-volve "joint consumption", but the converse is not necessarily true (Richard A. Musgrave, *The Theory of Public Finance*, New York, 1959, pp. 9–10).
§ It may be noted that this example indicates the inclusion within this category of the so-called Hotelling-case of production within the limits of indivisibilities that is discussed in the next chapter.

is simultaneously made available to many (in the sense of economic potential at any rate). To Professor Dickinson's second category there evidently belongs much, if not most, of public health provision and town planning and of educational and cultural facilities.

To this, however, Professor Dickinson added a third category of things that "are individually consumed and that might therefore be supplied through the market", but which for a variety of reasons may be better supplied communally. This is a rather miscellaneous category, with no single unifying characteristic to define it. In it there are included, apparently, cases of underestimation by individuals of what a particular good will contribute to their welfare and also (although not explicitly mentioned as such by Professor Dickinson) those where enjoyment of something is not solely the concern of the individual consuming it, because of repercussions, whether for good or ill, upon others. This, of course, brings in the kind of exceptions to 'market rationality' that we considered above, before introducing the specific (and overlapping) notion of 'public goods'; and it opens the door to the whole tribe of 'external effects' in consumption—which we have seen is to open a fairly wide door. What is interesting about Professor Dickinson's third category, however, is his suggestion that under socialism it might be extended to include the communal supply (free or at low prices) of the prime necessities of existence. "There seems to be no reason why bread, milk, simply cooked meals, clothing of a plain standardised type, and many other things should not be provided as free unrationed issues, leaving the more luxurious and varied qualities to be provided in response to market demand."*

In so far as there is an economic *rationale* in welfare terms for the inclusion of such things in this public category (*i.e.* apart from distribution-reasons), this would seem to be that when

---

* *Economics of Socialism*, p. 53. In this connection it may be of interest to recall that one of the proposals of the famous Beveridge Report at the end of the Second World War was the continuance in peace-time of a national nutrition policy, including bulk purchase of supplies and stabilised prices (to consumers) of essential foods : "The war has shown the advantages of a nutrition policy based on science and designed to ensure to every person in the community a supply of essential foods suited to his social needs" (William H. Beveridge, *Full Employment in a Free Society*, London, 1944, p. 161).

average income has reached a certain level these are things for which the price-elasticity and also income-elasticity of demand becomes very low, so that they are relatively easy to supply on a communal principle and not much waste is likely to be involved in doing so. Provided that the level of production is such as to supply a sufficiency, whether an economic price or no price is charged will make little difference to the extent to which resources are diverted from elsewhere to produce them; and some element of the communist principle of "to each according to his needs" could to this extent be combined with the existence of income-differentials dictated by the continued need for production-incentives. Indeed, reluctance to recognise, or to extend, this category of Dickinsonian communal consumption would seem to be more reasonably grounded in the possible effect on work-incentives than in any adverse effect it might directly have on welfare.

That demand-inelasticity in the case of primary wants is characteristic of higher-income groups today seems fairly clear. At what precise level of average income it is likely to characterise a large majority of consumers can only be guessed at, and is a question that must inevitably be left for experience to answer—an answer that need not be a uniform one for all countries. Once this level of productivity and of *per capita* income has been reached, the division between the two spheres of individual and of communal consumption and provision would seem to fall along a line of demarcation between 'luxuries' and so-called 'necessaries'—a line that would itself be a changing one over time, if demand-inelasticity (expressive of want-satiation) were to be accepted as the main criterion of distinction between the two.

There is some indication that this is the direction in which policy is likely to move. Already in the socialist countries discussion as to the practical content of the notion of a transition between Marx's two stages of socialism or communism ('lower' and 'higher') has led to an apparent consensus in favour of emphasising the growing share of elements of public or communal consumption, compared with individual consumption through the retail market, in determining the standard of life. In the degree that this share increases, and eventually perhaps becomes dominant, the welfare-economists' problem of a so-called 'top-level optimum' will manifestly have a diminishing rôle to play both in theory and in policy-making.

A reason why the maximising theorems of welfare economists appear unreal to many persons is that, when looked at in a dynamic perspective, the considerations with which such theorems deal seem to be dwarfed by the effects of change. The individual and his structure of wants or preferences is a creature of a social *milieu* that continually undergoes historical change and changes individuals with it. "Indeed, as time passes the consumers will tend to be different people from those present initially."* How then can the preferences of the latter be taken as the 'ultimate' of the welfare-problem? Changes in habit and custom may be more important for human happiness than whether individual wants as these exist at any given moment of time are satisfied to the maximum. Moreover, with new products come new wants—in that order of generation; so that with changing production and productivity the initiative rests essentially with the producer rather than the consumer. One is confronted, in other words, with producers' sovereignty rather than consumers' not from perversity of human choice and arrangement but from the nature of things. An incidental characteristic of producers' sovereignty to which Professor Scitovsky has drawn attention,† is its increasing tendency to ignore minority tastes and to cater primarily for what suits the majority (and this apart from what has been called the Gresham's Law of taste). Even if there were no such bias, a consumer could scarcely (at least very seldom) be said to have an innate want for something he has never experienced : until this object has first been created, consumers cannot be said to want it save by purely imaginative intuition, or in the same esoteric sense in which it might be said that desire for

* A. Bergson, *op. cit.* p. 154.
† "Today in the age of mass production, it usually seems more profitable to design every product for the majority, however saturated majority demand may be", and to rely on "moulding minority preferences through advertising . . . hence the secular increase in uniformity." He adds : "The individual consumer is still free to fill his shopping bag with whatever collection of goods he wishes. But the nature of the goods which he chooses is imposed upon him by the tastes and wants of the majority" ('A Critique of Present and Proposed Standards', in *American Economic Review*, vol. L, no. 2, May 1960, pp. 17–18; reprinted in T. Scitovsky, *Papers on Welfare and Growth*, London, 1964, p. 237).

television or moon-travel was latent in the inhabitants of England in the 10th century. When he first meets a new product, a consumer may treat it, of course, by analogy with something else from his past experience (as we may all tend to do with novelties of all kinds, whether material or spiritual). But this initial reaction will inevitably weaken with further acquaintance and familiarity, until the new object has acquired its own aura of associations (whatever these may be) and is reacted to *sui generis*. It has to be accepted, therefore, that change is continually altering not only products but also the structure of human wants, and thus modifying the data of our welfare problem.

As for the rate of development itself, we have mentioned reasons why the optimising theorems, at least in their conventional form and in their individualist interpretation, have little or no relevance; and decisions on such questions have to be taken on some basis other than the market, as collective policy-decisions. For one thing, decisions about change and growth concern the distribution of income over time and between generations: least of all in a dynamic context can income-distribution be assumed as given, or otherwise abstracted from, in order to derive optimising principles from the observation and summation of individual preferences. This is one reason why we earlier took the planned rate of growth as *a priori* to other economic decisions, such as choice of methods of production, and in this sense assigned it a pre-eminent rôle. Decisions about income-distribution over time are as inevitably 'political', and hence *a priori* to optimising procedures, as are any other decisions about income-distribution.

As Sir Alec Cairncross once very aptly stated: "To isolate individual buyers and sellers in some vacuum of choice . . . and discuss how industry can best maximise an ethereal utility is to misconceive the problem. . . . To substitute one assortment of goods and services for another may do far less for the people's welfare than the setting of new social standards or the direction of their energies into new and more acceptable channels."

"Nor is this all. For the act of substitution of itself *changes* social standards and creates new demands. If, for example, we provide cheaper wireless sets we may reduce the demand for theatre seats and increase the demand for coal, since more people will wish to stay at home and listen in. Thus the balance between value and cost is upset and no one can say with assurance whether it is upset for better or for worse. We cannot assume, therefore, that in fixing outputs so that prices are in a fixed ratio to marginal cost we are giving fuller satisfaction to the wants of consumers, for these wants are themselves affected by variations in output." To which he adds the further consideration: "Again, many of our wants are shaped by the very system of production which exists to supply them. A man's habits of living and of expenditure depends partly upon the work which he is called upon to do . . .."*

This last consideration introduces a certain amount of difficulty into the conventional analysis, if the maximising theorems are framed so as to include the disutilities involved in work as well as the utilities arising from consumption; since reaction of the nature of work upon the structure of wants creates a possibility of multiple equilibria, with the maximising conditions (*i.e.* the marginal equalities) being fulfilled at several positions and not only at one. How seriously this will affect any practical corollaries of those theories must remain a question for practical judgement and experience to decide. It is evidently right, if welfare is to be given any full meaning, that the consumption of an individual or a social group should be related to the work and conditions of work involved in producing the real income in question. Alike for an individual and for the community, to add to income by a relatively small amount at the expense of an inordinate lengthening of working hours or of a marked deterioration of working conditions would probably reduce rather than increase welfare, even if abundance of consumers' goods was enhanced thereby. Of two individuals with the same real income measured in terms of consumable goods, one might work much harder than the other or do much more disagreeable work, adversely affecting health and expectation of life. It would manifestly be absurd to say that the welfare of the two was equal. Such equality could only apply to them if the consumable income of the former was raised in the measure of the greater disutility of his work-effort.† In such a

---

* A. K. Cairncross, *Introduction to Economics* (1st edition, London, 1944), p. 213. (In the 4th edition of 1966 the relevant passages are on pp. 285–6.)

† Strictly speaking, fulfilment of the *marginal* conditions only (equality of disutility and utility at the margins of consumption and work respectively) would not here be enough. But it could be held to be the most that it was practicable to

case equality of welfare would not only be consistent with, but would require some *in*equality of real income. All this is as inescapable a conclusion as it is elementary. Nor does it essentially complicate the formal statement of the problem if one is willing to treat disutility as a simple negative of utility attaching to certain negatively valued goods. Formal statement, as well as its implications, *is*, however, complicated once one allows for wants (and the utilities attaching to the satisfaction of them) to be in any degree relative to the amount and nature of the work undertaken.

The sort of qualifications we have made in putting the problem of consumption in the setting of historical change are of crucial importance if we are to put the formal apparatus of optimum conditions (tangency conditions and the like) into proper perspective. One could regard them as an essential antidote to the myopia which the majority of welfare economists seem to develop in their preoccupation with individual preference scales as the irreducible atoms of their universe of discourse. As such these qualifications may well deserve more, rather then less, emphasis than they have been given here. Certainly they leave little standing of the individualist bias and precepts that have abounded in the traditional literature, generally in the form of the lauded optimal qualities of perfect competition. (The reason of course being, not only that income distribution has to be assumed to be somehow 'right'—the point we have already laboured so much—as well as the number and kind of goods in production, but that all the collective influences that shape wants and preferences, for good or ill, are ignored,* so that there is no reason for supposing an optimum position as defined to be an *optimum optimorum*.) To which one can add for good measure the consideration that if those external effects of which we have spoken are sufficiently general and important, e.g. pervading most luxury-consumption and durable consumers' goods, any optimum expressed in terms of purely

aim at; as well as being a condition for maximum possible attainment of welfare by each and all.

* *Cf.* Paul Streeten on the illusion that individual wants are "isolated, autonomous entities" cited above on p. 5n., and also Dr E. J. Mishan on the fallacy of "accepting people's wants as something given to us independently of the workings of the economic system" (*The Costs of Economic Growth*, London, 1967, pp. 109 *et seq.*)

market magnitudes cannot be at best more than a very rough *approximation* to a genuine welfare optimum, embracing both market and non-market magnitudes.

But when all this has been said, and a proper perspective restored to our vision, one cannot (at least *should* not—let us repeat it) deny that a not-important *niche* remains in any agenda of planning questions for the static problem of how best to adapt the pattern of supply of consumers' goods to the pattern of demand—in the absence of those specific reasons we have considered for refraining from doing so. This was the problem we considered in chapter 8 in the form of the comparative rates of change to be provided for various end-products within the horizon of any given planning period of medium length. Admittedly this problem will have a more modest place on the agenda than most welfare-economists to-date have assigned to it. But failure to assign a place at all could reduce consumers' welfare quite considerably—and in extreme cases by a large amount—below what this potentially could be at any given date. And although some might regard this as being of small moment, if change were sufficiently rapid, since in the long run everything would be raised to a higher level, it is well to remember that human life and welfare are composed of a succession of short-periods, even if these be powerfully affected by the long-term trend. The more extreme cases of damaging neglect that come to mind are those concerned with the complementarity of wants, such as the provision of dwelling accommodation but no furniture, or the converse, pens but deficient ink, too many razors and too few blades, motor vehicles more plentiful than requisite spare parts. But although there are precedents (perhaps too many) for such cases, they are also the most obvious in their baneful effects and hence most likely to be remedied when they occur. More serious are perhaps the less noticeable, but only in minor degree less damaging, cases where at a comparatively trifling social cost and re-routing of productive resources some serious deficiency could be eliminated; and this possibly by doing no more than marking-time for a limited period on the *increase* of various alternative consumers' goods catering for wants that are more plentifully supplied, or even approaching satiation. It is in such cases that planning decisions need to pay attention to, and accept more subtle guidance from, market indices : indices which may be quite simple, rather than complicated, to read. These consist, as we have seen, of the relation of retail- or demand-price ratios to cost-ratios, which, although requiring no rigid equalisation at any given date, should *tend* towards equality and not be allowed lightly to develop large *in*equalities without this being taken as a symptom of something being wrong and needing attention. What is simple, however, is not always obvious to those concerned with making policy, especially if they have grown too accustomed to focus attention on 'jam tomorrow' ; and what is surely necessary is that the relevance of this sort of question, shorn of exaggeration and set in realistic perspective, should be clearly appreciated. Then a proper place for the classical use-value in discussions of the market and of exchange-values, or prices, and the relation of these to planning output-quantities, may be found.

CHAPTER II

THE MARGINAL COST DISCUSSION
REVISITED

There was a time when discussion raged hotly over marginal cost as the basis for pricing policy; and this was regarded as an important, if not crucial, moment in the larger debate about economic rationality under socialism. More recently, in the fifties, the question of marginal cost obtruded itself into the Polish discussions of price-reform. Some attention to it, accordingly, seems to be called for here.

The case of extractive industries and of agriculture, which the Polish discussion seems chiefly to have had in mind, can be fairly quickly disposed of. Where additional output has to come from less favourable sites and sources, where the cost of producing a unit of output is higher than under intra-marginal conditions, there is an obvious reason for making this higher, or marginal, cost the basis of calculation, since this will represent the true social cost of *expanding* output by a small amount (or alternatively the cost that is saved by contracting output by a small amount). We took this as axiomatic above, in chapter 8, when considering prices and costs as affecting choice between alternative methods of production and the planning of relative outputs of end-products. If additional coal production must come from working less accessible or less productive seams, cost under these more difficult conditions is alone relevant to the choice of coal as a fuel in preference to rival fuels (at any rate when comparatively small changes are in question). The same is true of agriculture if extended cultivation of corn involves the cultivation of inferior soils (or soils relatively unsuitable to corn-growing) and/or the more intensive cultivation of existing land with enhanced expenditures of labour, manures, etc., per bushel. This idea is, of course, as old as Ricardo: appreciation of it being the basis of the classical theory of differential rent. If in these circumstances the pricing of coal or of corn were to be based on an averaging of the cost under more favourable and less favourable conditions, this would be in effect to use the rent arising from production under the former to subsidise an uneconomic extension of production under the latter, and consequently to encourage high-cost production of coal or corn at the margin in preference to using lower-cost substitutes.

In applying this elementary principle to particular cases, care needs to be taken, however, to see that production under high-cost conditions really is marginal in the *relevant sense:* namely, that it will be *the additional cost of producing* additional output. Here there may well be a conflict between marginal or incremental cost in the short period and in the longer period. This has been the occasion of some confusion in practical discussion of the matter; and although obvious enough once stated, the commonplace is not always observed. In other than stationary conditions it will by no means always follow, even in an extractive industry, that additional output in the quinquennium after this one will necessarily come from what happen to be the highest-cost sources today : *e.g.* coal from the oldest pits in the least favourable locations. Investment and the normal course of discovery and prospecting and transport-improvement may by then have opened new pits and new (and possibly richer) seams in what will ultimately prove to be more favourable locations.* The *dating* of the additional supply is crucial to finding what definition of incremental cost is *relevant* to the problem in hand. It is for reasons such as this that in ordinary industry (other than extractive) cost of additional output, when considered as a basis for economic calculation, has generally been taken as being the normal (average) cost of production in a 'representative', or typical, firm in the industry.† Yet there are always some simple-minded or statically obsessed enough to suppose that the so-called marginal principle requires prices to be fixed at the level of the highest-cost output of the highest-cost plant or firm in an industry at any given date.

* This consideration proved of some importance in the discussion of coal-pricing policy in this country following the Ridley Report of 1952 (*cf.* I. M. D. Little, *The Price of Fuel*, Oxford, 1953, pp. 14–15).

† In full competitive equilibrium (long period) this is, supposedly, equal to the marginal (full) cost of the same representative firm, and simultaneously equal to the short-period marginal cost of producing additional output from existing plant and equipment.

A more sophisticated way of looking at the principle of equating prices with marginal cost is to treat it as a direct corollary of the statement of optimum conditions : in particular of what in chapter 4 we called the second half of the Production Condition, about equalising the marginal yield of resources in all uses. Such a corollary it evidently is, at any rate of what we called the Stricter Version of that condition : we saw that equality of price and marginal cost is simply an alternative form of statement into which the condition can be translated. If, however, we reject this kind of 'top-level optimum', or at least do not take it too seriously, then it would seem that this condition and its alternative form of statement in terms of marginal cost must fall to the ground or be seriously weakened, leaving only extractive industries, as examples of increasing cost due to scarcity of a natural resource, in sole possession of the field. But lest this be a too hasty deduction, it would be wise to take a closer look at the special circumstances that cause marginal cost to diverge from average and to see what kind of problem these present. It is possible that these may share some characteristic that demands special attention.

The first type of case that has occupied discussion may be distinguished by calling it the short-period case. At any one time, owing to a temporary fall in demand or to an unanticipated change in demand (or its failure to expand as anticipated), there may be productive equipment installed which is incapable of being fully utilised. The charging of a 'normal' price, sufficient to pay the full cost, may preclude it from being as fully utilised as it otherwise might be. The additional cost that is here relevant to decisions as to how much output to produce from this equipment is evidently the prime or direct cost of so using it. This will include the cost of labour and raw materials used up, together with any additional repair and maintenance cost involved in producing as compared with not-producing (which may be classified as 'user-cost'). What is *not* here included is the capital-cost of the plant and equipment itself (*e.g.* interest-cost) and that part of its depreciation or amortisation which is attributable simply to the passage of time—which is not specifically due to use and would apply even if the equipment were idle. To this extent there is a difference between full cost (averaged over any given output) and incremental or marginal cost in a short-period context of already-installed durable equipment; and it is the latter which is evidently the social cost so far as immediate (and short-term) output-decisions are concerned. The commonsense of contending that in this situation price should equal marginal cost (only) and not average full cost is that, once plant is in existence, there is a social advantage in getting some use out of it rather than letting it stand idle (and in getting as much use out of it as possible), so long as the costs directly involved in use are adequately covered by the social utility of the output in question. To charge the full cost would restrict this use, and hence involve unnecessary wastage; whereas the inclusion in price of no more than the direct or marginal cost would result in an output that was 'just right' from a social point of view. (Like so much argument in this field, any strict interpretation of this contention implies, of course, the assumption that the demand-price is an adequate measure or index of social utility of the output in question.)

Such a principle extends beyond the frontiers of industry proper to various services, from which, indeed, many if not most of the familiar examples are taken. These include trains on an under-used permanent way or seats in a half-empty train, aeroplane or bus, hotel-rooms in the off-season, or electrical power from generating-plant with spare capacity. All such examples have the existence of spare capacity in some form as a common (indeed crucial) quality; and one can generalise them by saying that it is this existence of spare capacity that is needed to justify the charging of no more than marginal cost (temporarily at least) despite the industry or service being involved thereby in a loss.* Commonsense demands that excess capacity should be used rather than left idle if its use costs society nothing; and if some pricing principle stands in the way of using it, so much the worse for the pricing principle! This argument has special force, as Mr Little has justly emphasised, in all those cases (which he considers "very common") where marginal cost is "zero or near-zero".†

* One could sometimes say, however, that the loss is thus *minimised*, and not necessarily occasioned or increased by so doing; since if the alternative is no output at all, or a very much smaller output, a greater loss could be made.

† I. M. D. Little, *Critique of Welfare Economics* (2nd edition, Oxford, 1957), pp. 194–5. Bridges, roads, trams, buses, museums, parks, broadcasting and water supply are cited as leading examples; but it is added that lowering the price to

Granted, however, that this is correct and sensible as a short-period answer, it by no means follows that it remains so as an answer applicable to the long period. In the long period the question of the renewal, replacement or scrapping of the equipment itself will come on to the agenda. If continued use of the equipment in question cannot yield enough to cover its full cost, is this not presumptive evidence that it is wrongly placed, or that there is too much of it, that it should be economised upon and the investible resources embodied therein put to some other use where their social yield is greater? To continue to run the plant or service at a loss is, surely, to waste the limited invest-ment-potential of the economy by continuing the initial mis-take of misapplication to a sub-optimum use?

Here there are two cases to be distinguished : firstly where the equipment in question can be varied in comparatively small units or amounts, not only in a physical sense but also in the *economic* sense that this can be done without any seriously adverse effects on the productive process and its efficient operation ; secondly, where the plant and equipment in question can*not* be altered in supply continuously, but can only be varied in comparatively large 'jumps', because the instal-lation consists of fairly large, indivisible units. To the first of these cases the doubts expressed in the last paragraph justly apply. In the long period—in a period long enough for renewal or curtailment of the plant and equipment to come upon the agenda—the advantage of running the plant at a loss provided that marginal cost in its short-period context is covered no longer applies. This is sometimes expressed by saying that di-vergence between marginal and average cost only applies in the short-period interpretation of the former ; in the long period the divergence disappears if marginal cost is appropriately defined as the cost attributable to additional output (which, since the increase now being considered is permanent and not temporary, must include the cost of the additional equipment that has to be renewed and kept in being).*

zero "could hardly be done in the case of buses or trains. Everyone would wait to the last moment for the price to come down, when there would be a horrid scramble. It would obviously be impracticable to hold an auction at every station at which the train stopped."

* It is usually indicated that in this case 'ideal output' requires an equalisation of short-period and long-period marginal costs, so that there is no conflict between

In the second of our two cases, however, where plant and equipment are characterised by substantial *indivisibility*, the position is different. Since equipment is only discontinuously variable, it cannot always be adapted perfectly to the demand-situation, and some excess capacity in the indivisible unit (whether it be an automated assembly-line, a power-plant or a railway-track) may quite reasonably exist in the long period, as well as because of temporary irremediable maladjustment in the short run. This is the case where there are economies of scale *internal* to the production-unit or firm from spreading the fixed cost over a larger output. Nor does it necessarily follow in such a case that if the indivisible unit cannot be made to pay for itself, in the sense of selling its output or services at a price sufficient to cover full cost (including capital cost), that it ought not to be there at all, should be condemned from the stand-point of optimum allocation of resources and in the fullness of time withdrawn. It does not follow for reasons that have become familiar from the classic example of Dupuit's bridge :* namely, that when indivisible units of investment are involved the principle of *total benefit* supplants the marginal, and it is the total net benefit from its use that has to be compared with its cost. Where the indivisibility is fairly large, this total net benefit is likely to be significantly larger than any positive (and uniform) selling-price multiplied by output (net of prime cost).†

them; this being achieved by adapting the supply of installed equipment so as to enable each plant to be operated at optimum capacity, so defined that marginal (short-period) cost equals average cost (= long-period marginal cost).

* In the case of Dupuit's bridge it is usually assumed (if only for simplicity) that cost of use is zero. It follows that once the bridge is built maximum benefit requires toll-free use to anyone who would derive any individual benefit at all from using it (the total benefit being measured by the whole area under the demand curve). Construction of the bridge is justified *post facto* if this maximised benefit over its lifetime (suitably discounted) covers its cost. Any attempt to recoup the original cost, partly or wholly, by charging a toll would restrict the use of the bridge and hence the social benefit derivable from it. (*Cf.* J. Dupuit in *Annales des Ponts et Chaussées*, 2e serie, vol. 8, 1844, English translation in *International Economic Papers*, no. 2, pp. 97, 106–9; also H. Hotelling, in *Econometrica*, July 1938, pp. 242 *et seq.*)

† At least one writer on the subject would not agree, it would seem, about the long-period case without indivisibility as we have presented it. He has written as follows. "Marginal cost should include only *continuously* variable costs. It should exclude all fixed costs. Since the latter are increased only by output at the extensive margin, we can exclude them by measuring marginal cost at the *intensive margin, i.e.* where output is increased without any expansion in fixed plant. Those

The existence of substantial indivisibilities has, indeed, been used by some writers (notably Hotelling) as an argument for socialisation in all such cases, since private enterprise may be unwilling to undertake the investment where this is socially justified since total cost cannot be recovered by any system of uniform prices;* and that where the investment has already been undertaken, desire to cover average cost will cause the plant to be underutilised. To this it is added that if fixed costs have to be met (in part or in whole) by a subsidy, this is more feasible, both politically and economically, if the enterprise in question is State-owned and managed than if it is in private hands. Professor Lerner once roundly declared: "The only costs that are relevant are costs the incurrence of which is in question.

who believe that fixed costs should be included in marginal cost often claim that nearly all fixed costs eventually become variable costs. In reply we must emphasise that fixed costs become only *temporarily*, i.e. discontinuously, variable, and that marginal analysis can deal only with *continuously* variable cost . . . Hence, the smooth long-run marginal cost curves so often seen in books on imperfect and/or monopolistic competition cannot be based on this assumption. They imply that fixed costs are continuously variable, which is clearly not true" (B. P. Beckwith, *Marginal-Cost Price-Output Control*, New York, 1955, pp. 179–80). There seems to be a confusion here between discontinuously *in time*, which is not an objection *per se* to including fixed cost in marginal cost, and discontinuity in the sense of *indivisibility* of the actual units involved in the fixed costs. Only in the latter case does Mr Beckwith's contention apply. If there is perfect divisibility, then what appear as fixed costs in the short-period can be included in any calculation of additional cost *at the dates when decisions regarding them arise*.

Professor Peter Wiles, on the other hand, seems to regard long-run cases of divergence between marginal and average cost as quite exceptional, claiming that all "sunk costs" as he terms them (using this to cover all "past physical outlays") are properly "average cost" when viewed *ex ante* (*Price, Cost and Output*, Oxford 1956, pp. 287–8). Elsewhere he seems to deny that indivisibilities are practically important (*ibid.* p. 225).

* Some have suggested that a system of 'discriminating monopoly', with differentiated prices to different buyers or groups of buyers, having different intensities of demand, would here yield the socially desirable result. But (*a*) the operation of a system of differentiated prices requires special conditions to make it practicable (such as easily identifiable objective criteria of the group to which an individual buyer belongs, and criteria that are non-transferable between individuals) and differentiation at best can seldom be 'perfect'; (*b*) such price-differentiation will inevitably have pronounced distribution-effects which cannot be ignored and may be undesirable. On the additional dangers of using a 'consumers' surplus' measure of benefit (which should properly be restricted by the assumption of constant prices of alternative goods and services) *cf.* E. J. Mishan, *The Costs of Economic Growth* (London, 1967), pp. 98, 183–6.

The two-part tariff, where this is feasible, represents also a compromise solution for this type of case, collecting fixed costs by the fixed part of the tariff and charging a lower running cost for use.

They are therefore *all* prime. Supplementary (or overhead or fixed) costs are for us nothing but a useless carry-over from capitalistic book-keeping practices."*

It may be noted that cases of the kind we have been referring to are likely to be one-firm, or at most few firm (and hence oligopolistic), industries (or else sub-industries producing a differentiated product), where some form of monopolistic price-policy is likely to be pursued under capitalist conditions. In multi-firm industries, if anything approaching textbook-competition happened to prevail, price-cutting and output-expansion would proceed, possibly causing some firms to close down from insolvency, with the result that excess capacity as an enduring element in the situation would be eliminated.†

For analytical purposes, at least, this case of significantly large indivisibilities can also be held to cover (in part, at least) another chapter, or category, of the marginal cost discussion: that concerned with the existence of so-called external economies. These economies are external to the individual *firm* and are a consequence of expansion in the scale of the whole industry: they are not taken into account by an individual firm in deciding on expansion, because it will only realise in its own balance-sheet a small fraction of the resulting economies. Hence they will occasion a divergence between marginal cost to the whole industry and marginal cost to the individual firm. Two leading instances of this are specialisation among firms within an industry and a cheapening of the cost of subsidiary products as the demand for them from the industry in question (presumed to be the main user of them as components) expands. The former type of economy can be seen to depend on the existence of indivisibilities in certain production processes *within* the industry (setting a minimum limit to the scale on which specialised production or use of a certain process is

* A. P. Lerner, 'Statics and Dynamics in Socialist Economics', in *The Economic Journal* (June, 1937), p. 264.

† This implies a situation where demand is sufficiently large for all (or most) of the competing firms to produce and sell an output sufficiently large for average total cost to be at, or near, its minimum and for this cost to be recovered in the selling price. Thus the indivisibility would have ceased (in Professor Lerner's phrase) to be significant, in the sense of large in relation to the scale of output and of demand (*cf.* A. P. Lerner, *Economics of Control*, New York, 1944, pp. 176, 180–1).

practicable) ; the latter to depend on the existence of indivisibilities *outside* the industry (as narrowly defined), in other industries or plants producing the subsidiary products or components in question (textile machinery supplied to the textile industry affording the textbook-example of this case). The economy in this latter case arises from spreading the indivisible fixed cost over a larger output with a resulting fall in average cost per unit.*

It is a mistake, however, to suppose that the problem created by the existence of indivisibilities is confined to one of excess capacity: a mistake, moreover, that has been responsible for some myopic thinking about public utilities, especially electricity supply. It is quite possible for demand to be insufficient to call into existence (say) two indivisible units, but at the same time to involve *over-use* of the one unit—over-use in the sense of involving steeply rising prime costs of additional output (or in some cases breakdowns of equipment or delay due to bottlenecks) and absolute inability to meet additional demand (*e.g.* power-cuts in the case of electricity). In such a case a price is required sufficiently high to restrict demand within capacity. Marginal cost in these circumstances will be *above*, and not below, average total cost ; and unless price is also raised at least to this level, the degree of over-use may become intolerable.†

* For this reason it has been claimed on behalf of marginal-cost pricing that this principle, if applied universally, would cover this type of external economy (by excluding the possibility of falling selling-price of the subsidiary product), and hence to this extent would preclude disharmony between the social interest and the interest of an individual firm. But there are, of course, *other* sorts of external economy (and diseconomy) in the sense of financially unrecorded benefits or costs associated with expansion of an industry.

An analogous, though different, argument has sometimes been used to the effect that external economies are inconsistent with conditions of perfect competition since competitive equilibrium is inconsistent with unexhausted economies *internal* to the firm (and hence with a falling cost and price of any product that is used elsewhere in the system as an input). But to the extent that such economies are due to spare capacity within an indivisible unit, this is equivalent to saying that in many cases competition is inconsistent with the existence of an indivisible unit even where investment in such a unit is socially desirable. The question that this kind of apology for competition patently begs is whether the *number* of products (and services) can be assumed to be optimal. *Cf.* Joan Robinson, 'A Fundamental Objection to *Laissez-Faire*' in *The Economic Journal* (Sept. 1935), p. 581, with its reference to commodities not produced even though "the average utility would exceed the average cost".

† If at the full-capacity point the barrier to increased output becomes absolute (as with the so-called inverted-L-shaped cost-curve), marginal cost itself becomes

Nor does it *necessarily* follow that because the plant is more than normally profitable, the correct long-period answer is to bring into existence two (or more) indivisible units; since to do so may be at the expense of reintroducing a situation of excess capacity in both (or all) of them. (For which reason it seems wise to avoid saying, as some do, that in the over-capacity case marginal cost includes the capital cost.)

Public utilities also present us with more complex cases of alternating excess capacity and over-capacity use, according to the time of day (or week) or the season. This is the peak and off-peak problem, which particularly characterises transport and electricity-supply (and to a lesser extent gas and telephones). Here there is evidently a reason for differential charging according to time of day (*e.g.* by the time-of-day meter for electricity, or storage heaters) or season (*e.g.* seasonal differential with gas or hotel charges); higher prices at the peak-period being designed to discourage excessive pressure and over-use and price-concessions in the off-peak period to encourage demand when excess-capacity is available.* Unfortunately for such methods, demand at peak-periods often tends to be highly inelastic; and there is at least some indication that the effect of high peak-prices on consumers may be to encourage them perversely to economise not at the peak itself but at off-peak periods. This aspect of the problem, however, although it has figured fairly prominently in discussions of public-utility pricing in this country in recent years, does not illustrate any necessary conflict between social and individual interest, and has accordingly aroused less attention in this context.

What, then, of the arguments that have been used on the other side of the debate as grounds for rejecting the marginal-cost principle? These arguments have shown considerable variety

irrelevant (indeed meaningless), and what will be needed (unless demand is to be rationed) is a supply-demand equilibrium price high enough to restrict demand to the full-capacity level.

* Sometimes there is the additional complication, as in electricity, of different ways (and costs) of meeting a peak-demand of short duration and of long duration, raising the question whether the proper interpretation of marginal cost in the latter case is the cost of meeting it *minus* the cost of the former (*cf.* R. L. Meek, 'The New Bulk Supply Tariff for Electricity' in *The Economic Journal*, March 1968, pp. 49–63).

both in character and in weight. The ones that have exercised the most influence seem capable of being summarised under six heads.

First, it has been maintained that to base prices on average total costs has the advantage of administrative simplicity. It is simple to tell managers that they must cover cost and aim at making a profit, and to take the occurrence of a balance-sheet loss as *prima facie* evidence of inefficiency or of something being wrong with the scale or method of production. It has also been claimed that this notion is a familiar one—as familiar as the commercial notion of a balance-sheet. On examination, however, this contention seems to have less force than appears at first sight. Since some form of tax is probably included in the expenses side of the balance-sheet, even at times being included in the calculation of cost (notionally if not actually), there seems to be no convincing reason why a subsidy (as a negative tax) should not also be included. All that managers and accountants need in this case learn to do is to reverse a sign from *plus* to *minus*. In cases where marginal is below average cost a subsidy of some kind would necessarily be paid; and an obvious method of doing this would be to assess a fixed (annual) subsidy equal to the estimated difference, and to pay this to the enterprise or industry by writing-off fixed capital cost (possibly with the condition attached that selling-price should not be fixed above a certain level). In so far, however, as marginal-cost pricing is interpreted as an instruction to management to make a separate calculation of additional cost in each situation on a variety of occasions, and to fix price and output accordingly, some scepticism about administrative feasibility may be reasonable and the argument retain at least some force. This is a matter to which we shall return under another heading.

Secondly, average-cost pricing, it is said, does at least afford a conveniently simple investment-criterion which would otherwise be lacking: a balance-sheet profit yielding at least a *prima facie* case for expanding investment, and a loss for eventually contracting it. The weight to be attached to this objection seems to depend upon the importance one attaches to simplicity and convenience in a criterion as compared with 'correctness'. Some may well think that there is little point in having a convenient criterion for investment if it is more often than not a false one (we have seen that in the case of indivisibilities it is total benefit that needs to be balanced against total cost and not merely total receipts from selling at a uniform price).* Whether or not a reasonably full use of capacity can be made by selling to the public at a price equal to marginal cost (only) can probably claim to yield as good an approximation to a correct answer as whether total cost can be covered by any feasible system of pricing.

Thirdly, it has been contended (notably by Mr Coase)† that it is reasonable to expect those who benefit from a certain product or service to bear the full cost to society of providing it, including the cost involved in the original investment, and to do so in proportion to the use they make of it. If marginal cost alone is covered by receipts (in the case where it is below average cost) the difference (representing the original investment cost) will have to be borne by *some* section of the community, and if not charged to those who use it, this cost will fall upon others than the beneficiaries. As a moral principle in its own right, this Benefit Principle is manifestly capable of having a widely different appeal to different persons. The present writer can only say that he has never been convinced that great weight need be attached to it as an economic principle, however much political appeal it may have in special contexts. The Benefit Principle has not attained any very prominent place in Public Finance as a principle governing the distribution of taxation: to considerations of Equity or Ability to Pay it has generally, and quite properly, yielded second place. In price-policy generally it evidently cannot compete on an equal footing with considerations of income-distribution; and it can scarcely be given pride of place except by one who believes that existing income-distribution is ideal or divinely inspired. If, of course, those who employ this kind of argument intend merely to remind us that consideration of the effects on income-distribution of marginal-cost pricing should always be kept in mind,

---

* In a classic article Professor A. Lerner demonstrated analytically the several ways in which covering average cost would give the *wrong* answer with regard to investment-decisions (*The Economic Journal*, June 1937, pp. 261–4.)

† R. H. Coase, *The Economic Journal* (April 1945), p. 112: "It has been a commonplace for economists to argue that the consumer should pay the cost of any product which he buys"; otherwise "there would be discrimination". "It follows that the receipts from the sale of a product should equal its cost."

then no objection can be taken; and this is again a matter to which, under another heading, we shall return.

Fourthly, an objection voiced by Professor Arthur Lewis, among others, to marginal cost as a basis for pricing is that it has no unique definition, but rather a considerable variety of definitions, each of them contingent upon the special circumstances of a particular case. It is accordingly unsuitable as the basis for any general rule and accordingly impracticable of operation. "There is no such quantity", says Professor Lewis, "as the 'marginal cost of output'; there is not even a simple choice between two quantities, short- and long-run cost; there is a large variety of costs to choose from, depending merely on how far ahead you choose to look, and this collection of costs itself varies from day to day as current commitments alter."* To this Professor Lerner has again furnished an answer: namely, that this type of objection is based on a misunderstanding of the *modus operandi* of the marginal rule, which is to be regarded essentially, not as a rule for price-fixing, but for fixing *output*. All that is necessary is to tell managers when taking decisions about the scale of output to use that definition of marginal cost which fits the particular decision they are taking. What they should do in any particular case is simply to calculate the *additional* cost involved in the change or the activity under consideration (whether it be running an additional train or commissioning an additional track to be laid), and to compare this with the value of the additional output: if the latter exceeds the former, the increase of output should be undertaken, but not if the former turns out to be the larger of the two.

Evidently an assumption has been slipped into this way of formulating the problem: namely, that the price is somehow independently given, and that it is accepted as such by the taker of output-decisions. In other words, it is some kind of current supply-demand price, which although affected by output decisions is treated by decision-takers as essentially demand-determined; or else it is an administratively fixed

* W. Arthur Lewis, *Overhead Cost* (London, 1949), p. 12. Professor Wiles says that "the definition of 'marginal' is quite arbitrary" (*op. cit.* p. 287). (Professor Lewis thinks that "indivisible escapable costs" must be covered by the price, and even part of the cost of "non-renewable assets" if price-discrimination is possible; but apparently on Benefit Principle grounds.)

price determined by some price-fixing agency other than, or superior to, the management in question concerned with output and investment (although there remains the question in this case as to how the price-fixing decision is taken).

Where this is a realistic view of the situation, Professor Lerner's retort is both reasonable and adequate. Moreover, what he suggests is the only way in which such a rule can be applied to decision-taking. But it is less helpful and convincing as an answer to the objection in those cases where prices cannot be indefinitely flexible but have to take the form of 'announced prices' or 'list prices' or a 'tariff of charges' announced for some time ahead and stabilised over a considerable period of time (as is commonly the case with public utilities). Then whoever has to fix these prices or tariffs, whether it be the same authority as determines output or some other body, must be given some principle to guide his decision. He must be told on what basis to fix his prices. Here the Lerner-answer will not be much help to him; and if there really is an intention of using marginal cost as a basis in such cases, the difficulty mentioned by Professor Lewis seems to remain, and to constitute a quite serious obstacle in practice.* Economists who tend to be obsessed with prices as always flexible market prices often belittle the extent to which prices, for a variety of reasons, have to be of a fairly stable kind such as we have described as announced or list-prices. In these cases consistency in any rule for price-fixing and its application can be of prime importance, especially where competing and substitute products or services are involved.

Fifthly, it has been emphasised, and with good reason, that the marginal cost principle is essentially an all-or-nothing rule, in the sense that there is no advantage in applying it to one industry or service if it is not applied simultaneously to all others. Indeed, by applying it in one case when it is not applied elsewhere one might well be doing harm rather than good so far as the effect on the distribution of resources is concerned. A facile answer might be that what one needs to do in such a case is to make price in the individual case bear a relation to

---

* Perhaps a process of successive approximation of announced prices to marginal cost could be envisaged; but if so this process would take time and the approximation only operate in the long period.

marginal cost equal to the *average* relationship which it bears elsewhere, in all other industries. But even if one could discover what this average was, it is only on very special assumptions (*e.g.* about transferability of resources) that even this modified version of the rule would retain any validity. Some critics have gone so far as to assert that in such a situation nothing at all of a general nature can be said; and that whenever a large sector of industry is non-optimal (in the sense relevant to this discussion) there is no possible means of knowing in which direction a 'second-best solution' will lie. Such a degree of scepticism can probably be dismissed as an extreme counsel of despair. In a large number of actual cases it will evidently be possible to say more than this: for instance, within sectors or groups of industries that are characterised by a fairly high degree of transferability both of productive resources within the group and of demand for their products, while at the same time being comparatively isolated in both respects from other industrial sectors.* It would, of course, be pointless to take measures to reduce excess capacity of equipment in one industry if such a condition were universal and if labour and/or other prime resources were generally in short supply. But there could be an advantage in reducing excess capacity where this was exceptionally large or in concentrating available resources where marginal cost of additional output was relatively low at the expense of employments where it was relatively high.†

Sixthly, there is the objection that, since in the leading case we have considered, the marginal cost principle would involve running a number of industries or services at a loss, this would inevitably involve the subsidising of some groups of consumers at the expense of others and hence have significant effects on income-distribution. Such effects could not be ignored; if large enough they might well swamp the alleged beneficial effects of the marginal cost rule in the industry or service where it is

* *Cf.* I. M. D. Little, *The Price of Fuel* (Oxford, 1953), pp. xiii-xiv: "The importance of having relative prices and relative marginal costs equal depends clearly on substitutability . . . if there were zero substitutability it would not matter what the ratio was. Since fuels are far better substitutes for each other than any of them is for food, medicine or education, a change which gets relative prices and costs equal for the different fuels at the expense of greater inequality of price and cost between food and fuel may be reasonably judged a good one."

† *Cf.* H. Fiszel, *Investment Efficiency in Socialist Economy* (Warsaw and London, 1966), pp. 137 *et seq.*

applied ; if the effect upon distribution was seriously adverse, this might well be a sufficient reason for rejecting the principle altogether. It is clear that with this final objection we are really back to the point from which we started : that one can never divorce a supposedly optimum principle affecting pricing or output from the effect on income-distribution of applying it. If one could be sure that the latter was always likely to be beneficial, there would clearly be strong reason for applying it in all surplus-capacity cases, since its application would here result in giving one 'something for nothing'. But of this one can never (or seldom) be sure, and the possibility of an adverse distribution-effect must always qualify one's judgement, and in some cases, at least, be sufficient to cause one to suspend approval.

What conclusion, then, have we reached after this survey of argument? It should be sufficiently clear that equalisation of price and marginal cost as a universal imperative, as so many have used it, fails to make sense and is out of the question in practice. For one thing it shares what we have called the Perfectibility Fallacy of that general optimum principle from which it derives. On the other hand, there is much to be said for applying it, at least to the extent of waiving any 'covering-average-cost' rule, in any case of excess capacity, short-term or long-term, where this is not part of a universal condition of excess capacity in equal degree joined with an absence of any reserve of other (prime) resources, and where there is no reason to believe that the distribution-effect of so doing will be markedly unfavourable. The same applies to the external economies case where these economies arise from excess capacity in the production of some input or component. This disregarding of fixed costs in order to make fuller use of existing capacity is something that can be done in a socialist economy where it would not under capitalism, especially with any high degree of monopoly.

Even where the direct effect on distribution was likely to be adverse, there would be much to be said for taking measures to abolish or reduce the under-utilisation of capacity, if it were at all possible to counter the distribution effect in some other way, and in a way that would not have deleterious effects elsewhere (*e.g.* through money-wage adjustments enabling losers from the change to increase their purchases in some other direction).*

Similarly where production in any line has pronounced 'external effects', independently of indivisibilities and excess-capacity, whether these effects be classifiable as social economies or benefits (as with books or medicines) or social diseconomies (as with motor-cars), there is obvious sense in abandoning any rigid rule that ties price to average cost, at any rate so far as the price charged to the consumer is concerned. But although this is sometimes treated as an adjustment of price to *social* marginal cost, it is more properly regarded, perhaps, as re-laxing or abandoning a relation between price and cost in *any* of its interpretations (in order to allow for social effects), rather than sponsoring one interpretation of cost in preference to another.

For analogous, if opposite, reasons, in the over-use-of-capacity case, it is evidently reasonable to depart from an average cost rule in the opposite direction of adjusting price upwards (either temporarily or permanently), just as there is in extractive industries and agriculture for reasons of natural scarcity; also for differential pricing between peak and off-peak periods where there are marked fluctuations in demand and hence in utilisation of capacity.

One need hardly add that all this flows (or should do) from simple commonsense. A reader might be justified in saying that, since it does so, a sophisticated journey through the tortuous byways of the marginal cost discussion was scarcely necessary to reach so plain and easy a destination.

---

* The *limitation* on doing this is, of course, that if those whose money incomes are raised demand more of the things from the production of which labour and materials are being transferred to increase output in the surplus-capacity line of production, this will frustrate the intention of reducing price in the latter; just as it will also be frustrated if the potential purchasers of the product whose output is being increased have *their* money incomes decreased in an attempt to offset the distribution effect of the shift in relative prices. Again, the money-wage adjust-ments might have direct effects on the distribution of labour and/or the amount of work done. This illustrates once more the kind of difficulty to which glib talk about countering distribution-effects with money-transfers is so often obstinately blind.

CHAPTER 12

CONCLUSION

Since a Conclusion implies recapitulation and this in turn repetition, it inevitably invites tedium. As fruit, moreover, of longish argument the result may well seem meagre when seen *in parvo*. Hence those who have followed through and digested the argument of the preceding chapters may be advised that they can be spared this one. Perhaps the chief use of a Conclusion is for the sake of those who have the habit of reading books backwards or of browsing over peroration and index.

Precise formulation, moreover formulation that shows a meticulous regard for economic content, has particular importance in relation to propositions in welfare economics for two reasons. First, no part of economic theory has been so infused with controversial issues as has the analysis of the conditions for maximising utility or welfare. This is scarcely to be wondered at seeing that it bears so crucial a relation to economic policy. Policy-implications and ideological polemics have been to the forefront of the subject since Walras and Pareto, if not before; ranging from the identification of competitive equilibrium with the welfare optimum through the von Mises attack on socialism as a non-rational form of economy to more recent criticisms of socialist economies and of planning generally for their violation of optimum conditions. It could, indeed, be said that welfare economics, at least the 'new welfare economics', had itself become an ideology. Secondly, the subject deals with concepts that are supposedly applicable to different institutional contexts, and discussion of it is concerned with comparative evaluation of different economic systems. Since so much depends upon application of general concepts to concrete situations, care needs to be taken, accordingly, that the concepts do not change their meaning when translated from one context into another and different one.

It has emerged from our survey of welfare economics, old and new, that there are two essential precepts afforded by it, and perhaps only two, that can be enunciated in a precise and

unqualified form as demonstrable principles or theorems. One
of them is concerned with freedom of consumers' choice, which
enables consumers to get most satisfaction or utility for the
money income earned or allotted to them, given existing prices*
and available supplies of consumers' goods. The other is concerned with the choice of methods of production, among those
known and available, such as will maximise the production
obtainable from any given quantity of inputs for any given
product-pattern or output plan.† The first of these is a matter
of commonsense intuition rather than of analytical demonstration and has seldom, if ever, been seriously disputed, even if
there are occasions (*e.g.* wartime shortages which invite rationing) when it may be held to be overridden by considerations of
equity in distribution. It is equivalent to the dictum that the
housewife can generally be relied upon to make the most of her
shillings, and rests on the assumption that most housewives are
sensible enough to do so—at any rate when unbeguiled by the
wiles of high-pressure commercialised advertising and salesmanship. To allow her to do so does not usually involve any
cost to society and it enhances the incentive-effect of a given
money wage. The second is less obvious, and its application
may involve fairly complex calculation on the basis of an
appropriate system of costing. It is this, indeed, which gives
the question of what is a correct system of pricing of produced
inputs (such as was discussed in chapters 8 and 9) its central
importance as a basis for efficient decision, whether decision is
centralised or decentralised.

Reflection will easily show that the system of costing discussed in those chapters is a way of implementing the second
of the above-mentioned principles, since we saw that if methods
of production (and this includes the production and use of so-
called produced inputs, or capital goods) are chosen on this
basis‡ there is no alternative set of such methods that will

---

* This refers, of course, to the so-called 'parametric function' of retail prices
in relation to the choice exercised by each consumer. We have remarked above that
for such prices to equate total demand with the available supply in the case of
each commodity, they must at the same time be open to reciprocal influence from
total demand (whatever this may turn out to be as the net result of individual
choices and substitutions).

† It may be remembered that this was essentially the problem as posed by
Kantorovitch in his *Ekonomicheskii Raschot Nailuchshego Ispolzovania Resursov* (Moscow, 1959).   ‡ On the assumption that the cheaper method is always chosen.

involve as small an expenditure of labour to maintain the postulated level and rate of increase of output of end-products, or
consumers' goods (or alternatively will yield as high a level and
rate of increase of output with any given quantity of labour-
expenditures). Another way of expressing it is to say that if all
capital goods are reduced to terms of dated labour, the ratio of
marginal effectiveness of labour of any two dates will be
equalised in all lines of production when, in the costing of
capital goods, labour of any given date is uniformly priced
and the difference in pricing of labour of different dates* is
made equal to the average growth-rate over the period between
them. Such a system of costing, as we saw, does not depend upon
the operation of a market or quasi-market mechanism, as was
claimed to be a *conditio sine qua non* for implementing any such
principle in the famous *wirtschaftsrechnung* debate; although it
may well be facilitated in many cases by the *ex post* checks of a
trial-and-error process. But, if only because time as a factor is
crucially involved, it has to be viewed in a dynamic setting and
the appropriate pricing-principle cast in terms of a postulated
rate of economic growth. This has been obscured in the past by
formulating the problem within a static framework.

Both of the theorems we have mentioned can be regarded as
involving the much-canvassed notion of a Pareto-optimum.
They are both concerned with necessary conditions for maximising social welfare. But neither separately nor in combination
can they be regarded as *sufficient* conditions, since there is an
infinitely large number of output plans and sets of prices at
which they can be fulfilled. To define a unique position at
which (in given conditions) the welfare of the community will
be maximised has been the central preoccupation of the literature of welfare economics. Its postulation is only possible in
terms of a set of price-valuations of consumers' goods, and these
depend upon a certain structure of demand. It has been variously
expressed in terms of the equality of (social) marginal net products in all uses, or the equality of the ratios of product-prices
and marginal costs, or the equality of the consumers' rate of
substitution between any pair of final products and their production-transformation rate (this implying a common tangent

---

* The grading of this variation, of course, being according to the distance in
time of any labour-input from the emergence of the output in question.

to a collective indifference-curve and the production-possibility curve). But a position so defined is *not* a pure Pareto-optimum like the others, because it is not and cannot be independent of distribution, and cannot be uniquely defined without falling into contradiction. Some distribution-pattern, implicit or explicit, is crucial to aggregation, and aggregation is involved in any reference to collective or *social* welfare. Devices designed to give the notion of a general optimum necessary rigour by making it independent of distribution, whether this be the assumption that ideal distribution can be defined in terms of money income and can always be posited, or the illusion of appropriately offsetting and neutral 'lump-sum money-transfers', or the postulation of a 'social welfare function', turn out on scrutiny to be empty of content and unreal. Decisions about output are always and necessarily decisions about distribution so long at least as human tastes are non-uniform. Hence to put such an allegedly sufficient condition for an optimum on a par with the other two (even subordinating the latter to it) by calling it a generalised 'efficiency condition' is unwarranted and misleading. To derive from its postulation either a defence of competition or a categorical imperative for a socialist economy—an economic criterion by means of which the performance of the latter is judged and possibly condemned —has to be dismissed as obscurantism. Yet this has been a recurring theme of the professional literature and of long-drawn-out debate. Some may wish to defend such a theorem on the ground that it inculcates sound attitudes in policy-makers and administrators which without it would be lacking. At best this would be merely a temporary defence; and the history of the social sciences is rich in warnings of the dangers of letting excuses of this kind prolong and harden questionable dogma.

We have here (and in earlier chapters) laid primary stress upon income-distribution, and the difficulty of making precise formulations concerning it, as the reason why precision in for-mulating an overall optimum is impossible. In other words, maximising welfare has to be viewed in terms of a compromise between diverse ends; and to the extent that the ends are im-perfectly comparable, the 'best' solution in reconciling them cannot be read off from a system of equations. But there are other considerations as well as distribution that indicate the need to be content with a fairly rough approximation to any ideal, even when this has been formulated. First, there is the question of information, on the importance of which we have already had something to say in the context of planning. Any optimising procedure depends upon the collection of relevant information and its transmission in a manageable (preferably quantified) form to the actual decision-takers. But collection and transmission of information itself involves a cost (the cost of perfect information may often, indeed, be infinite).* It may simply not be worth while to pursue the process of reaching an optimum beyond a certain point because to do so becomes too costly, and what is lost by accepting a sub-optimum position is balanced by the saving on the additional cost of greater perfection (in a formal sense the cost involved in the means of attainment should be included in the equations defining the optimum itself—or, rather, the range of possible second-best optima as the result now becomes). Something analogous applies to the optimising process itself, whether this be a decentralised pricing-process, working *via* Walrasian *tâtonnement*, or some mathematical programming method operated centrally. A process of convergence, operating in actual time, may well be a slow one (limited as it necessarily will be by certain practical rules or conventions governing the 'stages' by which adaptations occur); and this very slowness constitutes a cost. Any planning must have a time-table, possibly a fairly strict one, if it is to be effective planning. It may well be preferable again to content oneself with some approximation to the final position rather than to wait for the convergence-process to be complete. (It is well known that some processes only converge asymptotically.) This kind of consideration acquires special importance in a dynamic context. Rigidities of various kinds may well occasion conflict between optimising and growth. Since time does not appear in the usual optimising equations,

---

* The most perfect information cannot remove (even if it can reduce) uncertainty with regard to the future; and the existence of uncertainty inevitably blurs the notion of optimising by introducing a dual element into choice: namely how much 'optimising' (in the usual sense) to forego in return for greater certainty (or alternatively for a given probability of gain). On the costs of information which "economists usually ignore", and the fact that "a large-scale iterative planning scheme generally cannot be run until the full optimum is reached", *cf.* Benjamin N. Ward, *The Socialist Economy: a study of organizational alternatives* (New York, 1967), pp. 65, 71.

sluggish mobility of resources may well mean that the quickest way to reach a certain future goal stands in conflict with optimum allocation within any given time-period. There are other practical considerations that may impose a preference for an approximation only rather than full and ideal attainment. As Malinvaud has said of planning, "the search for consistency is often of greater significance than the finding of an optimum".* At first sight it may not be easy to see why there should be any conflict between the two. The possibility can perhaps be illustrated by a very simple example. In the real world a number of the relevant functions, especially individual demand-functions, may be liable to oscillation or to high sensitivity (obviously, something must be accepted as 'data': not everything can be planned); and it is a well-known fact that a position where full-capacity working exists is apt to be highly unstable, since supply is inflexible in face of even the smallest demand-shift. Clearly in such a situation the conditions for easy convergence of provisional solutions may be absent. The more flexible position of some margin of reserve-capacity will be *per se* sub-optimal; yet it will probably be a situation more capable of yielding all-round consistency of plans *in esse* for most of the time.

To reject the notion of a simple and unique optimum is by no means to say that no welfare judgements are possible at all. It is often possible to say what is *better* without first postulating what is *ideal*. The conclusion by no means follows from what we have said that, with the aid of such a concept as utility, one cannot formulate precepts or rules that will enable us on numerous occasions (even a majority of occasions) to indicate the direction in which improvement in all probability lies. For example we may take the presumption that where large discrepancies between price-ratios and cost-ratios exist too little attention is probably being paid to market-indices of consumers' demand, in comparison with other policy-objectives, and that a reduction of these discrepancies would augment social welfare. A rule of this kind would at least require those other objectives

* In E. Malinvaud and M. O. L. Bacharach (eds.), *Activity Analysis in the Theory of Growth and Planning* (London and New York, 1967), p. 185. Professor Malinvaud also points out that in the case of methods of *tâtonnement* it is only possible "to establish convergence by making assumptions which taken all in all are pretty restrictive" (*ibid.*).

to be explicitly stated and defended and weighed in the balance against greater attention to the pattern of current demand. Viewed in this way—taking significant maladjustments as *prima facie* indication of something wrong, as opposed to the pursuit of a unique optimum—attention to such ratios and to demand-indices as guides to production no doubt deserves to be assigned a prominent place in a developed socialist economy. But in the course of such assignment it must have the status of one 'good' among a number of others, with optimising regarded as some compromise between them and not as maximum satisfaction of one of them alone. Even from the two necessary-but-not-sufficient conditions one can derive some quite important conclusions. From that affecting choice of methods of production we have seen that significant conclusions about the costing of produced inputs are to be derived; also the corollary that any investment-effectiveness ratio, as a calculating device for investment decisions, ought to be uniform and not differentiated.* Indeed, the theorem affecting methods of production seems the one to be singled out as being of prime interest and importance for a socialist economy, and as having manifest applications, as experience to-date has shown.†

What experience and reflection alike make clear, however, is that the problem of social welfare in such a society consists of judging between and reconciling a number of qualitatively distinct ends: for example, the ends of growth in productive power, of want satisfaction, of income distribution (and this in relation to incentives), of the formation of social standards and conventions and the calculation of only partially measurable (and certainly unmeasured by the market) 'external economies and diseconomies', or *social* benefits and costs. Decision between

---

* Unless the differentiation is designed so as to make appropriate allowance for differences in length of life of equipment. *Cf.* A. Lurie in *Voprosi Ekonomiki*, 1966, no. 7, p. 68, who urges a revision of the *Tipovaia Metodika* of 1960 in the direction of uniformity. On this, and on differentiation as a way of allowing for different 'life-spans' of equipment, *cf.* also M. Kalecki, *cit.* in the footnote below, (pp. 95-9). While Soviet practice has witnessed differentiated norms in various sectors, Poland and Hungary have adopted uniform norms.

† *Cf.* in this connection, Professor M. Kalecki's contribution to C. Feinstein (ed.), *Socialism, Capitalism and Economic Growth* (Cambridge, 1967), pp. 87-100. Also *cf.* D. M. Nuti, 'Material Incentive Schemes and the Choice of Technique in Soviet Industry', in *Australian Economic Papers* (Dec. 1966), pp. 183-98.

such ends is the province of economic planning *par excellence*. Even as regards price-policy itself we have seen that there is a problem of effecting a viable and satisfactory compromise between the several and possibly conflicting purposes and functions that prices are called upon to serve, such as short-period, clear-the-market prices and valuations as a basis for long-term calculation and decision. The problem is misconceived when it is viewed as the application of a single major theorem (or even cluster of major theorems), or as the reduction of all the main alternatives confronting planners' choice to the pursuit of a single quantifiable maximand—eminently satisfying as it would be to do so from the standpoint of formal economy and elegance. Any future generalisation along these lines or in this direction, arising from an appreciation of what kinds of conflicting purposes prove to be outstanding, and what in practice negligible or reducible to easy and obvious compromises—moreover, appreciation of what elements in social and economic change are modifiable by planning and what have to be accepted as 'objective' and as part of the data of planning—all this must wait upon fuller experience (including comparative experience) of the working of socialist economy than we have available to us to-date (at least, in a suitably sifted and classified form). To know what in practice are the constraints upon choice and decision is often of more moment than to possess an easy optimising formula for unconstrained choice. To this end we need to know the structure of decision-making and of feasible communication links. Generalisation about the pursuit of objectives, and the instruments of such pursuit, will be greatly facilitated by, if not actually dependent upon, knowledge of actual time-lags of any adjustment-processes (*e.g.* in decision-taking and decision-implementation and the feed-back flow of *ex-post* information about the results); and whether such processes exhibit quick or slow convergence, or the converse.

We have seen that one of the lessons of experience to-date relates to the constraints imposed by limited availability of information in quantifiable form, especially at the centre; and another the constraint upon the feasible degree of complexity of decision-making imposed by necessary planning time-tables, even if this constraint be relative to, and changing with, the speed and size of computers. Yet a further important lesson is the (differing) bias exerted upon lower-level decision by various types of incentives or of so-called 'success-indicators'.

It is, indeed, the expectation that the future may yield a sounder basis for generalisation to the end of forging a unified political economy of socialism that gives such a pronounced degree of intellectual fascination to current experiment and innovation in the economic mechanisms of socialist countries, especially as regards the relation between planning and the market mechanism, the rôle of prices and the scope and play (also the limitations) of production-incentives, both individual and collective. To such matured generalisation the present survey can be no more than prolegomenon.

INDEX

Advertising, 6, 31, 214, 215, 227 n., 251
Aggregation
    'illicit a.', 51, 69, 73, 253
    method of, determined by function and purpose, 136 n.
Affluence, 219, 222
Alienation, of labour, 124 n., 132
Allocation
    of productive resources, problem of, 28, 56, 73, 77, 111, 184, 188–9, 206
    of scarce durable consumers's goods, 219
    system of, 138, 141 n., 146 and n., 172–3
    centralised a. dismissed as too complex, 190
    and 'two-level planning', 206–7
    see also Marginal Productivity, Optimum
America, 222
American Economic Review, 79 n., 111 n., 222 n., 227 n.
Approximation, successive, 66, 169, 195, 204, 206, 207, 246 n.
Archiv für Sozialwissenschaften und Sozialpolitik, 183 n.
Arrow, Professor Kenneth J., 104 n., 113, 114, 115
Australian Economic Papers, 256 n.
Austrian School, of economists, 3, 154, 171, 198
'Automaticity', optimising, 76

Bacharach, M. O. L., 158 n., 206 n, 255 n.
Bagchi, Dr A. K., 167 n.
Baldwin, C. D., 189 n.
Barone, Enrico, 183 n.
Barter, 49
    determinate or indeterminate, 16 n.
Baumol, Professor William J.
    on lack of precision in consumers' preferences, 64–5, 220
    on social welfare function, 112
    on individual time-preference and investment-decisions, 217 n.
Beckwith, B. P., 238–9 n.
Beer, Max, 125 n.

Benefit
    mutual, in exchange, 10–12, 15–17, 20, 49
    total benefit compared with total cost, 238, 244
'B-principle' of pricing, 244, 245 n.
Bentham, Jeremy, 9 n.
    parable of Brahmin and Benthamite, 80
Bergson, Professor Abram (*alias* Birk)
    and prices to consumers in index-number comparisons, 51 n.
    and failure of prices in U.S.S.R. to conform to marginal cost, 61 n.
    and Social Welfare Function, 110 *et seq.*, 111, 115, 116
    and social dividend, 131 n., 223 n.
    on wage-differentials and disutility, 210 n.
    on individuals knowing what is good for them, 213 n., 214 n.
    and financing social expenditure, 223 n.
    and change of consumers with time, 227
Bettelheim, Professor Charles, 174 n., 206 n.
Beveridge, Sir William H., 225 n.
Böhm-Bawerk, E. von, 154
Boiarski, A., 137 n.
Bonus-payments, distorting effect when related to output according to certain dimensions, 131
Boulding, Professor Kenneth, 12
'Box-Diagram', 13 *et seq.*, 48
Brahmin, parable of, 80
Bread and wine, as example of real-income distribution, 51, 70–1, 93
Bureaucracy
    and socialism, 125 and n., 126, 132

Cairncross, Sir Alec K., 228–9
Cake, analogy of, for national income, 29
Capacity, *see* Spare Capacity
Capital
    as a *genus* composed of heterogeneous capital goods, 54, 171–2, 174–5, 189–90

Cost (*cont.*)
  'c.-plus', 135 n.
  c.-prices, 137, 157
  'real c.', 30
  'short-period c.', 145, 166, 235–6
  prime c., 235, 240
  wage-c., 157–8, 195, 200
  user-c., 235
  social c., 55, 145, 150, 165, 217, 249, 256
  Novozhilov method, 203–5
  average in 'representative' firm, 234
  overhead or fixed 238–9 n., 240, 248
  total c. and total benefit, 238, 241 n., 244
  inverted-L c.-curve, 241 n.
  average c. as basis for pricing, its administrative simplicity, 243
  of information, 254
  see also Marginal cost, Prices
Czechoslovak Economic Papers, 144 n., 175 n.
Czechoslovakia
  economic reforms of '65–66', 141 n.
  controlled and contractual prices in, 146 n.
  talk of plan and market in, 147
  prices in, 173 n.

Decentralisation, 122, 127, 133, 138 *et seq.*, 164 *et seq.*, 186 *et seq.*
  and inflation, 141 and n.
  and price-control, 150
  decision-taking on basis of prices or of quantities, 169
  blend of, with planning, 133–4, 140–2, 148, 188, 190, 205, 207
Demand
  as index of welfare, 30–1, 33
  inelasticity of, 49 n., 217–18, 225–6, 242
  income-elasticity of, 40 n., 58 n., 98, 225–6
  cross-elasticity of, 223
  sensitivity to variation, 255
  consumers' d., its influence, 49–50
  attention to consumers' d., 61–3, 140, 199, 209, 231, 255
  'derived d.', 188–9 and 189 n.
  as determinant of prices, 198 and n.
  joint or complementary, 219–20, 231
  fluctuations of, and peak-problem, 242, 249
  see also Consumers, Market, Prices

Demand-curve, 6, 16 n.
  L-shaped, of a market, 218
Democracy
  and socialism, 125
  'primitive d.', 125–6
  direct d. in industry, 125 n., 130
Depreciation, 160, 200 n.
Deus ex machina, 7, 111, 123
Development, economic, *see* Dynamic conditions, Growth
Dickinson, Professor H. D., 184 n., 186, 188, 223–6
'Dictatorship', 6, 114, 220–1 n.
Distribution, of income
  Walras and, 10
  Pareto and, 17–18, 22
  money and real, 23–6, 42
  attempt to separate from production, 18, 23, 25, 27, 41, 83, 103, 253
  Pigou and, 23 n., 28, 32, 77
  'ideal d.', 104, 108, 110, 209
  meaning of constant d., 25 n., 91
  assumed constant when measuring national income, 32, 40–2, 86, 103
  constant money-income wrongly assumed equivalent to constant d. in real terms, 23–4, 42
  and construction of a 'community indifference-curve', 46, 58, 69
  over time, 228
  effect of, illustrated from rich and poor consuming wine and bread, 51, 70–1
  its influence on demand and hence on prices, 57
  'd.-relative' character of an optimum, 57–60, 68 and n., 83 n., 252–3
  'd.-relative' nature of changes in social income, 91–2, 109, 121
  improving d. through the price-system, 61, 63, 209
  assumed to be 'ideal', 65–7, 112–13, 244, 253
  'getting rid of', 77
  and compensation criteria, 84–5 and n., 90–2, 102
  changes in, illustrated by Utility-Possibility Curve, 92–4, 109
  the Little-criterion and, 102–8
  comparison of, relative to goods-total distributed, 109–10
  according to need, 129, 210